EXPRESS TRACK

To SPANISH

A Teach-Yourself Program

SUSANA CHIABRANDO • FRANCISCO FERRERO
ANGELS VALERA

Translator/Editor of the English-Language Version:
ALLEN POMERANTZ, PhD

Illustrations: ALFONSO ORTUÑO

BARRON'S

Take-A-Break Illustrations: Xavier de Sierra
Graphic Design: Claudine Combalier
Cover Design: Zaü & Gaël
Picture Research: Altelier D'Image

First published in 1990 by Barron's
Educational Series, Inc.

The title of this original edition is *Voie
Express: Cours individuel d'Espagnol.*
Published by CLE International, Paris.

All inquiries should be addressed to:
Barron's Educational Series Inc.
250 Wireless Boulevard
Hauppauge, New York 11788

International Standard Book No. 0-8120-4574-2

Library of Congress Catalog Card No. 90-39249

Library of Congress Cataloging-in-Publication Data
Chiabrando, Susana.
[Voie express, cours individuel d'espagnol. English]
Express track to Spanish : a teach yourself program / Susana
Chiabrando, Francisco Ferrero, Angels Valera ; English language
version, Allen Pomerantz ; illustrations, Alfonso Ortuño.
p. cm.
ISBN 0-8120-4574-2
1. Spanish language--Self-instruction. 2. Spanish language--
Textbooks for foreign speakers--English. I. Ferrero, Francisco.
II. Valera, Angels. III. Title.
PC4112.5.C5513 1990
468.2'421—dc20
90-39249
CIP

PRINTED IN HONG KONG

67 490 987

WELCOME TO EXPRESS TRACK TO SPANISH!

Maybe you have never learned Spanish, and feel that now is the time to start. Maybe you learned Spanish years ago, and want to brush up. Maybe you're also interested in finding out about Spain and the Spanish, and, if you're going to the country, you'll also want to find your way around its customs and culture. Maybe you're going to work with Spanish speakers, and need the basis of a business vocabulary. Maybe you're just a traveler who likes to talk. . . . Whoever you are, the authors of Express Track to Spanish *wish you a warm welcome: in Spanish — Bienvenidos!*

They have carefully thought out a complete, step-by-step guide to the Spanish language.

What you will find in Express Track to Spanish

• *The Book contains dialogues, vocabulary lists, exercises, games, articles about Spain, a short story, a tourist guide, and a 1,500-word glossary.*
• *Four Cassettes with dialogues, exercises, and games.*
• *A Booklet with a complete transcript of what's on the cassettes and translations of the dialogues.*

Now you know the basic structure, it's up to you to use **Express Track to Spanish** *as you wish. Depending on your time, and your preferences, you can tailor* **Express Track to Spanish** *to fit your own specific needs.*

. . . For the serious student

Follow the **Express Track to Spanish** *method step-by-step. Each lesson begins with a* **Dialogue.** *Listen to simple, practical Spanish in everyday situations, practice your comprehension, and acquire vocabulary.*

All the dialogues are on cassette, with a selection of important phrases highlighted at the end of each dialogue. Listen for the sound signal, stop the tape, repeat, and practice your pronunciation and intonation.

Important words and expressions used in the dialogues, as well as other related vocabulary items, can be found under the headings **Vocabulary** *and* **How To Say It.** *Learn them all, and you'll go a long way!*

Notes *gives you a guide to some grammatical points, and some pitfalls not to fall into! And . . .*

. . . For those who like competition

even against themselves!
You can count up your scores at the end of each unit in the section **Test Yourself.**

If you have done all of the above, you might be ready for a bit of fun (in Spanish, of course!) So . . .

. . . For the more frivolous

You will find, in each unit: short, humorous accounts of all that's good and bad in Spain, and what awaits the unsuspecting traveler. A selection of famous Spanish songs, with their translations. Listening games, as well as word puzzles, quizzes, and crosswords to fill in on the page. A brief guide to Spanish slang, so you can communicate at street level, even if you haven't grasped how to say it the straight way.

. . . And, for the practical traveler

At the end of the book, **Practical Information** *tells you where to go, what to do, and how to get around. Useful addresses of hotels, restaurants, and museums, as well as prices, maps, and travel tips for when you first arrive in Spain. . . . And, of course, a 1,500-word glossary. So, whether you've been bitten by the language bug and want to really go for Spanish in the fast lane, or whether you want to take it easy and learn by listening and having fun, you'll find there's something for you in* **Express Track to Spanish.**

In any case, you're on the right track, or, as they say in Spanish: ¡Ustedes están en lo correcto!

The Authors

TABLE OF CONTENTS

TABLE OF CONTENTS

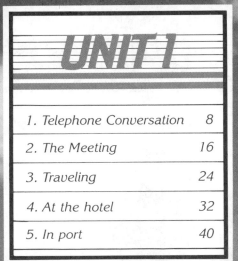

UNIT 1

MADRID : Plaza de Cibeles, Correo Mayor and Puerta de Alcalá

⊙⊙ LISTEN **TELEPHONE CONVERSATION**

Soledad Louveiro
Francisco Fernández
Paloma Montes

Paco Fernández, a photographer in Madrid, contacts Paloma Montes, actress and model, about a publicity job.

Paloma : *¿Diga?*

Paco : *¿Está Paloma, por favor...?*

Paloma : *Sí, soy yo. ¿Quién es usted?*

Paco : *Soy Paco Fernández, fotógrafo de «El Mundo». Y usted es modelo ¿verdad?*

Paloma : *Sí, soy modelo de una agencia de publicidad.*

Paco : *¿Está mañana en la agencia?*

Paloma : *No, mañana no.*

Paco : *Quiero hablar con usted. ¿Nos vemos en un café . . . ?*

Paloma : *De acuerdo. ¿Dónde?*

Paco : *En el Café Gijón.*

Paloma : *¿Dónde está?*

Paco : *Está en Recoletos.*

Paloma : *Bueno, hasta mañana.*

Paco : *Adiós. Hasta mañana.*

⊙⊙ LISTEN AND REPEAT
You will find the translation on page 1 of booklet.

Madrid : 1. Plaza Mayor
2. Gran Vía
3. Palacio de Oriente
4. Plaza de España

NOUNS

la conversación telefónica — telephone conversation
el teléfono — telephone
el fotógrafo — photograph
el sol — sun
el trabajo — work
el/la modelo — model
la agencia — agency
la publicidad — publicity
el café — cafe
el paseo — promenade
el/la periodista — journalist
el/la artista — artist
el profesor — professor
el/la estudiante — student
el/la contable — accountant
el ejecutivo — executive
el arquitecto — architect
el ingeniero — engineer
el escultor — sculptor
el secretario — secretary
el empresario — manager
el abogado — lawyer
el director — director
el pintor — painter
el/la comerciante — merchant
el escritor — writer
el médico — doctor

VERBS

estar — to be (with location; adjectives of condition)
ser — to be (origin; adjectives of characteristic)
querer — to want
hablar — to speak
ver — to see
descolgar — to take the phone off the hook
colgar — to hang up

MISCELLANEOUS

diga — hello
por favor — please
sí — yes
soy yo — It is I. (It's me.) *(1)*
¿ quién ? — who?
usted, ustedes — you *(2)*
y — and
¿ verdad ? — Isn't it so?
mañana — tomorrow
en — in
no — no
allí — there
con — with
de acuerdo — agreed
¿ dónde ? — Where?
del — of the, from the
bueno — good, O.K.
hasta mañana — until tomorrow
adiós — goodbye

1. INTRODUCING YOURSELF (YOUR NAME)

¡ Oiga ! — Hello
Soy Paco Fernández — It's Paco Fernández. I'm P.F.
Me llamo P.F. — My name is P.F.
Mi nombre es P.F. — My name is P.F.

2. ANSWERING A CALL

¿ Diga ?
¿ Dígame ? — Hello. Yes? (3)

3. ASKING TO SPEAK TO SOMEONE

¿ Está Paloma, por favor ? — Is Paloma there, please?
Quiero (Quisiera) hablar con P. — I would like to speak to P.
¿ Puedo hablar con P. ? — May I speak with P.?
¿ Se puede poner P. ? — Could you put P. on?

4. ASKING WHO IS CALLING

¿ Quién es ? — Who is it? Who's on the phone?
¿ Quién llama ? — Who's calling?
¿ Quién está al aparato ? — Who's on the phone?
¿ De parte de quién ? — Who shall I say is calling?

5. PUTTING THE CALLER ON HOLD

Un momento, por favor — Just a minute, please
No se retire — Don't hang up

NOTES . . .   NOTES . . .   NOTES . . .   NOTES . . .

(1) Literally: "It is I." — (2) "Usted" is one of two forms for "you" in Spanish; it is the polite or formal form. In Spanish it is the third person singular. Its abbreviation is "Ud." or "Vd." "Ustedes," for more than one person is the third person plural in Spanish. Its abbreviation is "Uds." or "Vds." — (3) You say "oiga" when you are making the call; say "diga" or "digame" when you are called.

1. MAKING A CALL

⊙⊙ LISTEN:

¿Diga?
• ¿Diga?

Listen and repeat according to the model:
¿Diga? — Hola — ¿Está Paloma, por favor?
¿Está el Señor Fernández, por favor? — Sí, soy
yo. — ¿Quién es usted? — Adiós — Hasta
mañana.

2. ASKING THE CALLER'S NAME

⊙⊙ LISTEN:

Señor Fernández
• ¿Usted es el Señor Fernández?

Continue following the model:
Señor Fernández — Señor Pérez — Señora Mar-
tínez — Señorita González — Señor García —
Señora Hernández — Señorita Perea.

3. ASKING SOMEONE'S PROFESSION

⊙⊙ LISTEN:

modelo
• ¿Tú eres modelo, verdad?

Continue following the model:
modelo — fotógrafo — profesor — dentista —
estudiante — ingeniero — secretario — ejecutivo.

4. GIVING YOUR PROFESSION

⊙⊙ LISTEN:

modelo
• Yo soy modelo ¿Y usted?

Continue following the model:
modelo — fotógrafa — profesora — dentista
— estudiante — ingeniera — secretaria —
ejecutiva.

5. ASKING ABOUT A LOCATION

⊙⊙ LISTEN:

café Gijón
• ¿Dónde está el café Gijón?

Continue following the model:
café Gijón — agencia de publicidad — universidad — restorán — París — bar La Paz — Hotel
Opera.

6. PRONUNCIATION

⊙⊙ LISTEN AND REPEAT:

El señor no es escultor, es pintor — ¿Está
Paloma, por favor? Está en el bar —
¿Puedo hablar con Salvador?

CAFÉS

If Spain aims to be mentioned in the Guiness Book of Records one day, it can claim one unquestionable title — that of having the greatest density per square foot of bars, cafés, taverns, and other bistros. The section on "bars" in the yellow pages of the telephone directory — for central Madrid only — extends to 16 closely printed pages!

Eminently sociable and an enthusiastic devotee of Latin conviviality, the Spaniard spends a fundamental part of his existence in bars, which have become the preferred place for social exchange. But, in contrast to what happens in other countries, drinking is never a solitary vice. Natives of Madrid are always accompanied (usually by office colleagues) when they enter a bar. There is always one conveniently located near the workplace.

The obligatory daily pilgrimage to the bar results in large part from the local schedule. When one doesn't eat lunch until 2 P.M., after having arrived at the office at 8, there is only one proven remedy to avoid hypoglycemia. Go down to the corner bistro. There, one can have a "cortado" (coffee "cut" with milk) or a "caña" (half-pint of beer), accompanied by the first "tapas" of the day. Tapas are those devilishly tempting hors d'oeuvres that invade

the counter of every self-respecting Spanish bar well before the lunch hour.

Don't try to call anyone around 10 A.M., even if he or she is supposed to have been at the office for at least an hour. You'd inevitably hear the answer, "Se fué a tomar café" (he left to get coffee). At first surprised, and then irritated, foreigners finally slip into the pattern. They'll observe that, in the final reckoning, the 10 A.M. "cortado" is not unpleasant and often permits people to resolve, in a more relaxed setting, small work-related problems that seemed so difficult at the office.

In the evening, cafés and bars are still in fashion. Like every inhabitant of a sunny country, the Spaniard loves to be out in the street until late at night. The national diversion consists then in "ir de copas," that is, in making the rounds of cafés. On the menu at each stopover — and they're often numerous — "cana" again, or better, "fino" (dry sherry), accompanied once again by those inevitable assorted "tapas," starting with small fish with olives, then proceeding to meatballs, croquettes, cheeses, and hams.

An itinerary to recommend? Why not begin by way of the venerable

Café Gijon on the Paséo de Recoletos, a café that is to Madrid what the Deux Magots is to Paris — a variegated meeting place of intellectuals and artists (real or presumed), politicians and film stars, and foreigners in search of the "real" Madrid.

Not far from there, on the way to the Plaza Mayor, there is Plaza Santa Ana, where "de copas" (the trendy youth) go. The human clusters that glue themselves around the bar at the Cerveceria Alemana virtually prevent access to the waiter. But, never mind — the important thing is not to have a drink, but to be seen. In the same style, the Cerveceria Santa Barbara in the square of the same name is the center of a mosaic of small streets filled with particularly lively "tapas" bars.

Stay then, and enjoy the Mediterranean privilege, the attractions of the open air. During the summer months, the Paseo de la Castellana — the big artery that crosses Madrid from north to south — and certain neighboring streets become filled with lively patios where Spaniards reform the world throughout the night. Join them, and the next morning after a brief sleep, recover your aplomb by taking your first "cortado" of the day in a nearby bistro.

N° 1   •• LISTEN

Listen carefully to what is said about these four people on the recording, and write the number representing the order of their description in the appropriate box.

Study the four sketches and find the order of responses in each conversation and the individuals who are speaking.

A _____

B _____

C _____

D _____

1	C	— ¿Diga...?
		— ¿Don Diego...?
4		— Soy Federico Hernández, el abogado. Estoy en el aeropuerto.
		— No. Soy su secretaria. ¿De parte de quién...?
		— Acabo de llegar de Barcelona.
	C	— ¡Ah! Es usted el abogado.

		— Tarde.
1	A	— Dígame
		— ¿María? Soy Pedro
4		— Estoy en el taller con Mariano.
		— ¿A qué hora vuelves?
	A	— ¿Dónde estás?

See solutions on page 2 of booklet.

🔊 LISTEN

THE MEETING

Paco and Paloma, who still have not met, arrange a meeting in a café in Madrid. But Paco greets the wrong person.

Paloma : *Perdone ¿ Ud. es el Sr. Fernández . . . ?*

Paco : *Sí, soy yo. Y tú eres Paloma, ¿verdad?*

Paloma : *Sí, encantada. ¿Cómo estás...?*

Paco : *Bien, gracias. ¿Y tú...?*

Paloma : *¡Es bonito este sitio!*

Paco : *Sí, es agradable. ¿Qué tomas...?*

Paloma : *Un café.*

Paco : *Tú vives en Madrid ¿no?*

Paloma : *Sí, vivo en Madrid pero soy de Sevilla.*

Paco : *¡Vaya! Modelo y andaluza.*

Paloma : *¿ Modelo . . . ? Yo trabajo de azafata en un banco francés.*

Paco : *¿Azafata? ¿No te llamas Paloma Montes?*

Paloma : *No. Yo me llamo Paloma García.*

Paco : *¡Qué confusión!*

. . . .

Paloma : *Perdone ¿Es usted el Sr. Fernández?*

Paco : *Y usted es Paloma Montes, modelo de la Agencia Marilluvia.*

Paloma : *Sí. ¿Por qué?*

Paco : *¡Uf! ¡Menos mal!*

🔊 LISTEN AND REPEAT
You will find the translation on page 2 of the booklet.

Madrid : 1. Plaza del Callao
2. Café Gijón (inside)
3. Café de Oriente (terrace)
4. Café Gijón (outside)

NOUNS

el encuentro — meeting, rendezvous
el señor — sir, gentleman *(1)*
la señora — ma'am *(1)*
la señorita — miss *(1)*
el sitio — place, spot
la azafata — hostess
el banco — bank
la confusión — confusion
el mar — sea
la lluvia — rain

---

la escuela — school
el colegio — (high) school
la universidad — university
el bufete — writing table
la empresa — (business) undertaking
la agencia de cambio — exchange agency
el despacho
la oficina — office
el taller — place of work, shop
la fábrica — factory
el laboratorio — laboratory

ADJECTIVES

encantado(a) — charmed
bonito(a) — pretty
agradable — pleasant
andaluz(a) — Andalusian
francés(esa) — Frenchman (woman) *(2)*

pequeño(a) — small
grande — large
bello(a) — goodlooking
viejo(a) — old
moderno(a) — modern

VERBS

tomar — to take
vivir — to live
trabajar — to work
llamarse — to be called

MISCELLANEOUS

perdone — excuse me
¿ cómo estás ? — How are you? *(3)*
¿ qué tal ? — How's it going?
bien — well
gracias — thank you
este (esta) — this (m), this (f)
¿ qué ? — What (is it)?
pero — but
¡ vaya ! — there you go!
¡ vaya confusión !
¡ qué confusión ! — What confusion!
¿ por qué ? — Why?
menos mal — fortunately

1. CONTACTING AN UNKNOWN PERSON

Perdone...
Disculpe... — Excuse me...

2. VERIFYING SOMEONE'S IDENTITY

¿ Tú eres Paloma ? — Are you really Paloma? Is it you, Paloma? *(4)*
¿ Usted es el señor Pérez ? — Are you Mr. P.? Is it you, Mr. P.? *(5)*
¿ Es Ud. la señora García ? — Are you Mrs. G.? Is it you, Mrs. G.?
¿ Es la señorita Sánchez ? — Are you Miss S.? Is it you, Miss S.?

3. ASKING HOW "THINGS ARE GOING" AND ANSWERING

¿ Cómo estás (tú) ? — How are you?
¿ Cómo está usted ? — How are you?
¿ Qué tal ? — How's it going?
Bien, gracias — Fine, thank you
¿ Y tú ? ¿ Y usted ? — And you? (informal) And you? (formal)

4. STATING YOUR NATIONALITY, PROFESSION, ETC.

Soy francés — I am French.
Soy de París — I'm from Paris
Vivo en Francia — I live in France
Soy fotógrafo
Trabajo de fotógrafo — I'm a photographer.
Yo trabajo en un banco — Me, I work in a bank *(6)*

| NOTES . . . | NOTES . . . | NOTES . . . | NOTES . . . |

(1) Abbreviations: "Sr.", "Sra.", "Srta". — (2) Pronouns of nationality are written without capital letters. — (3) Literally: "How are you?" — (4) In Spanish, using the familiar form is quite usual among young people after formal introductions. (5) "Señor (a/ita)": is always preceded by the definite article, except to address someone directly. — (6) The subject personal pronoun is generally omitted. But it is used in Spanish for emphasis or clarification.

1. STATING YOUR NATIONALITY

●● LISTEN

¿ Es usted francés ? (inglés)
• No, soy inglés
¿ Es usted alemana ? (española)
• No, soy española

Continue following the model:
¿ Es usted francés ? (inglés) — ¿ Es usted alemana ? (española) — ¿ Es usted italiana ? (francesa) — ¿ Es usted español ? (alemán) — ¿ Es usted sueca ? (suiza) — ¿ Es usted belga ? (holandés) — ¿ Es usted holandesa ? (belga).

Grammar: See C.

2. PRACTICING THE VERB "TRABAJAR"

●● LISTEN:

Yo trabajo en Madrid ¿ Y tú ? (agencia de publicidad)
• Yo trabajo en una agencia de publicidad

Answer the questions according to the model:
Yo trabajo en Madrid ¿ y tú ? (París) — Yo trabajo en un periódico ¿ y tú ? (agencia de publicidad) — Yo trabajo en una agencia de publicidad ¿ y usted ? (banco) — Yo trabajo en un banco ¿ y él ? (escuela) — Yo trabajo en una escuela ¿ Y vosotros ? (universidad) — Vosotros trabajáis en la universidad ¿ Y ustedes ? (empresa) — Ustedes trabajan en una empresa ¿ Y ellos ? (hotel).

Grammar: See K1.

3. PRACTICING THE VERB "VIVIR"

●● LISTEN:

francés, Madrid, yo,
• Soy francés pero vivo en Madrid

Continue by changing subjects (persons):
francés, Madrid, yo — alemana, París, tú — inglés, Berlín, usted — italianas, Lisboa, nosotros — portugueses, Estocolmo, ustedes — holandeses, Roma, vosotros — griego, Madrid, él — españoles, Atenas, ellos.

Grammar: See K1.

4. ASKING QUESTIONS

●● LISTEN

Me llamo José — Vivo en Madrid — Soy de Valencia
• ¿ Cómo te llamas ? ¿ Dónde vives ? ¿ De dónde eres ?

Continue according to the model:
Me llamo José — Vivo en Madrid — Soy de Valencia; Se llama Hernández — Vive en Tolosa — Es de Barcelona; Se llaman Dubois — Viven en París — Son de Burdeos.

Grammar: See G.

5. NATIONALITY; WORKPLACE

●● LISTEN:

Jacques Dubois — Francia — agencia de cambio
• Me llamo Jacques Dubois, soy francés, trabajo en una agencia de cambio

Introduce yourself as if you were each of the following people:
Jacques Dubois — Francia — agencia de cambio; Margareth Smith — Inglaterra — banco; Hans Vogel — Alemania — empresa textil; François Dupont — Francia — periódico; Pietro Germi — Italia — hotel; Soledad Montes — España — agencia de viajes.

6. PRONUNCIATION

●● LISTEN AND REPEAT:

La Señorita Pérez trabaja en una fábrica. ¿ Usted es fotógrafo ? No, soy escritor. Ella no es francesa, es griega. Nosotros somos empresarios. ¿ Dónde está el profesor de francés ? Con el ingeniero.

GREETINGS

Spaniards are warm and exuberant, even in their greetings. They prefer the "abrazo," which is quite unlike a cold handshake.

The "abrazo," a Spanish ritual that cannot be conveyed in all its warmth by the word "embrace," is preferably practiced in public — witnesses are actually an essential element. It consists of opening your arms in a wide and dramatic gesture, and placing them vigorously around the person you want to "abrazar." Then, you pound that person's back while leaning your head deliberately on one of his shoulders. Shifting shoulders necessitates a certain synchronization between the two participants; one acquires it easily after a few weeks south of the Pyranees.

The "abrazo" isn't the only example of Spanish warmth in introductions. Frequent recourse to kissing is another. Spaniards heap the opposite sex with kisses. A woman introduced to a man during an ele-

gant party (and whom he does not know from Eve) presents her cheek for a chaste kiss as soon as she has taken off her fur coat. Kissing a female minister or chief executive would become almost routine for a foreign newspaperman posted in Madrid.

In addition to embracing and kissing, the third point of informal Hispanic behavior is speaking in familiar terms. Unlike the widespread use of the formal French "vous," use of "Ustéd" is the exception rather than the rule when speaking Spanish. Speaking familiarly is common, no matter what age the conversationalists. Tradition only imposes use of the formal "you" on leavetakings. Otherwise, its use has not withstood the passage of time.

When Spaniards call one another by their first names, identification can become a rather tricky business. Half the Spaniards are named García, Rodriguez, Gonzalez or Mar-

tinez. In addition, it doesn't make things easier that half of the men's first names are Juan Carlos, Miguél, or José. (Avoid shouting out, when entering a café, to your friend Carlos Gonzalez whom you've just seen at the other end. A majority of those present may rise as one man to answer you!)

In writing, it has become fashionable to identify citizens by adding the family name of their mothers to that of their fathers. This enables you not to confuse Juan García Martinez and Juan García Gonzales. and also facilitates searches in the telephone book.

N° 1   ▭ LISTEN

After listening to the recorded information, write the corresponding number in the box adjacent to the correct map location.

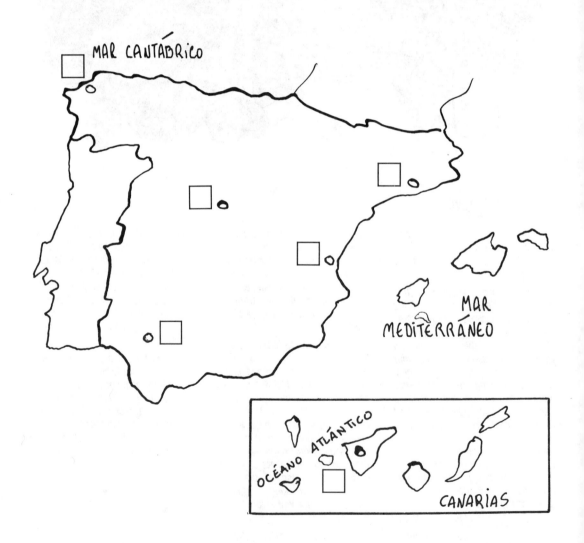

Match each person to his/her place of origin and profession.

Profesiones : *pintor · cineasta · futbolista · escritor · actor · actor y director de cine*
Países de origen : *americano · colombiano · argentino · italiano · francés · español*

1. Maradona es . . . . y . . . .
2. Jean-Paul Belmondo es . . . . y . . . .
3. Salvador Dalí es . . . . y . . . .
4. Federico Fellini es . . . . e . . . .
5. Charles Chaplin es . . . . y . . . .
6. G. García Márquez es . . . . y . . . .

By writing the nationality of each of these countries, you will arrive at the name of a famous Spanish painter in the vertical E column.

1. España
2. Italia
3. Francia
4. Alemania
5. Rusia
6. Austria
7. Portugal

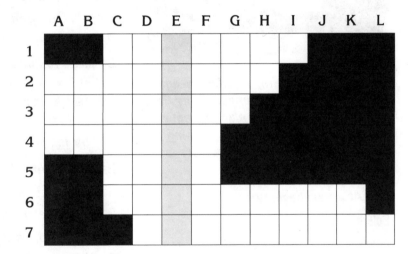

See solution on page 3 of booklet.

◉◉ LISTEN

TRAVELING

Soledad Louveiro, a publicity agent, goes to Barcelona accompanied by Paco and Paloma. There they plan to meet with the manager of an up-scale housing development to discuss a publicity campaign.

At a travel agency

Soledad : *¡Buenos días!*

Empleado : *¡Buenos días! ¿Qué desea...?*

Soledad : *Quiero tres billetes de avión para Barcelona.*

Empleado : *¿Para cuándo...?*

Soledad : *Para el viernes próximo.*

Empleado : *A ver... El viernes está completo, pero hay plazas libres en primera.*

Soledad : *De acuerdo. ¿Puedo pagar con tarjeta de crédito...?*

Empleado : *Sí, por supuesto.*

Soledad : *Gracias. Muy amable. Adiós.*

Empleado : *¡Hasta la vista!*

At the airport

Off : *«Iberia anuncia la salida de su vuelo 4.3.4. con destino a Barcelona...»*

Extranjero : *Perdone, no comprendo. ¿Qué vuelo es...?*

Paloma : *El vuelo 4.3.4. El embarque es por la puerta doce. Oye, Soledad, ya es la hora y Paco no llega.*

Paco : *¡Qué tráfico! ¿Llego tarde...?*

Paloma : *Tú siempre llegas tarde, Paco.*

Soledad : *Paloma, ¿llevas las tarjetas de embarque...?*

Paloma : *Sí, están en mi bolso.*

On the plane

Paco : *¿Fuma...?*

Señorita : *No, gracias; ahora, no.*

Paco : *¿Vive en Barcelona...?*

Señorita : *No, vivo en Ibiza ¿Y usted...?*

Paco : *En Madrid. Viajo a Barcelona por cuestiones de trabajo. Soy fotógrafo de prensa.*

Señorita : *¡Qué interesante!*

Off : *«Señores pasajeros, dentro de unos momentos tomaremos tierra en el aeropuerto de Barcelona».*

◉◉ LISTEN AND REPEAT
You will find the translation on page 3 of booklet.

1. *Chamartín Station (Madrid)*
2. *de Francia Station (Barcelona)*
3. *Atocha Station (Madrid)*
4. *Barajas Airport (Madrid)*

NOUNS

el billete — ticket
la plaza — plaza
la tarjeta (de crédito) — (credit) card
el aeropuerto — airport
el vuelo — flight
el extranjero — foreigner
el embarque — departure
la puerta — gate
la hora — hour
el tráfico — traffic
el bolso — purse
la cuestión — question
la prensa — press

el pasaporte — passport
la lista (de pasajeros) — (passenger) list
el asiento — seat
la tarde — afternoon
la noche — night, evening
el perro — dog

ADJECTIVES

bueno(a) — good
próximo(a) — next
completo(a) — complete, full
amable — amiable

VERBS

desear — to want
viajar — to travel
poder — to be able, can
pagar — to pay
comprender — to understand

llegar — to arrive
llevar — to carry

salir — to leave, to go out
entrar — to enter
reservar — to reserve

MISCELLANEOUS

de viaje — traveling
buenos días — good morning
para — for
cuando — when
el viernes próximo — next Friday (1)
a ver — Let's see
hay — there is, are
por supuesto — of course
muy — very
hasta la vista — see you soon
¡ oye ! — listen
ya — already
tarde — late
siempre — always
ahora — now
¡ qué interesante ! — How interesting! (2)

esta tarde — this afternoon (3)
esta noche — tonight, this evening
mañana por la mañana — tomorrow morning (4)
mañana por la tarde — tomorrow afternoon
pasado mañana — day after tomorrow
la semana próxima
la semana que viene — next week
hoy — today
el mes próximo — next month

1. GREETING SOMEONE COURTEOUSLY

Buenos días — Hello, Good day, Sir/Ma'am *(5)*
Buenas tardes — Good afternoon
Buenas noches — Good evening

2. GREETING SOMEONE IN A FAMILIAR WAY

Hola
Buenas — Hello. Good afternoon/evening

3. SAYING GOODBYE

Adiós — Goodbye
Hasta la vista
Hasta pronto — See you soon
Hasta luego — 'Till then

Hasta mañana — See you tomorrow
Hasta la tarde — Until this afternoon
Hasta la noche — See you tonight
Hasta el viernes — See you Friday *(1)*

4. ASKING SOMEONE WHAT HE/SHE WANTS

¿ Qué desea ?
¿ Que quiere ? — What do you want?
¿ Desea algo (alguna cosa) ?
¿ Quiere algo (alguna cosa) ? — Do you need something?

5. TELLING WHAT YOU WANT TO SOMEONE

Quiero un billete
Quisiera un billete — I would like a ticket
Un billete, por favor — A ticket, please

6. SAYING THANK YOU

Gracias — Thank you
Muchas gracias — Thank you very much
Gracias, muy amable — Thank you, you're very kind

NOTES . . .　　*NOTES . . .*　　*NOTES . . .*　　*NOTES . . .*

(1) Days of the week are always preceded by an article: "el" or "los." — (2) "Qué": unchanging exclamatory used before a noun or adjective. — (3) According to the situation, "tarde" may mean "afternoon" or "evening," and "noche" may mean "evening" or "night." — (4) "Por" is obligatory here. "Mañana," preceded by an article (la) means "morning"; if not, it means "tomorrow." — (5) Even in a very polite greeting, these forms are seldom followed by "Señor (a/ita)."

1. THE VERB "TO WANT"

⊙ ⊙ LISTEN:

un billete de tren (él)

* Quiere un billete de tren

Continue according to the model and changing the subjects (persons):

un billete de tren (él) — un billete de avión (yo) — la tarjeta de embarque (nosotros) — dos pasajes (tú) — el pasaporte (ella) — la lista de pasajeros (ellos) — un horario de trenes (vosotros).

Grammar: See K 1.

2. THE VERB "TO BE ABLE"

⊙ ⊙ LISTEN:

fumar (yo)

* Puedo fumar

Continue according to the model:

fumar (yo) — embarcar (él) — pagar con cheque (tú) — salir (nosotros) — entrar (usted) — desembarcar (vosotros) — entrar (ustedes) — reservar un pasaje (ellos).

Grammar: See K 1.

3. FINDING OUT THE DATE

⊙ ⊙ LISTEN:

avión (Barcelona)

* ¿Cuándo sale el avión para Barcelona?

Continue according to the model:

avión (Barcelona) — barco (Marsella) — tren (París) — autobús (Vigo) — expreso (Madrid) — vuelo (Sevilla).

Grammar: See I 2.

4. THE DATE

⊙ ⊙ LISTEN:

vuelo (lunes)

* Hay un vuelo el lunes

Continue according to the model:

vuelo (lunes) — autobús (martes) — tren (miércoles) — barco (jueves) — expreso (sábado) — vuelo directo (domingo).

5. REPEATING INFORMATION

⊙ ⊙ LISTEN:

vuelo

* Perdone ¿Qué vuelo es?

Continue according to the model:

vuelo — puerta de embarque — número de asiento — salida — compañía — ventanilla

6. PRONUNCIATION

⊙ ⊙ LISTEN AND REPEAT:

En el aeropuerto hay un restaurante. ¿Puedo viajar con el perro? En segunda no, pero sí en primera. Quiero reservar un billete para Pepe Parra. ¿Hay un tren rápido para París? ¿Puede repetir su nombre?

SELF-GOVERNMENT

Rather than a single country, there are actually several different Spains. Spain is overwhelming in its diversity and its distinctions; and this constitutes the main source of its cultural richness and of its political problems.

Is there another European country where intellectuals and historians get together so often to debate a similarly thorny problem as, "What is Spain?" This is an astonishing display of doubt and introspection for a country that was one of the first on the continent to establish itself on its present-day principles!

The problem of regional nationalism marks Spain's entire history. It is a problem of the perimeter confronting the center — the capital city that it has always had trouble accepting. Seen from the point of view of Barcelona or Bilbao, Madrid is a usurper, a lazy and unproductive city populated only by civil servants. The capital owes its title to Prince Philip II who decided to install the court there in 1561.

Industrialization further aggravated tensions. The weaving trades were established in Catalonia, metallurgy in the Basque country, and shipyards in Galicia — three regions that also have their own languages. "Peripheral" nationalism was born; Catalonians and Basques are well-founded in considering themselves engines that drive the national economy. Why still pay tribute to Madrid, "that mixture of Kansas City and village of la Manche, populated by subsecretaries?" according to the caustic description of author Camilio José Cela.

These separatist tendencies have never stopped weighing on the political life of Spain. Basque nationalism was at the bottom of three bloody conflicts (the Carlist wars in the nineteenth century). In a less aggressive, but equally resolute manner, the Catalonians (and in a smaller measure the Galicians) also demanded recognition by Madrid of their rights as a distinct minority.

They obtained it in the 1930s, in a short-lived way, with the Republic. Then Franco imposed 40 years of merciless, centralized rule on Spain. Centralization was imposed not by belief, but by fire and blood. The bitterness and resentment that developed during Franco's dictatorship has left deep scars to this day.

Under such conditions, recognizing the reality of many different Spains constitutes one of the prime tasks of rewon democracy. It is now a fact; Spain is divided henceforth into 16 autonomous "communities," each possessing an elected parliament and regional government. The prerogatives of the Basques and the Catalonians are the most extensive. They include, notably, an autonomous police force, a regional television channel, and important powers in educational and cultural matters. For the first time, they also have the right to levy taxes.

Of course, the peoples of the periphery think there is still insufficient autonomy, and cite the Confederate States of America as an example. This promises to be one of the liveliest debates in Spanish political life for many years to come. But thanks to democracy, spirited debate appears to have replaced force on all sides!

N° 1   ●● LISTEN

Listen to the recording, place in order and complete the schedule with the international departures.

CÍA	VUELO	DESTINO	SALIDA	PUERTA DE EMBARQUE
IB			8,20	
AF			10,40	
LH			13,10	
BA			17,15	
SR			20,00	

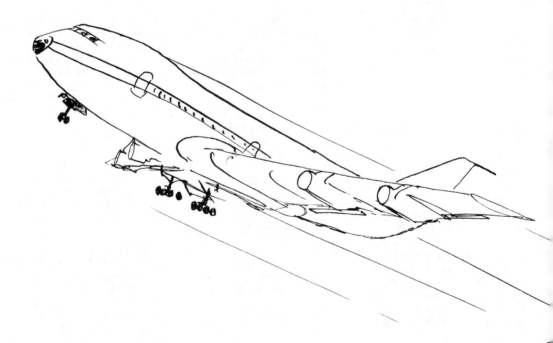

Read this announcement heard at the airport and complete Señor Dominguez's embarcation card.

Aviso urgente

«Se ruega al médico D. Juan Domínguez, español, que viaja a Barcelona con su hija María por asunto de negocios, llame a su domicilio en Aranjuez por asunto familiar grave o bien a los teléfonos 22.28.08.90 y 22.28.03.47»

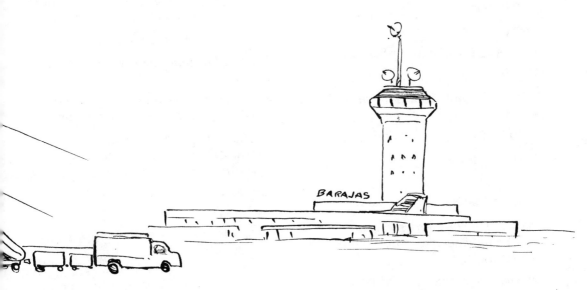

TARJETA DE EMBARQUE

Nombre ·

APELLIDOS ·

Nacionalidad ·

Profesión ·

Teléfono(s) ·

Motivos del viaje ·

Lugar a dónde se dirige ·

· ·

BARAJAS

See answers on page 4 of booklet.

●● LISTEN

AT THE HOTEL

Soledad, Paloma and Paco have arrived at Barcelona. They are staying in a downtown hotel.

In a taxi

Taxista : *¿A dónde van?*

Paco : *A la Calle Mayor n° 7, por favor.*

. . . .

Taxista : *Es aquí. Son, mil cuatrocientas pesetas.*

Soledad : *Tenga, el resto es para usted.*

Taxista : *Gracias.*

At the hotel

Soledad : *¡Buenas tardes! Tengo reservadas tres habitaciones a nombre de Soledad Louveiro.*

Conserje : *Un momento... No encuentro su nombre.*

Soledad : *Se escribe con «v». «L-O-U-V-E-I-R-O»*

Conserje : *¡Ah, claro! Aquí está. Habitaciones 521, 522 y 523. ¿Cuánto tiempo se van a quedar...?*

Paco : *Une semana. Hasta el martes.*

Conserje : *¡Muy bien!... El mozo sube con ustedes.*

Mozo : *¿Son éstas sus maletas...?*

Soledad : *No, mis maletas son aquéllas y también esta bolsa y ese paquete.*

Mozo : *Por aquí, por favor.*

Soledad : *¡Qué bonito ascensor!*

Mozo : *Sí, es muy antiguo. También el hotel.*

. . . .

Mozo : *Aquí tienen sus habitaciones... Hay una cafetería en la primera planta.*

Paloma : *¿Tiene restaurante el hotel...?*

Mozo : *El restaurante está en la segunda planta.*

Paco : *Tu habitación es muy alegre. ¡Mira! Esa es la Plaza de Los Patos.*

Paloma : *Hay mucha gente en la calle todavía. ¿Damos un paseo...?*

Soledad : *Yo no puedo, espero una llamada.*

●● LISTEN AND REPEAT:
You will find the translation on page 5 of booklet.

1. Hotel Palacio (Madrid)
2. Small hotel in Barcelona
3. 4. Parador de Sigüenza (inside and outside views)
5. Pueblo Indalo (Almería)

NOUNS

el taxista — taxi driver
la calle — street
el número — number
el resto — remainder, change
la habitación — room
la cama — bed
el nombre — (first) name
el apellido — family name
el conserje — concierge, receptionist
el momento — moment, instant
el mozo — bellhop, waiter
la maleta — suitcase
el equipaje — baggage
la bolsa — travel bag
el paquete — package
el ascensor — elevator
la planta — floor
el piso — floor *(1)*
la gente — people
la llamada — (telephone) call

---

la llave — key

sexto(a) — sixth
séptimo(a) — seventh
octavo(a) — eighth
noveno(a) — ninth
décimo(a) — tenth

VERBS

ir — to go
tener — to have
encontrar — to find
escribir — to write
quedarse — to remain *(2)*
subir — to go up
bajar — to go down
mirar — to look at
dar un paseo — to take a walk
esperar — to wait for, to hope

---

deletrear — to spell

MISCELLANEOUS

tenga — have *(3)*
a nombre de — in the name of
¡ claro ! — of course!
¿ cuánto tiempo ? — how long?
hasta — until
también — also
por aquí — through here
aquí tienen — here you have
mucho(a) — a great deal, much
todavía — still

ADJECTIVES

antiguo(a) — old
alegre — happy
primero(a) — first
segundo(a) — second
tercero(a) — third
cuarto(a) — fourth
quinto(a) — fifth

HOW TO SAY IT

---

1. GIVING YOUR ADDRESS

Voy a la Calle Mayor n°3 — I'm going to 3 Calle Mayor *(4)*
Vivo en la Plaza Mayor — I live on Plaza Mayor
Estoy en el Gran Hotel — I'm at the Grand Hotel

---

2. ASKING SOMEONE'S NAME

¿ Cómo te llamas ? — What's your name? (informal address)
¿ Cómo se llama (usted) ? — What is your name? (formal address)
¿ Cuál es tu (su) apellido ? — What is your last name? *(5)*
¿ Cuál es tu nombre ? — What's your name. . . . your given name? *(5)*
¿ Cuál es su nombre ? — What is your name? (formal address)

---

3. STATING WHAT FLOOR IT'S ON

Está en la planta baja — It's on the ground floor
Esta en la primera planta
Está en el primer piso — It's on the first floor *(6)*

---

4. STATING THE LOCATION OF SOMEONE OR SOMETHING

Es aquí — It's here
Está aquí
Aquí está — Here it is
Por aquí — Through here
Aquí tiene su habitación — Here's your room *(7)*
Aquí tienes tu maleta — Here's your suitcase (familiar address) *(7)*

NOTES . . .　　　　NOTES . . .　　　　NOTES . . .　　　　NOTES . . .

(1) "Piso," which means "(whole) floor" like "planta" can also mean "apartment" — (2) "To stay in a place" is expressed by the verb "quedarse," — (3) "Tener" usually means "to have." Here it has the sense of "to hold on to." — (4) In an address, the number is placed before the name of the street. — (5) "Apellido" indicates only the family name. "Nombre" indicates either the first name or the combination of the first and last name. — (6) When "primero" modifies a masculine singular noun, it becomes "primer." "Primera," before a feminine singular noun does not change. — (7) Literally: "Here you have."

1. SPELLING SOMEONE'S NAME

👂👂 LISTEN:

MARTÍN
* *M-A-R-T-I-N*

Spell the following names as in the model:
HENRÍQUEZ — CASTAÑEDA — RODRÍGUEZ
— BERLANGA — JARAMILLO — VALDEZ —
GUTIÉRREZ.

2. STATING AN ADDRESS

👂👂 LISTEN:

Calle Colón n° 460 (yo)
* *Voy a la calle Colón n° 460*
Avenida Castilla n° 115 (nosotros)
* *Vamos a la Avenida Castilla n° 115*

State the address changing the persons as in the model:
Calla Colón n° 460 (yo) — Avenida Castilla
n° 115 (nosotros) — Calle México n° 80 (yo) —
Calle León n° 13 (nosotros) — Avenida Repúbli-
ca n° 15 (yo) — Calle del Prado n° 7 (nosotros).

Grammar: See I 1.

3. DEMONSTRATIVES

👂👂 LISTEN:

Esta habitación es de Manuel
* *Ésta es la habitación de Manuel*
¿Esos bolsos son de Juan?
* *¿Ésos son los bolsos de Juan?*

**Change the sentences using the demonstrative pro-
nouns as in the model:**
Esta habitación es de Manuel — ¿Esos bolsos
son de Juan? — Aquella maleta es de los clientes — ¿Estas llaves son de Luis? — Ese coche es de María — ¿Esas maletas son de ustedes?   Grammar: See D 3.

4. PRACTICING THE VERB "TENER"

👂👂 LISTEN:

habitación (yo)
* *Tengo reservada una habitación*
dos billetes (nosotros)
* *Tenemos reservados dos billetes*

**Continue according to the model. Be careful! Don't
forget to make "reservado" agree with the noun it
follows: reservado, reservada, reservados or
reservadas.**
habitación (yo) — dos billetes (nosotros) — un
asiento (tú) — plazas (vosotros) — una mesa
(usted) — un pasaje (ustedes).

Grammar: See K VIII.

5. POSSESSIVES

👂👂 LISTEN:

habitación (yo)
* *¿Ésta es mi habitación?*
bolso (nosotros)
* *¿Éste es nuestro bolso?*

**Continue according to the model while using the
possessive adjectives:**
habitación (yo) — bolso (nosotros) — bolso
(vosotros) — maleta (ustedes) — billete (nosotros) — hotel (vosotros) — cliente (usted) —
llave (ustedes).

Grammar: See D 2.

6. PRONUNCIATION

👂👂 LISTEN AND REPEAT:
* *Yo me llamo Paco — Mi apellido es
Castillo — ¿Estas llaves son tuyas? —
No, son de Yáñez — Ya llega el avi-
ón — El hotel «Bayona» está en esta
calle.*

HOTELS AND INNS

Tourist country par excellence, Spain has a hotel network to satisfy the most demanding. From luxurious seaside palaces with two swimming pools and a half-dozen restaurants, to neat country inns, everyone can find something that fits his needs. Spain has more than 400 four- or five-star hotels, 10,000 that are three-star or less, and almost 12,000 inns.

There's a place for everyone — providing that you always remember to reserve in advance for the summer season. This is especially true if you want to be at the seashore. Some 50 million foreign visitors (more than one for each resident) come to Spain each year. Forty-five percent of those come between July and September. In the Canary Islands, however, the season lasts for the entire year; Scandinavians go there in winter, fleeing their frigid climate for an African-like warmth.

At the cost of a big chunk out of your vacation budget, how would you like to live the life of a pasha for a few nights? Why not do it at Puente Romano, the beautiful hotel in the luxurious seaside resort of Marbella? There, you can mix with the sheiks who have made it their gathering place. Or, perhaps rendezvous with the international financial elite at Hostal de la Gavina, near the smart S'Agaro beach on the Costa Brava. In Santiago de Compostela, at the sophisticated Hostal de los Reyes Católicos, (built by royalty as

a hospital in the sixteenth century and now renovated), you can abandon yourself to the arms of Morpheus in a canopied bed.

In a more affordable category, Spain offers you a type of hotel that has no equivalent in the rest of Europe. These are 86 "paradores" administered directly by the Secretary of State for Tourism. The first ones were constructed in the 1960s, just when the government began to realize that tourism would become the key to growth. For the most part, they were built at historic sites — in chateaux or monasteries that were fortuitously renovated for the purpose. Afterward, more modern paradores were built — mostly in the coastal regions.

As a group, paradores offer a better value for the money than their private counterparts — as well as a certain distinction. You can easily visit all four corners of the country, stopping at one every night. For those who visit Andalusia, Carmona Parador (not far from Seville) offers

fountains and a patio that reminds one of the Arabian nights. Arcos de la Frontera in the province of Cádiz is nestled in a castle overlooking one of the most beautiful and pristine Andalusian villages. The Grenada Parador allows you the rare privilege of falling asleep at the very gates of the Alhambra, opposite the peaceful Generalife gardens.

The Madrid area is surrounded by a string of historic paradores. Avila is set into the thick wall which encircles the city. Siguenza is in a twelfth-century palace, and Chinchón is in a restful convent. Toledo and Segovia have modern paradores.

Travelers crossing the Pyrenees can choose either the Viella Parador or Bielsa, at the foot of snowcapped peaks. As for those who wish to combine the pleasures of history with those of the sea, they would lean toward the splendid Bayona Parador, situated in a castle that juts out on a promontory on the Galician coast, south of Vigo.

N° 1 ●● LISTEN

Listen carefully to the recording and write, in the correct box, the number that corresponds to the place where the scene unfolds.

Read these ads and tell whether these statements are true or false.

EL SALER

El parador nacional de El Saler
está situado a 20 kms de Valencia.
Es moderno. Tiene más de 50 habitaciones dobles
y 25 sencillas.
Se encuentra situado cerca del monte
y no lejos del mar.

SANTILLANA DEL MAR

Es un bello parador, situado
a pocos kms de Santander.
Tiene habitaciones dobles a 9 000 pts
y sencillas a 5 000.
Es un parador tranquilo, aireado y cómodo.

SAN MARCOS

Este bello edificio, hoy parador,
recibe mucha gente en verano.
Las habitaciones son a 11 000 pts las dobles
y a 7 000 las sencillas.
Está en la ciudad de León, antiguo reino.

	SI	NO
1. El Parador Santillana del Mar está a 20 kms de Sevilla		
2. El Parador de San Marcos se encuentra en León		
3. El Parador nacional de El Saler está situado en Valencia		
4. El Parador de San Marcos tiene habitaciones dobles a 11 000 pts . .		
5. El Parador Santillana del Mar es tranquilo, aireado, cómodo		
6. El Parador de El Saler tiene 50 habitaciones sencillas		
7. El Parador de San Marcos es un edificio moderno		
8. El Parador de El Saler tiene habitaciones a 9 000 pts		
9. El Parador de Santillana del Mar está situado en Santander		

See answers on page 6 of booklet.

◉◉ LISTEN

IN PORT

Paco : *¿Dónde? ¡Ah, sí! Allí. Creo que es un avión.*

Paloma : *¡Estás tonto! Es el faro, la luz del faro.*

Paloma : *¿Quieres un cigarrillo...?*

Paco : *Después, ahora prefiero un café.*

During this time . . .

Conserje : *Una conferencia de Madrid para usted.*

Soledad : *¡Muchas gracias! ¿Diga...?*

Pablo : *Mamá, somos nosotros. ¿Cómo estás...?*

Soledad : *Bien. Estamos ya en Barcelona. ¿Cómo estáis vosotros...?*

Pablo : *Estamos bien, estamos estudiando francés con el nuevo método.*

Soledad : *¿Ah, sí...? ¡Qué bien! ¿Y tú, Nieves?*

Nieves : *Me aburro, estoy cansada y no quiero estudiar francés.*

Soledad : *¿No tienes un libro interesante...?*

Nieves : *No.*

Soledad : *Entonces, puedes mirar la tele. ¡Hala! Hasta mañana.*

Los dos : *¡Adiós, mamá!*

Paloma and Paco take a walk along Barcelona's port. Soledad stays at the hotel.

Paco : *¿A dónde vamos...?*

Paloma : *Al puerto, si quieres.*

Paco : *¿Vamos en taxi o a pie...?*

Paloma : *En taxi. Está lejos.*

. . . .

Paco : *¿Ves aquellos barcos...?*

Paloma : *¡Qué grandes!*

Paco : *Este puerto es muy importante. Llegan barcos de todo el mundo.*

Paloma : *¿Y aquella luz...?*

◉◉ LISTEN AND REPEAT

You will find the translation on page 6 of booklet

Barcelona: 1. Plaza Mayor
2. Statue of Columbus
3. Puerto
4. Las Ramblas

NOUNS

el puerto — port
el barco — boat
el mundo — world
la luz — light
el faro — lighthouse
el cigarrillo — cigarette
el cortado — coffee with a little milk
el café con leche — half coffee, half milk
la estatua — statue
la estación — station
la conferencia — telephone call between cities
el método — method
el libro — book
el beso — kiss

_____

el amigo — friend

ADJECTIVES

grande/gran — large/great *(1)*
importante — important
tonto(a) — silly
neuvo(a) — new
cansado(a) — tired

_____

contento(a) — happy
feliz — happy
triste — sad
joven — young
casado(a) — married
soltero(a) — unmarried

separado(a) — separated
divorciado(a) — divorced

VERBS

creer — to believe
preferir — to prefer
pasear — to take a walk
estudiar — to study
aburrirse — to be bored

_____

descansar — to rest
escuchar — to listen to
nacer — to be born

MISCELLANEOUS

¿ a dónde ? — where?
a pie — on foot
lejos — far
todo(a) — all
todo el mundo — the entire world, everyone *(2)*
después — after(wards)
antes — before
un poco — a bit, a little
junto a — next to
al lado de — alongside
cerca (de) — near
desde — (coming) from
¡ qué bien ! — Very good!
¡ hala ! ¡ hasta mañana ! — Get going, until tomorrow!
besos — (hugs and) kisses

1. STATING OWNERSHIP

Es mi maleta — It's my suitcase
Es la mía — It's mine
Aquí tienes tu bolso — Here's your purse
Aquí tienes el tuyo — Here's yours

Aquí está su habitación — Here's his room *(3)*
Aquí está la suya — Here's yours *(3)*

2. ASKING WHERE ONE IS, ONE GOES, FROM WHERE SOMEONE COMES

¿ Dónde estas ? — Where are you?
¿ A dónde vamos ?
¿ Dónde vamos ? — Where are we going?

¿ De dónde llegan ? — Where are they arriving from? Where are you arriving from?

3. SAYING WHERE ONE IS, GOES, AND FROM WHERE ONE COMES

Estoy en Valencia — I am in Valencia *(4)*
Viven en Portugal — They live in Portugal
Estudia en Argentina — She/He studies in Argentina
Se queda en la habitación — She/He remains in her/his room
Viajo a Barcelona — I'm traveling to Barcelona
¿ Vamos al puerto ? — Shall we go to the port?
Llegan de Madrid — They arrive from Madrid
Soy de Sevilla — I am from Seville

4. STATING A DATE

Madrid, 31 de enero de 1988 — Madrid, January 31, 1988 *(5)*
Nací el primero de mayo de 1954 — I was born on May 1, 1954 *(6)*
Llega el viernes 10 — She/He arrives on Friday the 10th
Estamos a dos — It's the 2nd (of the month)

| NOTES . . . | NOTES . . . | NOTES . . . | NOTES . . . |

(1) Placed before the noun, "grande" becomes "gran" and means "great." — (2) "Todos" or "toda la gente" are other Spanish equivalents for "everyone." — (3) The possessive adjective "su" can mean "his/her," "their" or "your." The possessive pronoun "el suyo/la suya" can mean "his/hers," "theirs" or "yours." — (4) The place in which one is located is introduced by the preposition "en," when it concerns a town, country, or some other place. The place to which one is going is introduced by the preposition "a." — (5) In a date, the day, month and year are separated by "de." — (6) The "first" of the month is expressed by the ordinal number "primero." All other days take cardinal numbers: "dos, tres, etc."

1. POSSESSIVE PRONOUNS

[● ●] LISTEN:

Éste es mi bolso.
- *Este bolso es mío*

Continue according to the model using the possessive pronouns:
Éste es mi bolso — Éste es tu pasaporte — Éste es·nuestro billete — Ésta es vuestra habitación — Éstos son mis libros — Ésta es nuestra casa — Éste es su coche — Éstos son sus amigos — Éstas son nuestras maletas.

Grammar: See F3.

2. "TO WANT" AND "TO PREFER"

[● ●] LISTEN:

cigarrillo · café · yo
- *No quiero un cigarrillo. Prefiero un café*

Continue according to the model using the verbs "querer" and "preferir":
cigarrillo · café · yo; té · café · nosotros; salir · descansar · él; dormir · pasear · ellos; estudiar · escuchar la radio · vosotros; ir en taxi · ir a pie · tú; leer · mirar la tele · ella.

Grammar: See KI.

3. LOCATING A PLACE

[● ●] LISTEN:

estación · hotel · lejos
- *¿La estación está lejos del hotel?*

Continue according to the model using "cerca de," "lejos de," "junto a." Careful: before a masculine noun you must use "del" or "al"
estación · hotel · lejos; aeropuerto · centro · cerca; restaurante · puerto · junto; plaza · estación · al lado; bar · recepción · junto; aeropuerto · lejos · ciudad.

Grammar: See I 1c.

4. NAME, DATE OF BIRTH

[● ●] LISTEN:

María Romero · 14 de enero de 1955
- *Me llamo María Romero. Nací el 14 de enero*

Continue according to the model:
María Romero · 14 de enero de 1955; Juan García · 15 de agosto de 1980; Pedro Alcázar · 11 de julio de 1973; Carmen de Sierra · 8 de diciembre de 1948; Julio Muñoz · 25 de mayo de 1948; Soledad Pérez · 11 de noviembre de 1982; Miguel Alfonsín · 11 de febrero de 1967.

5. CIVIL STATUS

[● ●] LISTEN:

Susana Louveiro · casada · dos hijos
- *Soy Susana Louveiro. Soy casada y tengo dos hijos*

Introduce yourself as if you were each of the following people:
Susana Louveiro · casada · dos hijos; Juan García · soltero; Pedro Alcázar · casado · 1 hija; Francisco Quesada · casado · 3 hijos; Laura Castillo · divorciada · 3 hijas; Patricia Márquez · soltera.

6. PRONUNCIATION

[● ●] LISTEN AND REPEAT:

- *Esta es su habitación. ¿Quiere un cigarrillo? El hotel está cerca de la ciudad. Al lado de la plaza, hay una estación. En la recepción reciben a los clientes. Me llamo Hernández y nací en marzo.*

YOUTH

Don't look for the word "pasota" in your Spanish dictionary because you won't find it there. It is also very difficult to translate. The adjective is, however, often used by Spaniards to define the critical manner of today's youth.

A young person described as "pasota" is one who is bored, apathetic, without ideals, depoliticized. Spaniards under the age of 20 are sometimes called that by their elders because the generation gap is very tangible south of the Pyrenees. An abyss exists between generations whose life experiences are as different from one another as you can imagine. In two decades, the nation has seen more spectacular change than any other European country.

Today's young Spaniards did not experience the Franco era their parents lived through, nor the Civil War that their grandparents lived through. Only in history books have they heard (often in a watered-down version) of the tragic fratricidal confrontations of the Civil War. They matured at the same time as democracy; they never knew Franco.

Yesterday's battles are no longer theirs. They see today's problems very differently from their elders. The most important concern is becoming part of society. Doing so is especially difficult in a country that has the highest unemployment rate in western Europe. The unemployment situation, above all, hits the young looking for their first jobs. Admission to high school, or even college, no longer guarantees them of being hired. Education expanded greatly in Spain after its baby boom of the '60s, but graduating from school opens fewer and fewer doors.

This preoccupation was at the center of demonstrations that occurred in Spain in early 1987. At that time, tens of thousands of students took to the streets for almost two months to express their unhappiness. Obviously, the youth were not as "pasota" as they would have their elders believe. Without trying to reform the whole world, they demanded that education become more democratic and more relevant.

Even if they are occasional protesters, today's young Spaniards are not prone to philosophical arguments. Above all, they want to live quickly and intensely. In this regard, the new generation has made a great leap compared to the one that preceded it. In a traditionalist country where the cultural influence of a still-conservative Catholic Church was predominant, a class of young people without hangups and with liberated morals suddenly appeared — ignoring the taboos of the elders.

Such young people would probably make Franco turn over in his grave. More than anything else, they symbolize the new Spain. In a mere 15 years, after a spectacular transformation, this new Spain has buried yesterday's ghosts and adjusted its structure and values to match those of western Europe — into which it is now fully integrated.

●● LISTEN

La Tarara

Traditional song
(Sung and arranged by Joaquín Díaz)

Tiene la Tarara unos pantalones	La Tarara has a pair of trousers
que de arriba abajo todos son botones.	from top to bottom only buttons
La Tarara sí, la Tarara no;	La Tarara yes, La Tarara no;
la Tarara, niña, que la bailo yo.	La Tarara, little girl, It is I who dance.
Baila la Tarara con bata de cola,	She dances, la Tarara, in a dress with a long train
y si no hay pareja, bailotea sola.	and, with no partner, she dances all alone.
La Tarara sí, la Tarara no...	La Tarara yes, la Tarara no . . .
Tiene la Tarara unos calzoncillos,	La Tarara has a pair of shorts,
que de arriba abajo todos son bolsillos.	from top to bottom only pockets.
La Tarara sí, la Tarara no...	La Tarara yes, la Tarara no . . .
Tiene la Tarara un vestido blanco,	La Tarara has a white dress
que sólo se pone en el Jueves Santo.	which she wears only on Holy Thursday.
La Tarara sí, la Tarara no...	La Tarara yes, la Tarara no . . .

IDIOMS

METERSE EN CAMISA DE ONCE VARAS
(Get into a shirt with eleven stays)

Filling your life with trouble

NO SOLTAR PRENDA
(Not let go of any valuables)

Don't give up a crumb

HACER DE SU CAPA UN SAYO
(Make a coat out of one's cape)

Making it all up in your head

CONOCER EL PAÑO
(Know the fabric)

Know the good from the bad

1.1

COMPLETE with SER or ESTAR : *Yo . . . . fotógrafa. Mi nombre . . . . Rosario. Ellos . . . . en Madrid. ¿ Vosotros . . . . . periodistas? ¿ Dónde . . . . . la agencia? ¿ Quiénes . . . . . ustedes?*

TRANSLATE : *It's Pablo Guzmán. His last name is Guzmán. His first name is Pablo. We are in Paris, and you? Who is it? Yes, it's me. Good morning. See you tomorrow.*
¿ Está Paloma, por favor? No, está en la agencia. Yo soy periodista. ¿ Y usted? Yo soy estudiante. ¿ Nos vemos en un café? ¿ Dónde está el café? De acuerdo. Adiós.

1.2

COMPLETE with the verbs in parentheses : *Nosotros . . . . (vivir) y . . . . (trabajar) en Madrid. Raúl . . . . (vivir) en Madrid pero . . . . (trabajar) en Barcelona. Ana y Paco . . . . (vivir) en Granada y . . . . (trabajar) en una empresa francesa. Yo . . . . (vivir) en París y . . . . (trabajar) en Oviedo.*

TRANSLATE : *¿ Qué tal? ¿ Cómo estás? Bien, gracias. ¿ Y tú? ¿ Qué tomas? Un café. ¿ Eres francesa y vives en Madrid? ¿ Cómo te llamas? ¿ Dónde trabajas?*
Excuse me, are you Mr. Fernández? Me, I am María López. I am Spanish. She lives in Paris and she works in a French firm. She works as a secretary.

1.3

COMPLETE with the verbs in parentheses: : *¿ . . . . (tener · usted) un billete para Bilbao? — ¿ . . . . (poder · yo) pagar con cheque? . . . . (querer · nosotros) el horario de trenes. Mañana . . . . (salir · yo) para Roma. ¿ . . . . (poder · nosotros) llamar por teléfono?*

TRANSLATE: : *¿ Qué desea? Un billete de tren para Zaragoza. ¿ Cuándo hay vuelos para Barcelona? Los lunes no hay. ¿ Quiere viajar el martes? Sí, por supuesto. Gracias, muy amable.*
Can I smoke? I would like a round-trip ticket for Toulouse. We arrive Saturday morning. Can I buy the ticket now? Of course. The train leaves Friday evening.

1.4

COMPLETE with EN / AL / A LA / DEL / DE LA : *Voy . . . . hotel Miraflores. Estoy . . . . el hotel. Nuestra habitación está . . . . el 5° Piso. Vengo . . . . banco. Vamos . . . . estación. Venimos . . . . agencia.*

TRANSLATE : *Aquí tienen sus habitaciones. ¿ Estos son sus bolsos? No, éstos no, aquéllos. No encuentro su nombre. Por aquí, por favor. ¡ Qué bonito ascensor! ¿ Cuánto es, por favor?*
I have reserved two rooms in the name of Pierre Loti. The restaurant is on the ground floor. It's here. The hotel is very comfortable. There are many people here. How long are you going to stay?

1.5

COMPLETE with SER or ESTAR : *Pierre . . . . francés. Usted . . . . cansado. Los franceses . . . . simpáticos. El hotel . . . . moderno. Gabriel . . . . en Lisboa. El puerto . . . . lejos de la estación. Jacques . . . . soltero.*

TRANSLATE : *Estamos aburridos. ¡ Qué bien! Besos a los dos. La parada de taxis está junto al banco. La habitación no tiene ducha.*
Where are you going? I believe that it's tomorrow. Do you prefer coffee? The port is far from here. Thank you very much. See you soon. We are already in Madrid.

See answers on page 33 of booklet

MORE VOCABULARY

THE DAYS OF THE WEEK

el lunes — Monday
el martes — Tuesday
el miércoles — Wednesday
el jueves — Thursday
el viernes — Friday
el sábado — Saturday
el domingo — Sunday

THE MONTHS

enero (m) — January
febrero (m) — February
marzo (m) — March
abril (m) — April
mayo (m) — May
junio (m) — June
julio (m) — July
agosto (m) — August
septiembre (m) — September
octubre (m) — October
noviembre (m) — November
diciembre (m) — December

SPAIN'S REGIONS

Andalucía (f) — Andalusia
andaluz(a) — Andalusian
Aragón (m) — Aragon
aragonés(esa) — Aragonese
Asturias (f pl) — Asturias
asturiano(a) — Asturian
Baleares (f pl) — Balearic Islands
balear — Balearic
Canarias (f pl) — Canary Islands
canario(a) — Canarian
Cantabria (f) — Cantabria
cántabro(a) — from Cantabria
Castilla y León (f) — Castille and Leon
castellano(a) · leonés(esa) — from Castile - Leon
Castilla La Mancha (f) — Castile La Mancha
castellano(a)·manchego(a) — Castilian from La Mancha
Cataluña (f) — Catalunia
catalán(ana) — Catalan
Extremadura (f) — Extremadura
extremeño(a) — from Extremadura

Galicia (f) — Galicia
gallego(a) — Galician
Madrid(m) — Madrid
madrileño(a) — Madrilenian
Murcia (f) — Murcia
murciano(a) — from Murcia
Navarra (f) — Navarra
navarro(a) — Navarrese
País vasco (Euzkadi) (m) — Basque Country
vasco(a) — Basque
La Rioja (f) — La Rioja
riojano(a) — from La Rioja
Comunidad valenciana (f) — Valencian Community
valenciano(a) — Valencian

NATIONALITIES

alemán(ana) — German
argelino(a) — Algerian
argentino(a) — Argentinian
australiano(a) — Australian
austriaco(a) — Austrian
belga — Belgian
brasileño(a) — Brazilian
búlgaro(a) — Bulgarian
canadiense — Canadian
checoslova-co(a) — Czechoslovakian
chileno(a) — Chilian
chino(a) — Chinese
colombiano(a) — Colombian
cubano(a) — Cuban
danés(esa) — Dane, Danish
ecuatoriano(a) — Ecuadoran
egipcio(a) — Egyptian
escocés(esa) — Scotsman (woman)
español(a) — Spaniard
estadounidense, americano(a) — American
filipino(a) — Filipino (Philippine)
finlandés(esa) — Finn
francés(esa) — French
británico(a) — British
griego(a) — Greek
holandés(esa) — Dutch
húngaro(a) — Hungarian
indio(a) — Indian
inglés(esa) — English
irlandés(esa) — Irish

islandés(esa) — Islandic
israelí — Israeli
italiano(a) — Italian
japonés(esa) — Japanese
libanés(esa) — Lebanese
libio(a) — Libyan
luxemburgués(esa) — Luxemburgian
marroquí — Moroccan
mexicano(a), mejicano(a) — Mexican
noruego(a) — Norwegian
pakistaní — Pakistani
peruano(a) — Peruvian
polaco(a) — Polish
portugués(esa) — Portuguese
rumano(a) — Rumanian
ruso(a) — Russian
sirio(a) — Syrian
sueco(a) — Swedish
suizo(a) — Swiss
tunecino(a) — Tunisian
turco(a) — Turk
soviético(a) — Soviet
venezolano(a) — Venezuelan
vietnamita — Vietnamese
yugoslavo(a) — Yugoslav

1. OMIT THE PRONOUN WHEN IT IS NOT NECESSARY

— **(Yo)** me llamo Alberto Fernández y **(yo)** soy español. ¿ Y **(tú)** ?
— **(Yo)** soy catalán y **(yo)** me llamo Caballé.
— **(Yo)** soy madrileño. ¿ Y **(tú)** también ?
— No, **(yo)** soy francés.
— ¿ Tú eres Pedro Álvarez, verdad ?
— Sí, soy **(yo)**.

2. CHANGE TO FEMININE FORM

Este es un amigo francés. . . . .
El cliente es muy simpático. . . . .
Nuestro fotógrafo es un hombre interesante. . . . .
El profesor de mi hijo es francés. . . . .
Es el amigo de su padre. . . . .
Mi colaborador es alemán. . . . .

3. CHOOSE THE CORRECT FORM OF "SER" OR "ESTAR"

. . . . cinco en el autobús. **(somos/estamos)** — Todo el mundo . . . .
contento. **(es/está)** — Ya . . . . en Madrid. **(somos/estamos)** — El hotel
. . . . completo. **(es/está)** — . . . . mil quinientas pesetas.
(son/están) — Hoy . . . . 5 de octubre. **(es/está)** — Nuestra habitación
. . . . muy grande. **(es/está)** — . . . . a 6 de noviembre.
(somos/estamos)

4. FOR EACH QUESTION, FIND THE NUMBERED RESPONSE

1. ¿ De quién es este billete ? . . . . A - Sí, son las nuestras.
2. ¿ Esta tarjeta es tuya ?. . . . . B - No, no es el nuestro
3. ¿ Es vuestro este pasaporte ? . . . . C - Es mío.
4. ¿ Estas llaves son las tuyas ? . . . . D - No, no es mío.
5. ¿ De quién son estos bolsos ? . . . . E - Sí, es mía.
6. ¿ Estas maletas son las vuestras ?. . . . F - Sí, son las mías.
7. ¿ Este hotel no es el nuestro ?. . . . . . . G - Son míos.

5. THESE ARE THE ANSWERS. WHAT ARE THE QUESTIONS?

Es Jacinta Perea. . . . .

Es de México. . . . .

Estamos bien, gracias. . . . .

Salgo el 23 de enero. . . . .

El restaurante está cerca de aquí. . . . .

Este bolso es de Pierre. . . . .

Me llamo Manuel. . . . .

6. COMPLETE WITH VERBS AND SUBJECTS IN PARENTHESES

— Buenas noches. . . . . **(tener - nosotros)** reservada una habitación a nombre del Señor Dupont.

— Voy a ver. Sí, aquí está. . . . . **(tener - ustedes)** la habitación 315.

— . . . . **(hablar - usted)** bien español.

— ¡Oh no! . . . . **(hablar - yo)** muy poco pero lo . . . . **(comprender - yo)** muy bien.

— ¿Cuánto tiempo se van a quedar?

— Dos días solamente. . . . . **(salir - nosotros)** el viernes para Málaga.

— Bien. ¿ . . . . **(querer - ustedes)** desayunar en el hotel?

— Sí, por favor. ¿ . . . . **(poder - ustedes)** subir las maletas a la habitación?

— Por supuesto. Enseguida . . . . **(venir)** el mozo.

7. MATCH THE RESPONSES OF THE SECOND COLUMN WITH THE FIRST

1. Este es mi asiento	**A** - Gracias, muy amable
2. Soy modelo y actriz	**B** - Sí, por supuesto
3. Aquí tiene la propina	**C** - ¡Qué interesante!
4. Este es el Señor Moliner	**D** - ¿Ah sí? ¡Qué bien!
5. Mañana salgo para París	**E** - De acuerdo
6. ¿Nos vemos en el café Rayuela?	**F** - Disculpe
7. ¿Puedo reservar un asiento?	**G** - Mucho gusto

Check your answers. See page 34 of booklet.

THE WAY TO EACH OTHER

Austerlitz Station. If I believe the sign, the train leaves at eight o'clock. Since there's no need to stamp international tickets, I go directly to Platform 13. It's really great: Bordeaux-Hendaye-Burgos-Madrid!

"You have cabin number 2, sir. Would you please fill out these two forms and give me your passport or your identity card. If you're having dinner on the train, the first service begins immediately and the second at ten-thirty. Here's your ticket for breakfast. *Gracias, Señor! Hasta mañana y buen viaje!*"

Why did I check off on the form "Spanish read, spoken, written"? I don't know how I'm going to manage there. Anyhow, I'll try to sleep while I'm waiting.

*
* *

Day breaks over a superb landscape of low, rocky mountains. The stones shine with a glitter of pink, lit unevenly by the capricious rays of the rising sun. The train never stops swaying. One wonders how the waiters have acquired the skill not to spill coffee on the clothes of the sleepy travelers.

We have barely crossed the mountains when the train enters the suburbs. Almost immediately the train arrives in the Madrid-Chamartin station.

"*Adiós, Señor. Le deseo una excelente estancia en España.*"

There's no lack of taxis in this country. "*Hotel Conde Duque, por favor.*"

Not so bad! I've managed to use a sentence! And now, old boy, open your eyes to what's around you. Here you are, finally, in this city that you've had so much trouble getting to.

Obviously, everybody wants a job in the European cities that are close by. To get a real change without going too far from France, makes Spain is an ideal place for work. The company's directors haven't had much trouble finding candidates to take charge of their new subsidiary. As for me, I don't think anyone knew what my real motivations were in applying for the job.

If only I succeed in finding her! Where can she be hiding? Behind one of these brick buildings? On one of the balconies overflowing with plants? Is she crossing the avenue in the middle of this group of passersby?

Good heavens! This lit-up sign says it's nine o'clock in the morning and four degrees celsius below! I didn't think it would be so cold. However, the sun's shining brightly on the city and the sky is pure blue. From inside this heated cab you'd think it was spring. It's amazing to see that the trees along the avenue still have their leaves.

« Purísima » Zurbarán

"Ya llegamos, Senor. Aqui está su hotel."

The window of my room looks out on a charming square. Some old people are already installed on the sunlit benches. The cafeteria across the way must do an excellent business. There are so many people coming and going from there! In fact, I think I'll join the crowd and buy myself a second breakfast to warm up.

"Qué le sirvo? Café solo, con leche o cortado? Tostada churros o croasán?"

I order a black coffee with a croissant so as not to make a mistake choosing. I have to find out eventually, however, what the other things on the menu are.

I have three weeks ahead of me before starting work. The company doesn't have an apartment for employees and I have to find somewhere to live before I start going to the office regularly. I'll take advantage of the time to buy myself one of those self-study courses with tapes to start learning the language. I should have done it long ago.

CONTINUED . . .

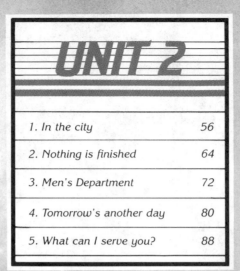

UNIT 2

BARCELONA: Sagrada Familia, de Gaudí.

⚫⚫ LISTEN   **IN THE CITY**

Paco wants to visit Güell Park and seeks information from the concierge of the hotel. Paloma prefers visiting the cathedral.

Paco : *¿Por favor? ¿Cómo puedo ir al Parque Güell...?*

Conserje : *Tiene que tomar un autobús, el 92 pasa muy cerca de allí.*

Paco : *¿Dónde está la parada más próxima...?*

Conserje : *Hay que caminar hasta el final de Las Ramblas. La parada está en La Plaza de Cataluña.*

Paco : *Muy amable. Gracias.*

. . . .

Paloma : *Oye, por favor. ¿Cómo hago para ir a La Catedral...?*

Un joven : *Mira el plano. Estamos aquí, en esta plaza... ¿ves...? Sigues todo recto; luego, en la segunda calle giras a la derecha, después a la izquierda y ya estás.*

Paloma : *¡Qué complicado!*

El joven : *¿Quieres que te acompañe...? Tengo tiempo libre.*

Paloma : *No, gracias. Prefiero ir sola.*

. . . .

Paloma : *¿Para ir a La Catedral, por favor?*

Un señor : *« Com diu...? »* *

Paloma : *Que... dónde está La Catedral.*

El señor : *Lo siento no soy de Barcelona.*

. . . .

Una pareja : *Señorita, por favor ¿Cómo hacemos para ir a La Catedral? No somos de aquí.*

Paloma : *¿A La Catedral...?*

*In Catalan: What are you saying?

⚫⚫ LISTEN AND REPEAT
You will find the translation on page 8 of booklet.

Barcelona: 1. La Pedrera of Gaudi
2.4.6. Details of the facades
3.5. Gaudi's Güell Park

NOUNS

la ciudad — city
el pueblo — village, town
el parque — park
la parada — (bus) stop
el final — end
la rambla — avenue, boulevard
la catedral — cathedral
la iglesia — church
el plano — plan
el tiempo — time, weather
la pareja — couple

---

la farmacia — pharmacy
los correos (m.pl.) — post office *(1)*
la telefónica — telephone company *(1)*
el estanco — tobacco store
el agente de tráfico — traffic policeman
la boca de metro — subway entrance
el barrio — area in the city
el tren — train
el puente — bridge
el semáforo — traffic light
la ida — departure
la vuelta — return
la avenida — avenue
el transbordo — transfer

ADJECTIVES

complicado(a) — complicated
derecho(a) — right
izquierdo(a) — left
solo(a) — alone

gótico(a) — Gothic
verde — green
rojo(a) — red
naranja — orange
intermitente — intermittent

VERBS

tener que — to have to, must
hay que — one must *(2)*
tomar el autobús
coger el autobús — to take the bus
pasar — to pass, to happen
caminar — to walk
hacer — to do, to make
seguir — to follow
girar — to turn
acompañar — to accompany
sentir — to regret

---

atravesar
cruzar — to traverse, to cross

MISCELLANEOUS

más — more
recto
todo recto — straight ahead
a la derecha — to the right *(3)*
a la izquierda — to the left *(3)*
luego — then, next

---

con cheque — by check
en efectivo — in cash

HOW TO SAY IT

1. ASKING DIRECTIONS

¿ *Cómo puedo ir al Parque ?* — How can I go to the Park?
¿ *Cómo hago para ir al P. ?* — What do I do to get to the Park?
¿ *Para ir al P., por favor ?* — To get to the Park, please?
¿ *Dónde está el P., por favor ?* — Where do you find the Park, please?
¿ *Está lejos el P. ?* — Is the Park far?

2. GIVING DIRECTIONS

Tienes que seguir todo recto — You must continue straight ahead
Hay que seguir de frente — One must continue straight ahead
Cruzas le plaza — You go across the plaza
Gira a la derecha — Turn right
Coge (Toma) la primera calle a la izquierda — Take the first street to the left.
Está al final de la avenida — It's at the end of the avenue
Está aquí cerca — It's near here

3. SAYING YOU DON'T KNOW

Lo siento, no sé — I'm sorry, I don't know   *No conozco el barrio* — I don't know
No soy de aquí — I'm not from here   this part of town

4. ASKING TO REPEAT

¿ *Perdón, qué dice?* — Sorry, what are you saying?
¿ *Cómo dice ?*
¿ *Cómo ?* — What are you saying?
¿ *Qué ?* — What?
¿ *Puede repetir, por favor ?* — Can you repeat (that), please?

NOTES . . .   NOTES . . .   NOTES . . .   NOTES . . .

(1) Both the post office and telephone, telegraph come under the direction of the Department of Tourism and Communication in Spain. — (2) "Hay que" + infinitive represents impersonal obligation, i.e., "one must";"tener que" + infinitive is conjugated according to varying subjects/persons like "tengo que" and represents strong physical obligation, translated as "I have to." — (3) The expressions are feminine, and the article must be used.

1. ASKING FOR INFORMATION

(• •) LISTEN:

una parada de autobús
• ¿Dónde hay una parada de autobús, por favor?
el banco
• ¿Dónde está el banco, por favor?

Answer using "hay" or "esta" as in the model:
una parada de autobús — el banco — la iglesia — una farmacia — Correos — un agente de tráfico — la Telefónica — un estanco — una parada de taxis — la boca del metro.

Grammar: See Q2, 3.

2. PRACTICING THE VERB "HACER"

(• •) LISTEN:

¿Para ir a la Catedral, por favor? (yo)
• ¿Cómo hago para ir a la Catedral?

Change as in the model:
¿Para ir a la Catedral, por favor? (yo) — ¿Para ir al barrio Gótico, por favor? (tú) — ¿Para ir al Parque Güell, por favor? (nosotros) — ¿Para ir al Pueblo Español, por favor? (ella) — ¿Para ir a la Plaza de Cataluña, por favor? (usted).

Grammar: See Q.

3. "TENER QUE" + INFINITIVE

(• •) LISTEN:

Debes girar a la izquierda
• Tienes que girar a la izquierda
Debo coger el tren
• Tengo que coger el tren

Continue according to the model using "tener que":
Debes girar a la izquierda — Debo coger el tren — Debéis atravesar el puente — Deben seguir todo recto hasta el final — Debemos coger el autobús — Debe caminar hasta el próximo semáforo — Deben cruzar la calle.

Grammar: See J 3.

4. "HAY QUE" + INFINITIVE

(• •) LISTEN:

¿Puedo ir a pie? (en taxi)
• No, hay que ir en taxi

Continue according to the model using: "hay que":
¿Puedo ir a pie? (taxi) — ¿Podemos pagar con cheque? (en efectivo) — ¿Puedo ir en barco? (en avión) — ¿Podemos girar a la izquierda? (a la derecha) — ¿Puedo coger el metro? (autobús) — ¿Podemos pagar mañana? (ahora).

Grammar: See J 3.

5. "GIRAR," "CRUZAR," "COGER"...

(• •) LISTEN:

girar a la izquierda · ir hasta el final de la calle
• Primero gira a la izquierda y luego va hasta el final de la calle

Continue according to the model:
girar a la izquierda · ir hasta el final de la calle; cruzar el puente · coger la avenida; tomar el metro · coger el autobús; subir en la Plaza de Cataluña · bajar en el Paseo Colón.

6. PRONUNCIATION

(• •) LISTEN AND REPEAT:

¿Dónde hay un agente? La iglesia es de estilo gótico. Tiene que coger un taxi, no puede seguir a pie. Debe girar a la derecha. ¿Cómo hago para pagar? ¿Puedo enviar un giro?

GETTING AROUND
IN THE CITY

How do you find your way and get around in a big Spanish city? It's an important matter in a country that attracts 50 million foreign visitors every year.

Let's talk first about finding your way. Road signs are relatively numerous on highways, but until a few years ago were a rarity in built-up areas. For the World Cup soccer game, which it organized in 1982, Spain succeeded in increasing them.

I advise people traveling through Spain to memorize the names of main highways ahead of time. Beyond Madrid, road signs — instead of telling you the way to Barcelona, for example — will often say N-II. For Valencia, they will say N-III. Toledo is known, in this outlandish system, as N-401, and Segovia by the similarly poetic C-607. For Avila, look for C-605.

You can, of course, ask for directions. Spaniards are both talkative and friendly. They're so friendly that, even when they don't know the place you want to go to, they will take great pleasure in pointing out another (even though it's far from the one you're looking for). As for their loquaciousness, especially in the villages, they'll describe not only the road to you, but also the surrounding countryside. Therefore, be sure not to ask directions on one of those small, narrow streets with a line of cars honking behind you and no room to pass. Patience is not the virtue most shared by Spanish drivers.

Next, let's talk about getting around. Spaniards have such a passion for their cars that to leave them for an instant — even to go 100 yards — seems like treason. This is true even if there's no place to move it. It's not surprising that traffic has become chaotic in most of the big cities, and that parking is total anarchy. In these conditions, why not get around by walking? It would be worth it in most of the big cities. For one thing, it's generally sunny; in this part of the world, rain is never more than a passing shower. For another, tourist attractions are usually very close to each other.

Such is the case in Barcelona, where everything seems to be concentrated in a few hundred square yards of the beautiful Gothic quarter — itself five minutes' walk from the famous Ramblas. It's the same way in Seville, where the Giralda, the Alcazar, and the Santa Cruz section are all in an area the size of a handkerchief. No doubt you'd have to walk a little further in Madrid, but the Prado — a thoroughfare that's a must for millions of tourists — is only 15 minutes' walk from the old section known as Madrid de los Austrias.

Finally, let's consider public transportation. Madrid and Barcelona have their metros or subways. But, in both cases, the systems are very crowded — especially on express trains. Buses go everywhere, but speed is not their main virtue. The lanes theoretically reserved for them are the ones automobile drivers prefer. For that reason, don't hesitate to use a taxi. They have the double advantage of being numerous and cheap — characteristics that are often closely linked.

N° 1 🔘🔘 LISTEN

After having listened to the information on the recording, write the number of order for each picture's description in the corresponding box.

Carefully study the plan below, then complete the sentences with the directions given above them.

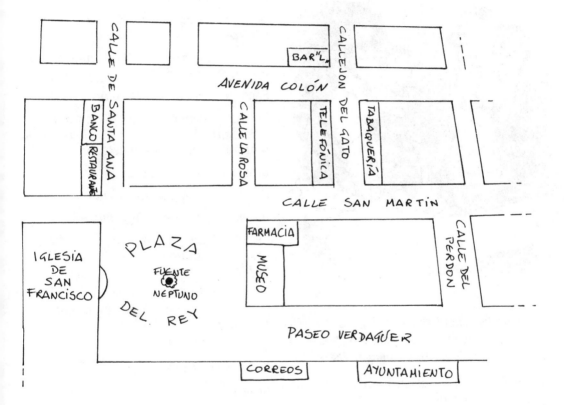

a la derecha de — a la izquierda — entre — al lado de — en — frente a

1. La Farmacia de don Cosme está . . . . del Museo.
2. La Tabaquería de Juanito está . . . . la Telefónica.
3. El Banco está . . . . del Restaurante.
4. El Bar L está . . . . la Avenida Colón y el Callejón del Gato.
5. El Ayuntamiento está . . . . el Paseo Verdaguer.
6. El Restaurante está . . . . del Banco.

See answers on page 9 of booklet.

[●●] LISTEN

NOTHING IS FINISHED

Soledad visits the housing development with Paco to get publicity photographs. They meet the manager there.

Soledad : *¿Conoce al Sr. Fernández? Es el fotógrafo de nuestra agencia.*

Gerente : *Mucho gusto.*

Paco : *Encantado.*

Soledad : *¿Todavía están en obras?*

Gerente : *Sí, estamos colocando las ventanas en el piso-piloto.*

Paco : *Entonces... no vamos a poder sacar fotos desde el exterior.*

Gerente : *Mañana va a estar terminado. Aquí tienen el salón.*

Soledad : *No está mal. Está bien iluminado.*

Paco : *Y además es amplio y agradable. ¿Y los muebles...?*

Gerente : *¿Los muebles...? Todavía no están.*

Soledad : *La chimenea queda muy bien en ese lugar. Me gusta.*

Paco : *¿Y el cuarto de baño...?*

Gerente : *Arriba, al lado de los dormitorios. Aquí abajo hay un servicio pequeño junto a la cocina, pero está sin azulejos.*

Soledad : *¿Y esa puerta...?*

Gerente : *Es la puerta del jardín.*

Soledad : *¿Esto es un jardín...?*

Gerente : *Mañana vamos a poner unos setos, una estátua y unas macetas... para la foto.*

Paco : *De todo esto tampoco voy a poder sacar fotos. Aquí todo está sin terminar.*

Later, in a café

Soledad : *Un vermut tinto con hielo.*

Paco : *Para mí, blanco.*

Gerente : *Yo, una cerveza bien fría y traiga, por favor, algo para picar.*

Camarero : *¿Unas aceitunas y unos tacos de jamón...?*

Gerente : *De acuerdo.*

[●●] LISTEN AND REPEAT

You will find the translation on page 9 of booklet.

Contemporary urban views: 1. Jávea (Alicante)
2. Walden 7 de R. Boffil (Barcelona) - 3. Las Rozas (Madrid)
4. Almería (under construction) Urban views of '50–'60:
5. Dehesa de la Villa (Madrid) - 6. Benidorm (Alicante)

NOUNS

el apartamento piloto — model apartment
la ventana — window
el salón — living room
el mueble — piece of furniture
la chimenea — fireplace, chimney
el lugar — place
el azulejo — tile
el cuarto de baño — bathroom
el dormitorio — bedroom
el servicio — bathroom
la cocina — kitchen
la maceta — flower pot
el hielo — ice *(1)*
la cerveza — beer
la aceituna — olive
el taco de jamón — "snack" of ham

la calefacción — (central) heating
el césped — lawn, grass
el cuadro — painting
la lámpara — lamp
la silla — chair
el armario — closet
la alfombra — rug
el espejo — mirror

ADJECTIVES

iluminado(a) — lit up
amplio(a) — ample
tinto — red *(2)*
frío(a) — cold

caro(a) — dear
arreglado(a) — arranged

roto(a) — broken
descuidado(a) — neglected
oscuro(a) — dark

VERBS

terminar — to finish
conocer — to know (to meet)
colocar — to put (to place)
sacar (hacer) fotos — to take photos
gustar — to please
poner — to put
traer — to bring
picar — to nibble (on cocktail snacks)

pintar — to paint
comer — to eat
barrer — to sweep
cortar — to cut
alquilar — to rent

MISCELLANEOUS

sin — without
mucho gusto — very happy (to meet you)
estar en obras — under construction
entonces — then
además — besides
todavía no — not yet
arriba — above
abajo — below
unos(as) — a few, some *(3)*
tampoco — either *(4)*
bastante — enough
para mí — for me

HOW TO SAY IT

1. INTRODUCING SOMEONE

¿Conoce al Sr. Fernández? — Do you know Mr. Fernández? *(5)*
Le presento al Sr. F. — I present to you Mr. F.
Permítame que le presente al Sr. F. — Let me introduce Mr. F.
Paco, nuestro fotógrafo — This is Paco, our photographer *(6)*

2. RESPONDING TO AN INTRODUCTION

Mucho gusto
Encantado(a) — It's a pleasure
Encantado de conocerlo — Very happy to meet you

3. SHOWING APPRECIATION ABOUT SOMETHING

No está mal — Not bad
Me gusta mucho — I like it (that) a lot
Me gustan los dormitorios — I like the bedrooms
Queda muy bien — That's done very well. Looks fine
Queda mal en ese lugar — Doesn't look right in that spot
Me encanta este jardín — I love this garden
¡Qué bonito apartamento! — What a lovely apartment!

4. POINTING OUT THE LOCATION

Está arriba (abajo) — It's up there (down there)
Está al lado de la cocina — It's on the side of the kitchen
Está junto a la cocina — It's next to the kitchen
Se ve desde el exterior (interior) — One can see (it) from the outside (inside)

NOTES . . .   NOTES . . .   NOTES . . .   NOTES . . .

(1) "Hielo" is "ice" and "helado" is "ice cream." — (2) "Red" is "tinto" only for red wine ("vino tinto"); otherwise use "rojo." — (3) The indefinite plural article, generally omitted, is sometimes used in the sense of "a few." — (4) "Tampoco" is used without negation when it precedes the verb. — (5) When the direct object pronoun is a person, it is "dignified" and preceded by the preposition "a." — (6) Giving only the first name is an informal way of introducing someone.

2.2 ORAL PRACTICE

1. BEING IN THE ACT OF . . .

⚫⚫ LISTEN:

¿Qué estás haciendo? (trabajar)
• Estoy trabajando
¿Qué está haciendo Adriana? (comer)
• Está comiendo

Answer as in the model, using "Estar" + gerund:
¿Qué estás haciendo? (trabajar) — ¿Qué está
haciendo Adriana? (comer) — ¿Qué están haciendo los niños? (escribir) — ¿Qué estáis haciendo? (pintar) — ¿Qué está haciendo usted?
(poner las puertas) — ¿Qué estás haciendo?
(hablar por teléfono) — ¿Qué estáis haciendo?
(discutir).

Grammar: See J4.

2. "IR A" + INFINITIVE

⚫⚫ LISTEN:

tomar una copa (nosotros)
• ¿Vamos a tomar una copa?

Ask questions as in the model:
tomar una copa (nosotros) — comprar una casa
(tú) — sacar una foto (él) — pasear por el parque
(vosotros) — ver la casa (ustedes) — colocar
las ventanas (los obreros) — alquilar un piso
(usted). Grammar: See J4.

3. "ME GUSTA" "NO ME GUSTA"

⚫⚫ LISTEN:

piso (yo)
• Me gusta este piso
cuadros (nosotros)
• Nos gustan estos cuadros

**Continue according to the model. Remember agree-
ment between the verb and the noun that follows:**
piso (yo) — cuadros (nosotros) — chimenea
(yo) — lámpara (vosotros) — sillas (yo) — ar-
marios (tú) — biblioteca (nosotros) — alfom-
bras (yo).

4. SHOWING APPRECIATION

⚫⚫ LISTEN:

El salón es espléndido (bien iluminado)
• Y además está bien iluminado
La cocina es pequeña (mal pintado)
• Y además está mal pintada

**Continue according to the model. Remember agree-
ment between adjective and noun:**
El salón es espléndido (bien iluminado) — La
cocina es pequeña (mal pintado) — Este piso
es muy caro (mal situado) — Los dormitorios
son amplios (bien decorado) — Los sillones son
bonitos (muy confortable) — El jardín es pequeño (muy descuidado) — La biblioteca es oscura (muy feo).

Grammar: See J1.

5. "TAMBIEN," "TAMPOCO"

⚫⚫ LISTEN:

Me gusta este piso
• A mí también
No nos gusta el edificio
• A nosotros tampoco

Continue according to the model:
Me gusta este piso — No nos gusta este edificio
— Me gusta esta casa — No me gusta esta calle
— Nos gustan estos muebles — No me gustan
los búngalos — Nos gusta la chimenea — Me
gusta el patio.

Grammar: See F1.

6. PRONUNCIATION

⚫⚫ LISTEN AND REPEAT:

Estoy trabajando. Me gusta la mesa
roja. ¡Qué bonitos azulejos! Ese espejo
no está mal. El jardín es acogedor. El
jamón es muy gustoso.

REAL ESTATE — HOUSING DEVELOPMENTS

Two words represent a nightmare for today's young newly married Spanish couples: "buscar piso" (to look for an apartment). It's with a bitter sigh that, day after day, most of them skim the list of brief real estate ads in the daily newspapers. Whether you're buying or renting, today's prices mean you have to be as rich as Croesus to live in Madrid or Barcelona.

The real estate market appears to have run away with itself in Spain after the last few years' boom. Spain's entrance into the European Community is pushing prices up to the levels of the most expensive capitals in neighboring countries. Unfortunately, from now on, the inhabitants of Madrid and Barcelona will no longer be envied by renters in Paris and London.

It won't surprise you that some spectacular fortunes were made during these last years, thanks to real estate. Many Spanish businessmen have left their traditional activities to devote themselves to the more profitable joys of building. Smelling a windfall, foreign investors in Kuwait, Great Britain, and elsewhere have also come en masse to take part in the feast, further accelerating the price spiral. A stable price is considered bad luck in today's market.

In the business quarters of Madrid, New York-style high-rise buildings mercilessly drive away the remaining individual houses, and office buildings are replacing apartment buildings. One has only to look at the Paseo de la Castellana, the big artery that crosses Madrid from north to south. The last small mansions and houses of those who somehow resisted are, one after the other, giving way to a groundswell of concrete and skyscrapers.

In addition, many families have left the central city for the more affordable surrounding areas — especially since, despite creeping urbanization, one can still live outside Madrid and commute there without losing much time. That's based on the premise that you make your home in one of the charming suburbs to the north, rather than in the more populous ones to the south. Madrid, like Barcelona, is encircled nowadays by a ring of "urbanizaciones," a Spanish term incompletely translated by the words "homes" or "housing development."

In Madrid, there are "urbanizaciones" for every taste and for every budget. From the crowded bedroom communities of Vallecas, south of the capital, where you can touch your neighbor's balcony across the way by stretching out your arm, to that of Puerta de Hierro, where Hollywood-type mansions are set in the middle of smooth lawns stretching as far as the eye can see.

The "urbanización," if it succeeds, aims at remedying the evils of urban inhumanity. Everything is closer and more accessible; people live as in a small community where everyone knows one another, greets each other on the street, and stops to chat. "Urbanización" aims to reconcile the irreconcilable — the virtues of the city and the countryside. It's a real challenge for the Spanish, a people that was rural such a short time ago and that has suddenly become city dwellers.

Listen to the tape carefully and complete the real estate agency's form.

FICHA DEL CLIENTE

Apellidos.....................................

Nombre.......................................

Profesión...............   Teléfono...............

Domicilio.......................................

Otros datos.......................................

	1	2	3	4	5	6
Dormitorios						
N°Mts.2	30	50	60	70	80	90	100	200	300
Garaje	sí	no				
Precio	2-3 millon.	4-6 mill.	6-8 mill.	10-20 mill.		
Zona preferida	Centro	Afueras	Barrio en concreto			
n° piso	1°	2°	3°	4°	5°	6°	7°	...	ático
Forma de pago						

Match the offers with the demands.

OFERTAS

Moratalaz-barrio Estrella, reformado total, planta onceava, todo exterior, 3 dormitorios enorme salón, garaje. 22.000.000. Condiciones inmejorables. Tel. 435.23.24

B Mirasierra, magnífico piso, urbanización cerrada, piscina, aparcamiento privado, 4 dormitorios, salón. 90.000. Tel. 431.66.19

C Urge vender interior a zona ajardinada, junto a Metro Valdillo, pequeño apartamento, 2 grandes dormitorios y salón. Moderno. 9.650.000. Facilidades. Tel. 276.64.08

D Salamanca. (Díaz Porlier), reformado. 2 dormitorios, amplísimo salón. Alquilo.mes: 35.000. Tel. 485.86.63

DEMANDAS

1 Alquilaría piso con 4 ó 5 dormitorios, salón, por la zona de Mirasierra o Majadahonda. Pagaría entre 80.000 y 100.000 pts.

2 Alquilaría piso por Zona Salamanca, entre 25.000 y 40.000 pts. A ser posible con garaje.

3 Compro piso o chalé en zona tranquila, con garaje, por Moratalaz. A ser posible con piscina. Pago en efectivo.

4 Urge comprar apartamento pequeño de 1 ó 2 dormitorios, entre 8.000.000 ó 12.000.000

See answers on page 10 of booklet.

(● ●) LISTEN:

MEN'S DEPARTMENT

Paco and Paloma are going to shop in the large department stores.

Paco : *¿Qué haces mañana...?*

Paloma : *Por la mañana quiero ir al Museo Picasso, pero por la tarde no sé todavía.*

Paco : *¿Por qué no te vienes conmigo...? Quiero ir de compras.*

Paloma : *¡Vale! Y aprovecho para comprar un pantalón. ¿A qué hora nos vemos...?*

Paco : *A las cinco, delante de la puerta del hotel.*

Paloma : *De acuerdo. Ahora me voy a dormir. Estoy cansada. ¡Buenas noches!*

Paco : *¡Hasta mañana!*

. . . .

Paco : *¿Dónde vamos a ir primero...?*

Paloma : *A la sección de caballeros. Creo que hay rebajas. ¿Qué quieres comprar...?*

Paco : *Un bañador y dos camisas.*

Paloma : *¿Qué te parece ésta?*

Paco : *¿Cuánto vale...?*

Paloma : *Cuatro mil setecientas.*

Paco : *No está mal, pero la quiero en verde y una talla más grande.*

Paloma : *Mira, aquí tienes una.*

Paco : *No es tan moderna como la otra.*

Paloma : *Sí, pero es más barata.*

Paco : *Voy a ver cómo me queda. ¿Dónde está el probador?*

Paloma : *Ahí, detrás de la caja.*

Paco : *¿Dónde...? No lo veo.*

. . . .

Paco : *¿Me queda bien...?*

Paloma : *Muy bien. Te hace más joven.*

Paco : *Bueno, no lo pienso más. La compro.*

Paloma : *¿Vemos los bañadores...?*

Paco : *¿Qué hora es...?*

Paloma : *Las siete y media.*

Paco : *Es muy tarde. Van a cerrar dentro de media hora.*

Paloma : *¿Vamos a cenar con Soledad...?*

Paco : *No, con ella no. Solos.*

(● ●) LISTEN AND REPEAT
You will find the translation on page 11 of booklet.

1. Calle Serrano (Madrid)
2. Commercial center of La Vaguada (Madrid)
3. Suckling pig and shellfish
4. Street vendor
5. Tenderete (Andalusia)
6. Valencia market

NOUNS

la sección — section
el caballero — man, sir
las rebajas (fpl) — sales
el bañador — bathing suit
la camisa — shirt
la talla — size
el probador — fitting room
la caja — cashier
_____

el traje — suit, dress
la chaqueta — jacket
la blusa — blouse
el zapato — shoe
la bota — boot
la falda — skirt
el calcetín — sock
la zapatilla — slipper
el ejercicio — exercise
las noticias (fpl) — news
la tienda — store
el color — color

ADJECTIVES

barato(a) — inexpensive
_____

corto(a) — short
largo(a) — long
oscuro(a) — dark
claro(a) — clear, light

azul — blue
blanco(a) — white
amarillo(a) — yellow
negro(a) — black

gris — gray
marrón — brown
rosa — rose-colored, pink
pálido(a) — pale

VERBS

ir de compras — to go shopping
aprovechar — to take advantage
ir a dormir — to go to sleep (1)
parecer — to seem
pensar — to think
cerrar — to close
cenar — to have supper
_____

empezar — to begin
abrir — to open

MISCELLANEOUS

conmigo — with me (2)
¡ Vale ! — Agreed!
delante (de) — in front (of) (3)
primero — first
¿cuánto vale? — how much is it worth?
tan . . . como — as . . . as
ahí — there
detrás (de) — behind (3)
dentro — within
dentro de — inside of

NOTES . . .   NOTES . . .   NOTES . . .   NOTES . . .

(1) "To go" + infinitive is translated by "ir a" + infinitive. — (2) After a preposition the pronouns "me, you (familiar), him, her, yourself" are expressed by "mi," "ti," "si." But "with me," "with her/him/yourself" we have "conmigo," "contigo," "consigo." — (3) "In front of" and "behind" are translated as "delante de" and "detras de" respectively. — (4) "'Son las' + hours" becomes "'Es la' + hour" when the time is between one and one thirty. — (5) Comparison of equality is expressed by "tan" + adjective, "tanto" + verb. "Tanto, tanta, tantos, tantas" + noun must be followed by "como."

HOW TO SAY IT

1. ASKING AND ANSWERING QUESTIONS ABOUT TIME

¿Qué hora es? — What time is it?
Es la una — It's one o'clock
Son las siete y media — It's seven-thirty *(4)*
¿A qué hora nos vemos? — At what time do we see each other?
Vamos a llegar dentro de media hora — We are going to arrive within a half hour
Espera aquí un cuarto de hora — Wait here for a quarter of an hour

2. COMPARING QUALITY AND QUANTITY

Es más cara que la tuya — It's more expensive than yours
Hay más camisas que bañadores — There are more shirts than bathing suits
Aquí hay menos artículos que allí — There are fewer articles here than there
Trabajas menos que yo — You work less than I
Es tan barato como el otro — It is as cheap as the other one *(5)*
Trabajo tanto como tú — I work as much as you *(5)*
No hay tantas rebajas como el año pasado — There are not as many sales as last year *(5)*

3. ASKING AN OPINION

¿Qué te parece esta camisa? — What do you think about this shirt?
¿Cómo la ves? — How does it look to you?
¿Me queda bien?
¿Me sienta bien? — Does it look good on me?
¿Me va bien?
¿Te gusta? — Do you like it?

4. ASKING THE PRICE OF SOMETHING

¿Cuánto vale esta falda? — How much is the skirt?
¿Cuánto cuesta esta falda?
Dos mil pesetas — Two thousand pesetas
¿Cuál es su precio? — What's the price?
¿Cuánto es? — How much is it?
Son quinientas pesetas — It is five hundred pesetas

1. PARECER, QUEDAR

(●●) LISTEN:

camisa
• ¿Qué te parece esta camisa? ¿Me queda bien?
pantalones
• ¿Qué te parecen estos pantalones? ¿Me quedan bien?

Continue according to the model making "parecer" and "quedar" show singular or plural forms:
camisa — pantalones — traje — chaqueta — zapatos — blusa — botas — medias — calcetines.

2. MAKING COMPARISONS

(●●) LISTEN:

Esta falda es muy bonita
• No es tan bonita como la otra
Estos pañuelos son muy baratos
• No son tan baratos como los otros

Continue according to the model using the correct form of "el OTRO":
Esta falda es muy bonita — Estos pañuelos son muy baratos — Estos calcetines son muy grandes — Este libro es muy interesante — Estas zapatillas son muy bonitas — Este restaurante es muy bueno — Este ejercicio es muy fácil.

Grammar: See E.

3. ASKING THE HOUR

(●●) LISTEN:

cerrar (restaurante)
• ¿A qué hora cierra el restaurante?
salir (vuelo 905)
• ¿A qué hora sale el vuelo 905?

Continue according to the model:
cerrar (restaurante) — salir (vuelo 905) — abrir (las tiendas) — llegar (tren de Burdeos) — comer (los empleados) — ser (el espéctaculo).

4. TELLING THE HOUR

(●●) LISTEN:

banco (11 horas)
• El banco cierra a las 11 de la mañana
estanco (19.30 horas)
• El estanco cierra a las siete y media de la noche

Continue and use "de la mañana," "de la tarde," or "de la noche":

banco (11 horas) — estanco (19.30 horas) — restaurante (23 horas) — oficina (13.15 horas) — bar (2.30) — biblioteca (11 horas) — tienda (10.30 horas).

Grammar: See I 2.

5. PRACTICING PRONOUNS

(●●) LISTEN:

¿Te gusta este pantalón? (corto) (largo)
• Es muy corto. Lo quiero más largo

Continue according to the model replacing the nouns with pronouns:

¿Te gusta este pantalón? (corto) (largo) — ¿Te gustan estas camisas? (caras) (baratas) — ¿Te gusta esta chaqueta? (oscura) (clara) — ¿Te gusta este traje? (amplio) (estrecho) — ¿Te gustan estos zapatos? (alto) (bajo) — ¿Te gustan estas botas? (caro) (barato).

Grammar: See E.

6. PRONUNCIATION

(●●) LISTEN AND REPEAT:

Este vestido me va bien. ¿Cuánto valen estas botas? Son muy baratas, debes aprovechar. Vamos de compras, hay muchas rebajas.

MARKETS, STORES

It's not an exaggeration to say that Spain knows how to preserve the human element in trade. Those who've seen the law of the jungle rule in shopping areas elsewhere can't help but be pleasantly surprised by the relaxed, friendly atmosphere here.

You won't find scowls here or daggers figuratively drawn in battle against fellow customers. The Spanish custom is that everyone "pide la vez," that is, ask where the end of the line is and wait his or her turn. The Spanish are very sociable, and lines in front of shops are good places to start a conversation with a neighbor. You can begin by talking about the quality of the merchandise, and end with the health of your children.

The marketplace is still a meeting place in Spain — a reminder of "ferias" of former times, those rural free-for-alls where villagers did business with one another. The "feria"

has been transformed since then into the "mercadillo," or open-air market. Each city and town has one once a week at a special time. It's a colorful and noisy spectacle. Spaniards generally have loud voices, and the market is a favorite place for raising the decibel count.

Visitors from the outside can't resist stopping before baskets of seemingly inexhaustible riches, such as the cold meats and "chorizos," assorted and savory sausages twisted all around the butcher's stall. Or the tempting hams dangling in front of the faces of passers-by.

Big cities like Madrid also have "mercadillos," sometimes covered, where the din is usually deafening, the sounds reverberating back from the roof. Right in the midst of the capital, these small markets, where everyone seems to know one another, give off an agreeable countryside flavor that makes one momentarily

forget the pollution and traffic jams outside.

The best "mercadillo" in Madrid is Rastro — a sort of flea market in a little street south of Plaza Mayor called "Ribera de Curtidores," (tanners' row). Every Sunday morning there is an unbelievable display of old items of all kinds — valuable and rare antiques alongside jumbled piles of junk. You can hear the heartbeat of old Madrid amid a motley and picturesque crowd.

Of course, in today's Spain, the "mercadillo" has learned to survive alongside large supermarkets. In addition, department store chains like El Corte Inglés and Galerias Preciados compare favorably with their counterparts in other western European countries. Sometimes, though, in their antiseptic atmosphere, a visitor surprisingly misses the pleasant disorder and din of "mercadillos" that symbolize the warmth of Old Spain.

N° 1   ●● LISTEN

Doña Juana and Martita meet in the street. They are going to the market. It is 11 A.M. and they chat for a long time. Listen to the cassette and answer "yes" or "no."

	SÍ	NO
1. Doña Juana planchó de 2 a 4		
2. Martita : «Me levanté a las 9»		
3. Martita : «A las 7 me vienen unos amigos»		
4. Doña Juana : «A las 7 empieza la película»		
5. Luis se fue a trabajar a las 7.30		
6. Doña Juana : «Mis hijos no vienen hasta las 3»		

Here's the diary of Don Camilo, custodian of a residential building, who spends his time watching the tenants. He maintains a log where he indicates the hour at which they leave and the hour at which they return.

• *Luisito, el del 4° piso, se levanta a las 7 y sale de casa a las 8.00. Regresa a las 5 todos los días.*
• *Antonio, el del 2° piso, no madruga. Sale a las 10 y regresa a las 3, durante toda la semana.*
• *María, la del 1ᵉʳ piso, sale a la 7 de la mañana. Vuelve a las 7 de la tarde.*
• *Juana, la del 3° derecha, está jubilada. Sale a las 10.00.*
• *Don Bernabé, el del 3° izda, no sale casi nunca. Sólo de vez en cuando, entre las 4 y 6 de la tarde.*
• *Manolín del 5°, sale a las 8. Regresa a la 1. Por las tardes sale a las 3 y vuelve a las 5.00.*

	MANOLÍN	LUISITO	DON BERNABÉ	JUANA	ANTONIO	MARÍA
PISO →						
7 h						
8 h						
9 h						
10 h						
11 h						
12 h						
13 h						
14 h						
15 h						
16 h						
17 h						
18 h						
19 h						

See answers on page 12 of booklet.

◉◉ LISTEN

TOMORROW'S ANOTHER DAY

After having finished their work in Barcelona, Paco and Paloma head toward Andalusia together. Soledad returns home.

Soledad : *¡Qué bonita camisa tienes, Paco!*

Paco : *¿Te gusta...?*

Soledad : *Sí. Me gusta mucho el color. ¿Qué váis a hacer ahora...?*

Paco : *Yo iré a Sevilla un mes. Tengo que trabajar en un reportaje sobre La Feria.*

Soledad : *¿Y tú, Paloma...?*

Paloma : *Voy a Granada. Tengo una propuesta para actuar en el cine.*

Paco : *¡Ah, sí! ¡Qué interesante! ¿Con quién vas a trabajar?*

Paloma : *Con un director joven. No lo conozco todavía. Le telefonearé esta noche para concretar.*

Paco : *¿De qué tratará la película...?*

Paloma : *No sé. Creo que es histórica, con moros, cristianos y guerra santa...*

Soledad : *¿Y cuál será tu papel...?*

Paloma : *Haré de cautiva. La hija menor de un comerciante muy rico. ¡Oye, Paco! ¿Por qué no alquilamos un coche y vamos juntos...?*

Paco : *¡Buena idea! ¿Cuándo tienes que estar en Granada?*

Paloma : *Antes de fin de mes. Creo que el rodaje empezará en el mes de mayo.*

Paco : *¿Y tú, Soledad?*

Soledad : *Primero iré a la playa con mis hijos, les sentará bien el sol y el mar. Luego, los llevaré al campo.*

Paco : *¡Qué suerte tienes! Yo también voy a tratar de descansar unos días, antes de ir a Sevilla.*

Camarero : *¿Qué les sirvo...?*

◉◉ LISTEN AND REPEAT
You will find the translation on page 12 of booklet.

Arab and Christian Andalusia:
1. Patio de las Muñecas (Alcazar of Seville)
2. Plaza de los Reyes (Seville)
3. Gardens of La Alhambra (Grenada)
4. Iglesia de San Cayetano (Cordova)
5. Mezquita (Cordova)
6. La Alhambra (Grenada)

NOUNS

el reportaje — report, reporting
la propuesta — proposition
el cine — movies
el director — director
la película — film
el cristiano — Christian
la guerra — war
el papel — role
el cautivo — prisoner
la hija menor — younger daughter
el hijo mayor — older son
el coche — car
la idea — idea
el fin — end
el rodaje — filmmaking
la playa — beach
los hijos (mpl) — children, sons *(1)*
el campo — country

_____

el chico
el niño — child *(1)*
el reloj — watch, clock
el periódico — newspaper
el guardia — policeman
la esquina — (street) corner
el cenicero — ashtray
el hermano — brother
el vino — wine
la dirección — address
la mesa — table, desk
el colaborador — collaborator

ADJECTIVES

histórico(a) — historic
santo(a) — saint
menor — smaller, younger *(2)*
mayor — bigger, older *(2)*
rico(a) — rich
pobre — poor

VERBS

actuar — to play (a role)
concretar — to make concrete
telefonear — to telephone
tratar — to try *(3)*
hacer de — to play the role of
sentar bien — to fit well (clothing)
sentar mal — to not fit well
servir — to serve

MISCELLANEOUS

sobre — on, over
¿cuál? — which (one)?
¡qué suerte! — what luck

_____

en frente (de) — in front (of)
encima — over, above
encima de — on, over
en el medio — in the middle

1. ASKING SOMEONE'S PLANS

¿ *Qué vas a hacer ahora ?* — What are you going to do now?
¿ *Qué harás el año próximo ?* — What will you do next year?
¿ *Qué piensas hacer ?* — What do you intend to do?

2. STATING YOU ARE UNSURE OF YOUR PLANS

No sé qué hacer — I don't know what to do
Ya no sé qué hacer — I don't know what to do now
No sé todavía (Todavía no sé) lo que voy a hacer
No sé aún (Aún no sé) lo que voy a hacer — I still don't know what I'm going to do

3. MAKING A SUGGESTION

¿ *Por qué no vamos juntos ?* — Why don't we go together?
¿ *Por qué no ir juntos ?* — Why not go together?
Podemos descansar un poco, si quieres — We can rest a bit, if you wish
¿ *Quieres que te acompañe ?* — Do you want me to accompany you?
Te propongo ir de compras — I suggest going shopping

4. STATING THE ORDER OF ACTIONS

Primero, iré a la playa
En primer lugar, iré à la playa — First, I will go to the beach
Luego, al campo
Más tarde, al campo — Afterwards, to the country
Después, al campo

NOTES . . .   NOTES . . .   NOTES . . .   NOTES . . .

(1) "Chico" and "niño" refer to a child in general; "hijos" are someone's children. — (2) "Mayor" and "menor" respectively have the meaning of "bigger, older, elder" and "smaller, younger, youngest" — (3) Other meanings of "tratar": "tratar de tú (usted)" = "use of 'tú (usted)'"; "tratar de" = infinitive = "to try to"; "se trata de" = "it's a question of, deals with."

2.4 ORAL PRACTICE

1. PRACTICING PRONOUNS

●● LISTEN:

¿Ves la estación? (enfrente)
- Claro que la veo. Está enfrente.

Answer the questions by replacing the nouns with the pronouns:
¿Ves la estación? (enfrente) — ¿Ves a Juan? (detrás de María) — ¿Ves a los chicos? (en el banco) — ¿Ves el reloj? (sobre el piano)— ¿Ves a Carmencita? (en el medio) — ¿Ves el periódico? (en la biblioteca) — ¿Ves a los turistas? (delante del museo) — ¿Ves el cenicero? (debajo de la mesa).

Grammar: See F.

2. PRACTICING PRONOUNS

●● LISTEN:

¿Vas a llamar a los Pérez?
- Sí, los voy a llamar por la tarde
¿Vas a escribirle a Juan?
- Sí, le voy a escribir por la tarde

Continue according to the model using "lo/la/los/las" when replacing the direct object and "le/les" for the indirect object:
¿Vas a llamar a los Pérez? — ¿Vas a escribirle a Juan? — ¿Vas a telefonearle a tu hermana? — ¿Vas a esperar a los niños? — ¿Vas a visitar a los Pérez? — ¿Vas a hablarles a tus padres?

Grammar: See F.

3. DO YOU KNOW . . . ?

●● LISTEN:

¿Conoces a Martín? (hermano)
- No, a Martín no lo conozco pero a su hermano sí

Continue according to the model:
¿Conoces a Martín? (hermano) — ¿Conoces a Alberto? (padre) — ¿Conoces a los Pérez? (hijos) — ¿Conoces a Antonio y Elena? (padres) — ¿Conoces a Silvia y Diana? (hermanos).

Grammar: See F.

4. SPEAKING ABOUT THE FUTURE

●● LISTEN:

¿Vas a trabajar? (Por la tarde)
- No, ahora no, trabajaré por la tarde

Continue according to the model. Watch out for irregular verbs ("salir: saldré; venir: vendré")
¿Vas a trabajar? · por la tarde; ¿Ustedes van cenar? · más tarde; ¿Juan va a venir? · esta noche; ¿Usted va a comer? · luego; ¿Los niños van a ir al zoológico? · mañana; ¿Vas a escribir? · por la noche; ¿Vamos a festejar? · más tarde.

Grammar: See M.

5. "CUÁL/CUÁLES"

●● LISTEN:

papel (tú)
- ¿Cuál es tu papel?
clientes (usted)
- ¿Cuáles son sus clientes?

Continue according to the model using "cual" or "cuáles." Remember to change the possessive according to the subject:
papel · tú; clientes · usted; dirección · vosotros; amigos · usted; profesores · ustedes; mesa · yo; patrón · vosotros; trabajo · tú; colaboradores · él; coche · ellos.

Grammar: See G.

6. PRONUNCIATION

●● LISTEN AND REPEAT:

¿Conoce a ese chico? Es amigo de los Chávez. Es chileno. ¿Tomas una horchata? ¿Quieres un cuchillo o una cuchara? ¿Te han dicho que tengo un chalé en Chivilcoy?

AUTOMOBILE TRAVEL

Impulse is important to many Spanish drivers. With a few happy exceptions, logic seldom plays a part in their behavior behind the wheel. The Spanish, like drivers elsewhere, are also quick to answer you back.

Use of the signal is often considered optional. The horn, on the other hand, is a must. Lovers of noise in general, Spaniards love it equally well when they're behind the wheel. Be warned that in Spain a red light is no deterrent. Those who drive through them, however, have the good grace to slow down first. However, on the other hand, many drivers on four-lane roads refuse to go more than 30 miles an hour; at the same time, they insist on staying in the left lane. And there are some people who consider it a personal affront if others pass them.

It's true that too few penalties can encourage crime. Fines are light in Spain, and there is little radar in use on the roads. Police on the highways and in the villages can be strict, but those in the big cities won't trouble you in the same way. It's not unusual in Madrid, in fact, to see police cars set a bad example by running red lights.

In any case, driving in Spain is no more dangerous than elsewhere on the Continent. The number of auto fatalities (190 per million inhabitants) is close to the average.

The roads might be more to blame for the number of accidents than the behavior of the drivers. The road system hasn't kept up with the rest of the country. It represents a bottleneck right now when Spain is experiencing rapid growth. Of course, the days when travelers who left the main road found themselves on dirt tracks are a thing of the past. All the roads are now paved, but national roads are often narrow and winding. (They say that, after Switzerland, Spain is the most mountainous country in Europe.) Because one can't see far ahead under such conditions, passing can be hazardous.

Highways are still rather rare. Most of them were designed for the needs of foreign tourists rather than for the Spanish. They link the frontiers with the coastal areas popular with tourists, ignoring, for example, Madrid — one of the very few European capitals still not linked by highway to the others.

Hopefully, this description of automobile travel will not deter you from driving in Spain. Of course, if you plan only on visiting a big city, don't drive. On the other hand, it is the only means of travel that permits you to leisurely make stops in villages and the countryside — where you find the real and most fascinating side of Spain.

Two important fashion designers talk about their models, Pepita Soriano and Rocio Pineda, and the designs they are going to present. Listen carefully and complete the columns.

	PEPITA	ROCÍO
1. Falda	. . . .	. . . .
2. Zapatos	. . . .	. . . .
3. Sombrero	. . . .	. . . .
4. Combinación	. . . .	. . . .
5. Medias	. . . .	. . . .
6. Joyas	. . . .	. . . .

If you find the place of each article of clothing, you will have a surprise in column E.

Pantalón · Bufanda · Falda · Botones · Zapatos · Cinturón · Jersey · Sombrero · Combinación · Medias · Traje.

	A	B	C	D	E	F	G	H	I	J	K	L	LL	M
1								T						
2				Z										
3										R				
4						M								
5								Y						
6							D							
7						R								
8	M													
9			F											
10		O												
11				J										

See answers on page 14 of booklet.

87. *ochenta y siete*

🔊 LISTEN

WHAT CAN I SERVE YOU?

Before finally separating, Paco, Paloma and Soledad get together for a farewell dinner.

Soledad : *Queremos cenar.*

Paco : *¿Nos trae la carta, por favor...?*

Camarero : *¿No prefieren comer abajo, en el comedor...? Van a estar mejor que aquí arriba.*

Paloma : *No, no. Estamos bien. Nos gusta este sitio. Desde la terraza se ve el jardín y la ciudad.*

Camarero : *¡Como quieran!... Bueno ¿qué les sirvo...?*

Paco : *Para mí un plato combinado, el 13, y una cerveza.*

Camarero : *¿La cerveza, bien fría...?*

Paco : *Sí, la quiero fría.*

Camarero : *¿Y usted, señorita...?*

Paloma : *¿Qué me aconseja...? No tengo mucha hambre.*

Camarero : *El pescado está muy bueno y es fresco.*

Paloma : *Bueno, pues una ración de merluza con patatas fritas.*

Paco : *Muy bien. Para la salud el pescado es mejor que la carne.*

Soledad : *Pero yo no lo puedo comer. Me sienta mal.*

Camarero : *¿Y para usted...?*

Soledad : *Mire, sólo un filete y una ensalada mixta con poca sal.*

Paco : *Es más sano comer sin sal; y no se engorda.*

Camarero : *¿Para beber...?*

Soledad : *Agua mineral sin gas, para mí.*

Camarero : *¿Quieren otra cosa, los señores?*

Paco : *Unos calamares fritos y unos taquitos de queso para empezar.*

Camarero : *Bien, señores. Lo de picar, lo traigo ahora mismo.*

🔊 LISTEN AND REPEAT
You will find the translation on page 14 of booklet

Handicrafts: 1. Sausage makers
2. Chinchón bakery
3. Ceramics
4. Tiles
5. Furniture maker
6. Alfarero Potter

NOUNS

la carta — letter, menu
el comedor — dining room
la terraza — terrace
el plato combinado — combination plate
el hambre (f) — hunger
el pescado — fish
la ración — portion
la merluza — hake
la patata — potato
patatas fritas — French fries
la salud — health
la carne — meat
el filete — steak
la ensalada — salad
la sal — salt
el agua (f) — water
el calamar — to calm
el queso — cheese
las tapas (fpl) — snacks before dinner
_____
el limón — lemon
la horchata — orgeat *(1)*
el refresco — soft drink
el zumo — (fruit) juice
la naranja — orange
la fruta — fruit
las vacaciones (fpl) — vacation
el postre — dessert
la tarta — tart, pastry
la manzana — apple
el arroz — rice
el tomate — tomato
el plátano — banana

el mejillón — mussel
la cuchara — spoon
el tenedor — fork
el cuchillo — knife
el vaso — glass

ADJECTIVES

fresco(a) — fresh
sano(a) — clean
_____
rico(a) — delicious
relleno(a) — stuffed
congelado(a) — frozen

VERBS

aconsejar — to advise
engordar — to get fat
beber — to drink
_____
elegir — to choose

MISCELLANEOUS

mejor — better
pues — then, well
sólo — only
poco(a) — a little
otro(a) — (an) other
ahora mismo — right now

NOTES . . .   NOTES . . .   NOTES . . .   NOTES . . .

(1) A refreshing drink, a favorite, made from cultures of plant tubers ("chufa"). — (2) The partitive in Spanish is often expressed by the absence of the adjective: "¿Tienes dinero?" = "Do you have any (some) money?" — (3) "Mejor" is, at the same time, an adjective and the adverb "better." — (4) Literally: "I have a lot of thirst," "I have a little hunger." "Tener" is the equivalent of "to be" in expressions of condition: "to be cold" = "tener frío"; "to be careful" = "tener cuidado."

HOW TO SAY IT

1. ASKING SOMEONE WHAT SHE/HE WANTS TO ORDER

¿ Qué les sirvo ? — What (shall) I serve you?
¿Qué desean para empezar? — What do you want to begin with?
¿Qué van a tomar de entrada? — What do you want as a main course?
¿Y de primer plato? — And as a first course?
¿De postre? — And for dessert?
¿Y para beber? — And to drink?
¿Quieren otra cosa?
¿Alguna cosa más? — Do you want something else (more)?

2. ORDERING THE MEAL

Queremos comer — We wish to dine
Quiero cenar — I would like to have dinner (supper)
¿Nos trae la carta, por favor? — Please bring us the menu
Una ración de merluza, por favor — An order of hake, please
La cuenta, por favor — Check, please

3. ASKING ADVICE

¿Qué podríamos tomar? ¿ Carne o pescado? — What should one eat? Meat or fish? *(2)*
¿ Qué nos aconseja? (recomienda? propone?) — What do you advise us? (recommend? suggest?)

4. EXPRESSING AN OPINION ABOUT THE MEAL

El pescado es mejor que la carne
El pescado es más bueno que la carne — The fish is better than the meat *(3)*
Es mejor comer sin sal — It's better to eat without salt *(3)*
Es la mejor cerveza — It's the best beer
Es aquí donde se come mejor — One eats better here
El agua con gas me sienta mal — Soda water does not agree with me
El pan engorda — Bread makes you fat.

5. EXPRESSING HUNGER OR THIRST

Tengo hambre — I'm hungry
Tengo sed — I'm thirsty

Tengo mucha sed — I'm very thirsty *(4)*
Tengo poca hambre — I'm not too hungry *(4)*

1. ASKING FOR ADVICE

●● LISTEN:

No sé qué pedir
• ¿Qué me aconseja?
No sabemos qué hacer
• ¿Qué nos aconseja?

Continue according to the model. Remember to vary the pronouns after the persons:
No sé qué pedir — No sabemos qué hacer — Paco no sabe qué comer — María no sabe qué leer — Los clientes no saben qué comprar — Las chicas no saben qué elegir.

2. THE SUPERLATIVE

●● LISTEN:

Esta comida es muy rica
• ¿Rica? ¡Es riquísima! Es la más rica de todas
Este restaurante es muy bueno
• ¿Bueno? ¡Buenísimo! Es el mejor de todos

Continue according to the model. Watch the superlative of "bueno": MEJOR and "malo": PEOR:
Esta comida es muy rica — Este restaurante es muy bueno — Esta botella es muy bella — Este pescado es muy fresco — Este café es muy malo — Esta chica es muy linda — Este ejercicio es muy difícil.

Grammar: See E.

3. ORDERING: "Y DE POSTRE . . ."

●● LISTEN:

ensalada mixta (helado)
• Quisiera una ensalada mixta y de postre un helado

Continue according to the model:
ensalada mixta · helado; patatas fritas · tarta de manzana; calamares con arroz · ensalada de frutas; tomates rellenos · un plátano; mejillones · flan.

4. ORDERING: "PARA MÍ / TI / ÉL . . ."

●● LISTEN:

Yo quisiera un helado de limón
• Para mí, un helado de limón
Paco quisiera una horchata
• Para él, una horchata

Continue according to the model varying the pronouns after the persons:
Yo quisiera un helado de limón — Paco quiere una horchata — Tú quieres una cerveza — Los chicos quieren una limonada — Nosotros queremos un refresco — Montserrat quiere un vino tinto — Ana y Susana quieren un zumo de naranja.

Grammar: See F.

5. "NO MÁS QUE . . ."

●● LISTEN:

Yo sólo tomaré una ensalada
• No tomaré más que una ensalada
En este restaurante hay sólo paella
• En este restaurante no hay más que paella

Continue according to the model using "No más que...":
Yo sólo tomaré una ensalada — En este restaurante hay sólo paella — Pediré sólo una fruta — Paco come sólo carne — Saldré sólo tres días de vacaciones — Tú ves sólo películas policíacas.

Grammar: See H2.

6. PRONUNCIATION

●● LISTEN AND REPEAT:

El mes próximo trabajaré de extra — Tengo que pasar un examen — El director es muy exigente — Exige al máximo pero tiene mucho éxito. Tú exageras, es exigente pero no tanto.

DINING

Spanish cuisine does not consist totally of gazpacho and paella. That is, however, a widely held stereotype and doesn't do justice to the diversity of rich eating pleasures that can be found in Spain.

There's really no single cuisine, but many types of Spanish cuisine. According to a well-known formula, Spaniards in the north cook with sauces; in central Spain, they roast; and in the south, they fry. The varying customs reflect varying climates and gastronomic tastes.

Let's begin by talking about paella, since that is what has carried the reputation of good Spanish cooking beyond its borders. Whether it's made with fish, seafood, chicken, or a combination of all these things, true paella comes from the region of Valencia where rice is king. The Spanish eat it only at lunch, generally on holidays or weekends to give their stomachs time to digest it. If you see a group of guests in a restaurant seated around a paella dinner in the evening, you can be sure they're tourists unacquainted with local custom.

From Valencia, let's go to the opposite side of Spain, rainy and maritime Galicia — fish and seafood paradise. There's a reason that Galician fishermen are renowned on the seven seas: Fishing is second nature to them. There is undoubtedly no other region of Europe where lobster and other shellfish are so affordable. As for nonmaritime specialties, Galicia is famous for "lacón con grelos" (pork shoulder and turnip greens).

In the Basque country, where the cuisine is among Spain's most imaginative, fish is also king. Experts there, graduates of nouvelle cuisine, simmer intricate sauces to cover their dishes. Traditional dishes are also popular — fish in green sauce, or cod Biscay style with seafood sauce.

In the center of the country, Castille, with its harsh continental climate, has given birth to a plain popular cooking style especially rich in protein. This is the well-known "cocido" of Madrid — a Spanish stew where boiled beef is combined with bacon, vegetables, chickpeas, and puddings of all kinds. Between Segovia and Burgos stretches the area known for mutton and suckling pig, served in giant portions with an unpretentious rugged wine.

Catalonia also has its culinary customs, such as "butifarra" (sausage eaten with beans). As for Andalusia, it's the home of fried fish. You can lean on the bar and taste it along with "fino," a glass of dry sherry that seems to have been created to go with it.

Your only problem will be in making a choice when you dine in Spain. Remember that the Spanish eat a lot and often, beginning with "tapas" (cocktail snacks) at 10 A.M., and ending with a big dinner that finishes at midnight. You'll see that dieting is a science that, happily, has not yet crossed the Pyrenees.

● ● LISTEN

La Melitona

Traditional Song
(Sung and arranged by Joaquín Díaz)

Hoy voy a cantar la copla *del pan de la Melitona*	Today I'm going to sing of the bread of la Melitona.
Quedose sin levadura *porque la tiene Pamplona*	It had no leavening for the yeast was in Pamplona.

Mi tía Melitona ya no amasa el pan

que le falta el agua, la harina y la sal

Y la levadura la tiene Pamplona ⎫

por eso no amasa mi tía Melitona ⎭ *bis*

My aunt Melitona no longer kneads the bread

which needs, water, flour and salt

And the yeast is in Pamplona ⎫

That is why she does not knead, my ⎭ (REPEAT)
aunt Melitona

Eso de pelar la pava *tiene mucho que entender*	In the business of plucking the turkey (flirting) There is much to understand
Unos la pelan sentados *otros la pelan de pie*	Some do it sitting down others do it standing up

Mi tía Melitona...

My aunt Melitona . . .

¿Ursula qué estás haciendo? *Que te estamos esperando*	Ursula what are you doing? We have been waiting for you
Hemos matado la pava *y ahora la estamos pelando*	We have killed the turkey and now we are plucking it

Mi tía Melitona...

My aunt Melitona . . .

IDIOMS

(Pluck the turkey)

To flirt, to woo

(Give pumpkins)

To jilt, to give the cold shoulder

(Hang the sanbenito* on someone)

To make (call) things what they are not

(Expect pears from an elm)

To ask for the impossible

*A garment stigmatizing an accused and penitent heretic in the Inquisition.

2.1

COMPLETE with HAY/ESTÁ or ESTÁN : ¿ Dónde . . . . la parada más cercana? ¿ Qué . . . . en el bolso? ¿ Dónde . . . . los cigarrillos? En el centro . . . . una oficina de turismo. Los niños . . . . en la habitación.

TRANSLATE : Disculpe, Señor, el barrio Gótico ¿ está lejos de aquí? No, hay que seguir todo recto hasta la avenida. ¿ Tengo que cambiar de autobús para ir a la estación? ¿ Qué línea tengo que tomar para ir al centro?
Excuse me, sir, which bus must I take to go to Güell Park? I'm sorry, I don't know the area. It's 100 meters from here. I would like to go down to Cibeles. To go to the station, please?

2.2

COMPLETE with ESTAR + gerund : La señora no está, ... (trabajar). ¿ Dónde . . . . (vivir) tú? Te llamamos esta noche, ahora . . . . . . (comer). ¿ Qué . . . . (hacer) vosotros? ¿ Qué . . . . . . (beber) Ustedes? Ahora no puedo, ... (leer) el periódico.

TRANSLATE : No está mal. La chimenea queda bien aquí. Ahora no puede, está mirando la tele. Los dormitorios están arriba.
Here you have the living room. Here, this is the bathroom. I would like to rent an apartment. I don't like these pictures. We are in the middle of eating. I am going to leave.

2.3

COMPLETE with TAN/TANTO/TANTA/TANTOS or TANTAS : Aquí hay . . . . gente como en la otra tienda. Este vestido es . . . . .·. . caro como el otro. Tienes . . . . . . bolsos como yo. La chaqueta roja no es . . . . . bonita como la verde. Yo no llevo . . . . . dinero como tú.

TRANSLATE : Quiero una camisa para esta falda. ¿ Puede enseñarme ese vestido que está en el escaparate? Quisiera un par de botas de cuero. ¿ En qué puedo ayudarle? ¿ Algo más?
I would like a cotton blouse. I don't like the color. Do you have size 38? Where is the fitting room? That looks (goes) well on you. How much does this cost? No, thank you, that is all. What time is it?

2.4

COMPLETE with LO/LA/LOS/LAS or LE/LES : Este trabajo no . . . . puedo hacer sola. ¿ . . . . das esta carta a Juan? ¿ Me explicas este problema? No . . . . comprendo. A los niños no . . . . gustan los payasos. ¿ Te acuerdas de Juanita? . . . . voy a ver esta noche. Voy a llamar a Juan. . . . . . . diré que estamos aquí.

TRANSLATE : ¡ Qué suerte! ¡ Qué bien! ¿ Cuándo tienes que empezar el rodaje? Saldremos la semana próxima. ¿ Por qué no trabajamos juntas?
Do you like this director? This automobile is very expensive. I am not going to rent it. What is your address? I will take them to the mountains; that will do them good.

2.5

COMPLETE with the verbs in parentheses : El mozo . . . . (servir) a los clientes. Los niños . . . . . . (pedir) helados. Nosotros . . . . (servir) a nuestros invitados. María . . . . (despedir) a sus amigos en la estación. ¿ Vosotros . . . . (pedir) lo mismo? Nosotros . . . . (despedir) a nuestros amigos.

TRANSLATE: : ¿ Alguna otra cosa? No, nada más, gracias. ¿ Puedo ver la carta, por favor? La carne poco hecha, por favor. ¿ Puedo pagar con cheques de viaje? ¿ Dónde están los servicios?
For me, fish with French fries. I don't feel like having dinner. I am hungry. I would like dessert. Is the service (tip) included?

See answers on page 33 of booklet.

MORE VOCABULARY

GETTING DRESSED

las prendas de vestir (fpl) — garments

la ropa — clothing

el tejido — fabric

la lana — wool

el algodón — cotton

la seda — silk

el cuero — leather

el abrigo — overcoat

la gabardina — raincoat

el vestido — suit, dress

el conjunto — set, ensemble

la cazadora — blouson, loose blouse

los vaqueros (mpl) — jeans

el chandal — overgarment

el suéter
el jersey — pullover, sweater

el chaleco — vest

el cinturón — belt

el sombrero — hat

la bufanda — scarf

el pañuelo — handkerchief

el guante — glove

la corbata — tie

las gafas (fpl) — eyeglasses

el calzoncillo — men's briefs

las bragas (fpl) — women's panties

el sujetador — brassiere

las medias (fpl) — stockings

el camisón — nightshirt, nightgown

la bata — bathrobe

las playeras (f) — tennis shoes, sneakers

el paraguas — umbrella

la toalla — towel

la servilleta — napkin

el botón — button

la aguja — needle

el hilo — thread

las tijeras (fpl) — scissors

EATING

los alimentos (mpl) — foods

la vaca — beef

la ternera — veal

el cerdo — pork

el cordero — lamb

la chuleta — cutlet, chop

el pollo — chicken

el pavo — turkey

el pato — duck

el conejo — rabbit

el salchichón — large sausage

el embutido — pork sausage

la sopa — soup

el caldo — broth

la salsa — sauce

las verduras (fpl) — (green) vegetables

las legumbres (fpl) — vegetables

las judías verdes — green beans

la col — cabbage

la coliflor — cauliflower

la zanahoria — carrot

el puerro — leek

el rábano — radish

la lechuga — lettuce

el pepino — cucumber

la cebolla — onion

el ajo — garlic

los guisantes (mpl) — peas

los garbanzos (mpl) — chickpeas

las lentejas (fpl) — lentils

la pera — pear

la cereza — cherry

el melocotón — peach

la ciruela — prune

la sandía — watermelon

el pomelo — grapefruit

la piña — pineapple

la uva — grape

la almendra — almond

la nuez — nut

el caramelo — caramel

la galleta — biscuit, cookie

el helado — ice cream

el azúcar (m/f) — sugar

la mantequilla — butter

el aceite — oil

el desayuno — breakfast

el almuerzo — lunch

la comida — meal, dinner

la merienda — light meal, snack

la cena — dinner, supper

la bebida — drink

la gaseosa — soda

2. TEST YOURSELF

1. WRITE THE CORRECT FORM

Esta chaqueta no me queda bien. Voy a llevar la roj. . . . ¿Qué te parecen estos pantalones azules? A mí me gustan más los blanc. . . . ¿Qué camisa vas a llevar? ¿La gris. . . . o la amarill. . . . ? ¡Qué bonita esta falda negr. . . . ! La verd. . . . está mejor. ¿Puedo probarme estos zapatos gris. . . . ?

2. MAS/MENOS/MÁS. . .QUE/MENOS. . .QUE/TAN. . .COMO/TANTOS. . .COMO

— El pescado es . . . . sano . . . . la carne.
— Tienes razón, pero a mí me gusta . . . . la carne.
— Tu piso es . . . . pequeño . . . . el mío.
— Claro, en este edificio los pisos son todos iguales.
— En este restaurante hay . . . . gente . . . . en el otro.
— Es que es . . . . caro.
— En España hay muchos tipos de quesos.
— Sí, pero no hay . . . . como en Francia.

3. COMPLETE WITH MUY/MUCHO/MUCHA

El ambiente es . . . . acogedor. Me gusta . . . . comer aquí. La comida es . . . . sabrosa. Hay . . . . gente en este restaurante.

4. FIND THE MATCHING QUESTION

1. Son las seis
2. Es Juan
3. El azul me queda mejor
4. Con Juan
5. A las seis
6. La chaqueta más larga
7. De Juan

A - ¿De quién hablas?
B - ¿Cuál prefieres?
C - ¿A qué hora salimos?
D - ¿Con quién hablas?
E - ¿Qué color prefieres?
F - ¿Quién habla?
G - ¿Qué hora es?

5. COMPLETE WITH THE OBJECT PRONOUN

A mí . . . . gustan los mariscos. ¿Y a ti?
Quisiéramos comer pescado. ¿Qué . . . . recomienda?
Ya sé que te gusta el jerez pero . . . . sienta mal.
¿Dónde están las llaves? No . . . . encuentro.
¿Estáis cansados? ¿Qué . . . . parece si volvemos al hotel?
¿Quiere la carta? Aquí . . . . tiene.
¿Quién es aquél chico? No . . . . conozco.
Mis amigos quieren comer paella. ¿Qué . . . . recomienda?
¿Dónde están los papeles ¿No . . . . veo.

6. LOOK AT MR. RAMIREZ'S SCHEDULE . . .

and write what he must do on Tuesday. You must use TENER QUE + infinitive.

10 hs : desayuno con editor francés . . . _A las diez tiene que desayunar con un editor francés._
11 hs : visita de la editorial Nathan . . . .
13.15 hs : almuerzo con el director general . . . .
15 hs : telefonear a Diana . . . .
16 hs : visita del Louvre . . . .
19 hs : cena con amigos . . . .

7. CHANGE THE VERBS IN PARENTHESES TO THE FUTURE

Mañana . . . . **(desayunar - nosotros)** _temprano y luego_ . . . .
(ir - nosotros) _de tiendas._ . . . . **(coger - ellos)** _el primer avión, así_ . . . .
(tener - ellos) _tiempo para visitar la ciudad. Si sube por esta avenida,_ . . . .
(encontrar - usted) _la celle que busca. Si puedo,_ . . . .**(venir - yo)** _con el_
coche. ¿Qué . . . . **(hacer - tú)** _para las vacaciones? No_ . . . . **(poder -**
yo) _salir de vacaciones, tengo mucho trabajo._

8. CHANGE THE VERBS IN PARENTHESES TO THE CORRECT FORM

— _¿Qué estás_ . . . . **(hacer)**_?_
— _Estoy_ . . . . **(mirar)** _el horario de trenes._
— _¿Te_ . . . . **(ir)** _de viaje?_
— _Sí,_ . . . . **(salir)** _esta tarde para Castellón y_ . . . . . . **(volver)** _el lunes._
— _¿Dónde_ . . . . _ese sitio?_ **(estar)**
— _Cerca de Valencia,_ . . . . . . **(tener)** _que ir hasta allí y luego cambiar de tren._
— _Te conviene tomar el nocturno._ . . . . **(llevar)** _coches-cama y es más barato que_
el Talgo.
— _Y ¿qué harás en Castellón?_
— **(Pasar)** . . . . _unas vacaciones allí, en casa de mi hermano._

9. MATCH THE REACTIONS IN THE SECOND COLUMN WITH THE FIRST

1. _¿Y si vamos a cenar?_
2. _Me gustan estas botas_
3. _¿Quieres una naranjada?_
4. _Mira esos pañuelos_
5. _¿Qué te parece esta corbata?_
6. _Este salmón está muy bueno_
7. _No hay más asientos_
8. _¿Algo más?_

A - _¡Qué bonitos!_
B - _No, no tengo sed._
C - _No está mal_
D - _¡Qué mala suerte!_
E - _¿Por qué no?_
F - _A mí no me gustan nada_
G - _Sí, es exquisito_
H - _No, nada más_

Check your answers on page 34 of booklet.

THE WAY TO EACH OTHER

The choice was extremely difficult. An apartment in the heart of old Madrid tempted me very much. To live there would have allowed me to have an aperitif at nightfall on one of the terraces of the Plaza Mayor, then to wander aroud the nearby streets tasting all sorts of tapas. Each bar has its specialty: *el Mesón de la tortilla, el Méson del champiñon, el de los mejillones* . . . I don't know if my stomach could have taken it in the long run. Well, the apartment was in very bad shape and it would have required spending enormous amounts of money to make it liveable.

The one that was in the Barrio de Salamanca was another story. The Prado and the Retiro almost within walking distance. The principal art galleries right at hand. The most stylish stores for clothes. But all these wonderful things at the price of terrible noise all day and all night. The insane traffic never stops on Velazquez Avenue. Pity!

To find quiet, I could have chosen the little town of Majadahonda, a fairly agreeable little suburb. But frankly, all the houses were so much alike that I'd have been afraid of going to sleep in the wrong one when I came home at night after a little too much to drink!

There were also the northern districts, above Bernabeu Stadium. There you'd be surrounded by Americans and Argentinians. Beautiful apartments, however, and well designed. A way had even been found to surround them with gardens. What a pleasure to come home through these leafy walkways!

I think that in the end my choice was good. Chamberi is an agreeable district. Formerly considered the north, it has now become entirely central — so much has the city spread out on all sides. It has good connections, and the charm of traditional Madrid with its shopkeepers, its bars, its old and new restaurants. Exactly as it should be. And it's a central point. Looking at the map I see that from here I can systematically go all over the city.

The people of Madrid love to go out. At least one out of every three meals is eaten out, either *la merienda*, in the middle of the afternoon, or *la copa por la noche*. It will be difficult, but with a little luck, I'll run across Rosa one day or another. There are also the Vip center for the night owls. The regulars all meet there around three o'clock in the morning. Fortunately these Vip centers, with cafeteria, bookshop, grocery store, and gift shop aren't very numerous.

I just have to find the places where people like her get together. I've found out that in Madrid it works in waves — fads started by groups with the same interests. You can make the rounds quickly. The letter that Rosa left for me when she went away sets up a real treasure hunt now. At the time I had to give it to someone to translate, and even then I hadn't understood very much. For her farewell, she had been forced to write in her own language — a perfect way to communicate the break, underlining it by the gulf that had always separated us. She had understood everything about my world and my language, but I knew nothing of hers. The idea of discovering it had never even occurred to me.

« Portrait » Picasso

Querido mio:

Me voy. Estoy harta de Paris, de los esfuerzos y de la vida tan rápida. Añoro mis antiguas costumbres comunitarias, los amigos numerosos, los de siempre y los de la vispera, el chocolate con churros, las charlas en el cafe Gijon, el cocido de los lunes en Casa Anselmo, los chotis en la Plaza del Dos de Mayo seguidos de la copa de la madrugada en La Manuela. Tú no sabes de eso y no lo puedes entender. Perdóname. Un beso y adios:

Rosa

She couldn't have any doubt now that I was here to try to understand.

CONTINUED . . .

UNIT 3

"ANDALUSIA:" Castillo de Vélez Blanco.

⟦•• ⟧ LISTEN

ON THE ROAD

algunas nubes que se convertirán en chu-
bascos durante la tarde. En el Norte se
esperan temperaturas más frías. Estado
de la mar: marejadilla a marejada.
Soplará una ligera brisa y el termómetro
alcanzará, al mediodía, los 21 grados. Por
la tarde, refrescará. Mañana se espera
buen tiempo en todo el litoral medite-
rráneo».

Paloma : *¡Qué pena! Va a llover y no*
podremos bañarnos. Habrá que cambiar
de planes.

Paco : *¡Qué le vamos a hacer...! ¿No te*
gustaría comer en un restaurante de El
Saler...?

Paloma : *¿De El Saler...?*

Paco : *Sí, mujer. La playa más conocida*
de Valencia. Luego podríamos dar una
vuelta por la ciudad.

Paloma : *¿Dónde me llevarás...?*

Paloma and Paco, en route to Andalusia, pass through the area of Valencia.

Paloma : *¿Cuál es el camino hacia Va-*
lencia...?

Paco : *En la gasolinera se lo preguntare-*
mos al empleado.

Paloma : *Me gustaría comprar fruta.*

Paco : *En la carretera venden. Podremos*
comprarla más tarde.

Radio : *«Aquí radio Valencia, emisora*
F.38, La Voz del Mediterráneo. Emitimos
para todos los oyentes el programa "Viva
la Fiesta." Podrán escucharnos todos los
días desde las 11.30 a las 14 horas.
Información meteorológica: cielo cubierto,

Paco : *¡Ah! Tengo una sorpresa. ¿Te la*
digo...? ... Te llevaré a Los Viveros, a re-
correr la parte más antigua y a visitar el
Museo Fallero.

Paloma : *¡Gracias, corazón! Eres un cielo.*
Me encantará.

⟦•• ⟧ LISTEN AND REPEAT
You will find the translation on page 16 of booklet.

Views of Spain: 1. Pyrenees (Huesca)
2. Castillo de Peñafiel (Valladolid)
3. Patones de Abajo (Madrid area)
4. Cádiz countryside
5. La Rioja
6. Highway in Guipúzcoa (Basque Country)

4

6

NOUNS

la carretera — road, highway
el camino — road
la gasolinera — gas station
el/la empleado(a) — employee
la voz — voice
el/la oyente — listener
la fiesta — party
el cielo — sky, Heaven
la nube — cloud
el chubasco — shower, storm
el estado — state
la marejada — groundswell
el mediodía — noon
el grado — degree
la mujer — woman
la sorpresa — surprise
el corazón — heart

_____

el deporte — sport
el calor — heat, warmth
el viento — wind
el dibujo — picture, design
el asiento — seat
el cuaderno — notebook
el supermercado — supermarket
la gasolina — gasoline

ADJECTIVES

cubierto(a) — covered
ligero(a) — light
conocido(a) — known, famous

_____

despejado(a) — clear, cloudless

VERBS

preguntar — to ask
comprar — to buy
vender — to sell
convertir(se) — to change (into)
soplar — to blow, to breathe
alcanzar — to reach
refrescar — to refresh
llover — to rain
bañarse — to bathe
cambiar — to change
decir — to say
llevar — to lead, to bring
recorrer — to travel through

_____

gastar — to spend
nevar — to snow
enseñar — to show, to teach
mostrar — to show
devolver — to return (something)
firmar — to sign
comunicar — to communicate
leer — to read
enviar — to send

MISCELLANEOUS

hacia — toward
algún(a/os/as) — some *(1)*
que — who, that *(2)*
durante — during
¡ qué pena! — what a pity!
¡ qué le vamos a hacer! — What are we going to do?

_____

en tu lugar — at (or, in) your place
demasiado — too much

HOW TO SAY IT

1. SPEAKING ABOUT THE WEATHER

¿ Qué tiempo hace? — What's the weather?
Hace buen (mal) tiempo — It's good (bad) weather *(1)*
Hace calor (frío) — It's warm [hot] (cold) *(3)*
Hace viento — It's windy
Llueve a mares — It's raining heavily, It's really coming down

2. EXPRESSING REGRET

¡ Qué pena!
¡ Qué lástima! — What a pity!
Es una pena (lástima) — It's a shame!
¿ Qué le vamos a hacer? — What are we going to do?

3. MAKING A SUGGESTION

¿ No te gustaría bañarte? — Wouldn't you like to go bathing?
Podríamos salir, si quieres — We could leave, if you want to
¿ Y si empezáramos sin ellos? — And if we start without them? *(4)*
¿ No tienes ganas de caminar? — Don't you feel like walking?

4. EXPRESSING TENDERNESS

Eres un cielo (un amor) — You're Heaven (a love)
Eres un encanto de mujer — You are feminine charm personified
Gracias, cariño — Thank you, dear
Adios, corazón — Goodbye, my love (heart)
¡ Qué tal, preciosa? — What's new, my lovely?
¡ Tesoro mío! — My treasure!
¡ Cariñito! ¡Cielito! — My love! Dearest! *(5)*

| NOTES . . . | NOTES . . . | NOTES . . . | NOTES . . . |

(1) Placed in front of a masculine singular noun, "uno," "alguno," "ninguno," "bueno," "malo," "primero," and "tercero" drop their final "o." — (2) The relative pronoun "que" has the English equivalents of "who," "which," "that" and is written without an accent, contrary to the "qué" in exclamatory and interrogative sentences. — (3) "Hace calor" is literally "It's making heat (or, warmth)." — (4) The past subjunctive is more commonly used in Spanish. — (5) The diminutive "ito(a)," very common in familiar, informal language, most often expresses smallness in size, but also affection at times.

1. CONDITIONAL TENSE

🔊 LISTEN:

Trabajas mucho
- *Yo en tu lugar trabajaría menos*
Come poco
- *Yo, en su lugar, comería más*

Continue according to the model. Watch out for IRREGULAR VERBS!
Trabajas mucho — Come poco — Descansa poco — Sales mucho — Hace poco deporte — Bebe mucho — Fumas demasiado — Duermes poco — Gasta mucho — Lees poco — Vas mucho al cine.

Grammar: See N.

2. TALKING ABOUT THE WEATHER

🔊 LISTEN:

El cielo está despejado
- *Mañana el cielo estará despejado*

Change as in the model using weather expressions and verbs in the future tense:
El cielo está despejado — Hace mucho calor — Soplan vientos del norte — Nieva en la Sierra Nevada — Llueve en San Sebastián — Hay vientos fuertes en Galicia — Hace frío en Barcelona — La temperatura alcanza los 30° en la costa mediterránea.

Grammar: See M.

3. DOUBLE OBJECT PRONOUNS

🔊 LISTEN:

¿Me envías el paquete? (mañana)
- *Te lo voy a enviar mañana*
¿Nos reservas una localidad? (más tarde)
- *Os la voy a reservar más tarde*

Answer using the two pronouns as in the model:
¿Me envías el paquete? - mañana; ¿Nos reservas una localidad? - más tarde; ¿Nos enseñas tus dibujos? otro día; ¿Me reservas un asiento? - esta tarde; ¿Nos das los billetes? - enseguida; ¿Me escribes una carta? - esta noche; ¿Me explicas este ejercicio? - más tarde; ¿Nos subes las maletas? - enseguida.

Grammar: See F.

4. DOUBLE OBJECT PRONOUNS

🔊 LISTEN:

¿Le das la entrada a Carlos? (teatro)
- *Sí, se la daré en el teatro*
¿Les compras los cuadernos a los niños? (supermercado)
- *Sí, se los compraré en el supermercado*

Continue according to the model replacing the noun with the pronoun. Remember "le" becomes "se" when it is followed by another third-person pronoun beginning with "l":
¿Le das la entrada a Carlos? - teatro; ¿Les compras los cuadernos a los niños? - supermercado; ¿Le devuelves el libro a Juanita? - casa; ¿Les pagamos la gasolina a los Pérez? - restaurante; ¿Les muestras los cuadros a los señores? - estudio; ¿Le firmas el contrato al nuevo empleado? - oficina; ¿Le comunica su dimisión al presidente? - reunión. Grammar: See F.

5. PRONOUN WITH THE INFINITIVE

🔊 LISTEN:

¿Estás leyendo el periódico?
- *No, voy a leerlo más tarde*

Continue according to the model. Remember to place the pronoun after and attached to the infinitive:
¿Estás leyendo el periódico? — ¿Estás despidiendo a los clientes? — ¿Estás sirviendo a los señores? — ¿Estás discutiendo el contrato? — ¿Estás mirando la tele? — ¿Estás enviando el télex? — ¿Estás haciendo las cartas? Grammar: See F.

6. TRANSLATION OF "on" = "se"

🔊 LISTEN:

¿Qué venden en ese puesto? (pan)
- *Se vende pan*
¿Qué venden en esa tienda? (frutas)
- *Se venden frutas*

Continue according to the model. Remember number agreement between the verb and noun that follows:
¿Qué venden en ese puesto? (pan) — ¿Qué venden en esa tienda? (frutas) — ¿Qué alquilan en esa agencia? (pisos) — ¿Qué fabrican aquí? (zapatos) — ¿Qué compran aquí? (ropa) — ¿Qué compran en esa joyería? (oro). Grammar: See F.

WEATHER

There's a good reason why hordes of tourists sweep down each summer onto the Iberian peninsula — Spain means sun and warmth. This claim requires some explanation. There is sun and warmth, but not everywhere nor all the time.

It's true that most of the atmospheric depressions that cross western Europe tend to dissipate rapidly below the Pyrenees. About 80 percent of the Iberian peninsula has more than 2,500 hours of sunshine a year, a privilege shared with Spain and Portugal by only one other European country — Greece. In certain areas of the Costa del Sol or in the Seville region, there are an average of 300 days of sunshine annually. That's enough to make anyone happy.

Nevertheless, it's not all sunshine in Iberia. You can find some gray and rainy corners that can contribute to rheumatism. This is true of Galicia and its eastern extension — the Cantabrian cliff road and the Basque country. The countryside there is a vision of green valleys and pasturelands rich enough to make Castilian cows, condemned to the arid "meseta" of the central plateau, moo with envy.

Throughout the entire heart of Spain, aridity prevails. Vegetation that is often yellowed and scrubby, with occasional evergreens, is a reminder that it seldom rains and that the land is barely fertile.

Aridity in the central portion does not guarantee warmth. Castile's climate is one of the most continental in western Europe, with tremendous swings of temperature from day to night and between winter and summer. "Nine months of winter, three months of Hell," say Madrid natives

to describe it. It's a climate of extremes in which you go without transition from the last cold winter day to the first warm summer day and swimsuit weather. Some cities in Castile are among the continent's warmest in summer and, at the same time, among the coldest in winter.

Altitude contributes a great deal to this climate. Did you know that Madrid, which is more than 2,000 feet above sea level, is the highest capital in Europe? While not far away in Avila, Cuenca, and Segovia, winterlong Siberian cold even surprises tourists from the north.

To find a climate less schizophrenic, you must leave harsh Castile and go first toward the Mediterranean, then toward the south. In Barcelona, it can still be cold in

winter, but much less so than in Madrid. In Valencia, it's a lot warmer. In Málaga, hardly any of the average monthly temperatures are below 55° F (13° C). It's not unusual on Costa del Sol beaches to enjoy a privilege that's rare in Europe — getting a little suntan at Christmas or the New Year when Parisians and New Yorkers are skidding on ice-covered roads.

To complete this rapid survey of the mosaic Spanish climate, there's just one more unique phenomenon to describe. That's the climate of the Canaries. These islands are planted in the mid-Atlantic Ocean more than 600 miles south of any part of Europe, but just over 60 miles from the Saharan coast with which it shares the beneficence of the sun's rays 12 months a year.

N° 1 ●● LISTEN

Listen carefully to the announcer and choose the right answer to the questions.

1. ¿Quién encontró a quién?

El perro Kala encontró a su dueño Julián . . ☐

El dueño encontró a su perro Kala . . . . ☐

Julián dijo encontrarse muy guau . . . . ☐

2. ¿Cómo se llama el libro?

Barry Hughes . . . . ☐

El Guiness . . . . ☐

El Turmalet . . . . ☐

3. ¿Cuántos años tenían el novio y la novia?

Tomás 97 y María del Rocío 68 . . . . ☐

María del Rocío 86 y Tomás 91 . . . . ☐

Tomás 97 y María del Rocío 86 . . . . ☐

Identify who has asked for what during the radio program by looking at the illustrations.

1. *Tengo una muñeca vestida de azul* ☐   **4.** *Anima mea . . . .* ☐

2. *No me dejes . . . .* ☐   **5.** *Recuerdos del ayer . . . .* ☐

3. *Somos novios . . . .* ☐   **6.** *Mahler : Sinfonia nº 2 . . . . . .* ☐

A _____

B _____

C _____

D _____

E _____

F _____

See answers on page 17 of booklet.

⊙⊙ LISTEN

OLD VALENCIA

Upon arriving at Valencia, Paco and Paloma take a walk. This city evokes in Paco memories of his childhood.

Paco : *Mira, Paloma, por estas calles iba yo al colegio. Allí, junto a la torre, estaba la heladería y, al lado, había un reloj de sol.*

Paloma : *¿Caminabas por estas calles tan oscuras...?*

Paco : *¡Claro! Era el camino más corto. Me despertaba tarde y tenía que venir corriendo por aquí.*

Paloma : *A mí me pasaba lo mismo, pero el colegio estaba al lado mismo de mi casa.*

Paco : *¿Ves ese supermercado...? Antes había un cine : «El Avenida». Solíamos ir allí todos los sábados. Veíamos películas de indios, de guerra. Lo pasábamos muy bien.*

Paloma : *A mí, mis padres no me dejaban ir al cine, pero yo me escapaba algunas veces.*

Paco : *¿Cómo se llamaba aquella actriz rubia y pequeñita que tanto nos hacía reír...?*

Paloma : *¡Ah, sí...! ¡Qué horror! ¡Era malísima!*

Paco : *¡No había otra cosa!*

Paloma : *Yo coleccionaba cromos de actores. Los tenía casi todos.*

Paco : *Bueno, vamos. Te llevaré a una calle medieval, la calle de los Cordeleros.*

Paloma : *¿De qué...?*

Paco : *De los Cordeleros. En la Edad Media las calles llevaban los nombres de los oficios : cerrajería, cordelería, bolsería...*

⊙⊙ LISTEN AND REPEAT
You will find the translation on page 17 of booklet.

Valencia: 1.2. Fallas
3. Valencia oranges
4. Plaza de la Virgen

NOUNS

la *torre* — tower
el reloj de sol — sundial
el reloj de pared — wall clock
el reloj de pulsera — wristwatch
el despertador — alarm clock
la casa — house *(1)*
el indio — Indian
los padres (mpl) — parents *(2)*
el actor/la actriz — actor/actress
el cromo — picture
el oficio — trade
la Edad Media — Middle Ages

_____

el regalo — gift
la película del oeste — western
los dibujos animados (mpl) — animated cartoons
el teatro — theater
las cartas (fpl) — (playing) cards
la obra — (theatrical) work
el/la cantante — singer
la canción — song
el bigote — mustache

ADJECTIVES

rubio(a) — blond
moreno(a) — dark, olive-complected
castaño(a) — chestnut-colored
pequeñito(a) — very small
malo(a) — bad
malísimo(a) — very bad *(3)*
buenísimo(a) — very good *(3)*

_____

guapo(a) — handsome

feo(a) — ugly
rizado(a) — curly
concurrido(a) — frequented
soso(a) — insipid, flat

VERBS

despertar(se) — to wake up
correr — to run
pasar — to spend; to pass (time)
soler — to be accustomed to
pasarlo bien (mal) — (not) to have a good time
dejar — to leave, to permit
escaparse — to escape
reír — to laugh
referirse — to refer to
coleccionar — to collect

_____

jugar — to play (a game) *(4)*
tocar — to play (an instrument) *(4)*

MISCELLANEOUS

tan — so
algunas veces — at times, sometimes
tanto — so much
¡ qué horror! — how horrible!
casi — almost

_____

cada vez — each time
cada vez más (menos) — more (less) each time
a menudo — often
con frecuencia — frequently

HOW TO SAY IT

1. EXPRESSING A POSITIVE OPINION ABOUT A PERFORMANCE

La película era buenísima (muy buena) — The film was very good
La obra era divertida (entretenida) — The play was entertaining
¡ Qué maravilla de concierto ! — What a marvelous concert!
Me encanta esta música — I love this music
Los trajes son preciosos — The costumes are splendid
Este payaso me hace reír siempre — This clown always makes me laugh

2. EXPRESSING A NEGATIVE OPINION ABOUT A PERFORMANCE

La película era malísima (horrible) — The film was very bad
La obra era aburrida (sosa) — The play was boring
¡ Qué horror de concierto ! — What a terrible concert!
No me interesa mucho — It doesn't interest me much
No soporto el ballet clásico — I can't stand classical ballet
Es un fracaso — It's a failure

3. GIVING SOMEONE'S PHYSICAL DESCRIPTION

Es pequeñito y más bien feo — He's quite short and rather ugly
Es alto para su edad — He's big (tall) for his age
¡ Qué guapa ! — How pretty she is!
Parece agradable — He looks like a nice person
Se parece a un cuadro de Picasso — He looks like a Picasso painting
La encuentro más delgada que antes — I find her more slender than before
Este traje la hace más joven — This dress makes her look younger
Se hace cada vez más preciosa — Each time she becomes lovelier

4. EXPRESSING AN OPINION ABOUT SOMEONE'S CHARACTER

Es muy simpático (antipático) — He's very nice (disagreeable)
Me da lástima — I feel sorry (for him/her/it)
La veo aún más amable que de costumbre — I find her friendlier than usual

---

NOTES . . .   NOTES . . .   NOTES . . .   NOTES . . .

(1) For "my" (your) house, one says "mi = (tu) casa." — (2) "Padres" = "parents" or "ancestors." "Hijos" = "sons" or "son(s) and daughter(s)" or "children." — (3) The superlative with the suffix "ísimo(a)" often has a stronger meaning than the combination of "muy" + adjective or adverb. — (4) "To play a game" is "jugar a" + article + game: "jugar al béisbol"; to play a musical instrument is "tocar" + article + instrument: "tocar el piano."

1. THE IMPERFECT TENSE

⊙⊙ LISTEN:

Cada vez que viene, me trae regalos
• Cada vez que venía, me traía regalos
Los sábados vemos películas del Oeste
• Los sábados veíamos películas del Oeste

Change the verbs in the following sentences to the imperfect:
Cada vez que viene me trae regalos — Los sábados vemos películas del Oeste — Siempre me espera a la salida del cine — Todos los días voy al colegio — Nunca la dejan salir — Cuando puedo, voy al teatro — A veces vamos al teatro — Algunas veces nos reunimos con amigos.
Grammar: See L.

2. TO BE ACCUSTOMED TO...

⊙⊙ LISTEN:

El director llega a menudo tarde
• El director suele llegar tarde
María venía a vernos con frecuencia
• María solía venir a vernos

Continue as in model, changing "a menudo," "siempre," and "con frecuencia" for the present or imperfect of the verb SOLER:
El director llega a menudo tarde — María venía a vernos con frecuencia — Yo actúo siempre en este teatro — Tocabamos a menudo el piano — Mis padres nos leían siempre estos libros — Con frecuencia nos quedamos en casa — Los vecinos nos invitan con frecuencia — Siempre compraban el periódico aquí.
Grammar: See J.

3. EXCLAIMING AN OPINION

⊙⊙ LISTEN:

Estas calles son muy oscuras
• ¡Qué calles tan oscuras!

Continue according to the model:
Estas calles son muy oscuras — Este cine es muy pequeño — Esta sala es muy bella — Esta chica es muy simpática — Este hombre es muy tonto — Esta actriz es muy mala — Esas películas eran muy divertidas — Este espectáculo es muy soso — Esa obra era muy aburrida — Este chico es muy feo.

4. "AQUEL/LA, LOS, LAS"

⊙⊙ LISTEN:

actriz rubia (hacer películas cómicas)
• ¿Cómo se llamaba aquella actriz rubia que hacía películas cómicas?

Continue according to the model. Remember to put the verb in the imperfect tense.
actriz rubia (hacer películas cómicas) — presidente francés (tener una nariz muy larga) — señora tan guapa (llevar el pelo rizado) — chicos tan simpáticos (vivir en Torremolinos) — cantante moreno (cantar canciones románticas) — actor andaluz (ser divertido).
Grammar: See F.

5. "EL/LA DE"

⊙⊙ LISTEN:

¿Conoces a ese chico? (gafas)
• ¿Cuál? ¿El de gafas?
¿Conoces a esa chica? (ojos verdes)
• ¿Cuál? ¿La de ojos verdes?

Answer the questions as in the model:
¿Conoces a ese chico? (gafas) — ¿Conoces a esa chica? (ojos verdes) — ¿Conoces a ese señor? (traje oscuro) — ¿Conoces a esos periodistas? (bigotes) — ¿Conoces a esas actrices? (minifalda) — ¿Conoces a ese actor? (pelo largo) — ¿Conoces a esa cantante? (pelo corto).
Grammar: See G.

6. IT'S THE MOST . . .

⊙⊙ LISTEN:

el más antiguo (teatro)
• Éste es el teatro más antiguo. Es uno de los más antiguos teatros de la ciudad
la más estrecha (calle)
• Ésta es la calle más estrecha. Es una de las calles más estrechas de la ciudad

Follow the model:
el más antiguo (teatro) — la más estrecha (calle) — la más bonita (sala de conciertos) — el más concurrido (cine) — la más importante (plaza) — el más elegante (café) — la más conocida (plaza de toros). Grammar: See E.

OLD CITIES

To talk about old Spanish cities presents a serious problem — one of choice. How can we list them without doing the unforgivable by leaving one out. Spain's vast number of historic sites is, along with those in Italy, the greatest in Europe.

Where should we begin? Why not with Santiago de Compostela in the heart of Galicia? The Place d'Espagne, surrounded on all sides by splendid buildings like the cathedral, town hall, and royal hospital, is undoubtedly one of the most beautiful main squares in the country. Nearby, you can stroll around searching for remembrances of past eras in the lively little streets of the old city, with their rows of fine old homes.

From northwestern Spain, let's travel to the northeast. You will marvel at the Gothic quarter of Barcelona. Its cobblestoned streets between the cathedral and San Jaime Square swarm with museums and old buildings. Centuries of history are encompassed in a few hundred square yards.

Castile mustn't be left out. The old quarter of Madrid is sadly reduced, but within a radius of 60 miles around the capital, historic sites thrive. There's old Toledo, with its many churches, its Alcázar, and its El Greco paintings. Segovia is also in that area, with its aqueduct, its cathedral, and its Alcázar as well. Avila has its ramparts and cathedral, and in each of these cities are marvelous old quarters where, with a few long strides, you can leave the twentieth century!

What about the south? When you think about Andalusia, you think about historic sites. There are some dazzling ones there, like the Cordova mosque, the sumptuous Alhambra in Grenada, the Giraldo in Seville — shining witnesses of the Moslem past that left to Spain some of its most beautiful masterpieces. Histo-

ry is everywhere. You see it in the old quarters, in the little streets in Cordova that wind past the mosque, and in the Santa Cruz quarter in Seville with its lanes bursting with dazzling white flowers.

To list them all is almost impossible; there's always one more. Salamanca is one — a city built around its famous university, one of the oldest on the continent. Then there's Cáceres in Estremadura, with its historic quarter surrounded by old walls. Or in the Basque country, there's the astonishing old quarter of San Sebastian with its streets full of noise, and savory smells of fish and the sea.

Of course, Spain's monuments can be found not only in the cities, but also in the villages. From villages of stone houses hanging on the

side of the Pyrenees, to the untouched hamlets of Andalusia, visitors who allow themselves to become lost among the hilly lanes are bewitched by what they see. Many of these have been declared national historic sites. Albarracín, not far from Teruel, is one of these, situated in bare mountains and looking as if it's right out of the sixteenth century. Alberca, south of Salamanca, is another, evoking a rural Spanish town at the close of the Middle Ages.

Let's not forget the string of Andalusian villages between Ronda and Arcos de la Frontera, winding among hills where sparkling little towns rise, one above the other, in the sun.

Are you afraid you'll forget this long list? Don't worry — that will let you discover others for yourself.

LISTEN

Study the photos and conclude from the conversations of the four individuals when and where they will take their vacations.

1. ¿Cuándo tomará Julio sus vacaciones? . . . . ¿Dónde? . . . .
2. ¿Cuándo se irá Mila de vacaciones? . . . . ¿Dónde? . . . .
3. ¿Dónde irán don Pedro y doña Rosa? . . . . ¿Cuándo? . . . .
4. ¿Dónde irá Teresa? . . . . ¿Cuándo? . . . .

Study the definitions and complete the crossword puzzle.

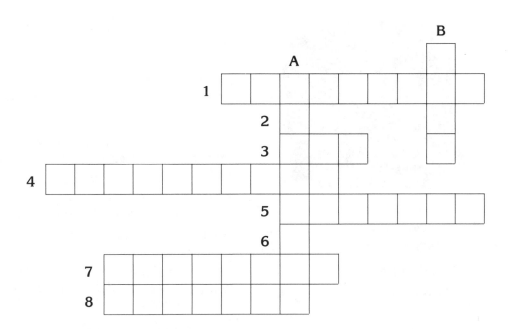

Horizontal
1. En ese lugar se vende algo que refresca la boca en verano.
2. Vocal
3. Lugar donde se juega a las cartas, se bebe café, se charla, se toma el aperitivo...
4. Lugar en el que se llena el combustible del coche, camión o moto.
5. Ahí van los niños y el maestro. Unos a aprender y el otro a enseñar.
6. Consonante.
7. Ahí puedes comprar peras, manzanas, uvas, melones y otras frutas.
8. Ahí acuden algunos fieles a rezar, cantar y suplicar a Dios.

Vertical
A. Lugar donde se venden los libros.
B. En donde los espectadores van a ver películas en pantalla grande.

See solution on page 18 of booklet.

LISTEN

AT THE FAIR IN SEVILLE

Paco and his colleague are at the fair in Seville. They have been drinking wine.

Paco : ¿Quieres otra copa, Ramón...?

Ramón : No, no. Ya tomé muchas y tú no deberías tomar más.

Paco : ... La última... ¡Camarero! ¡Camarero...!

Camarero : ¿Sí...?

Paco : Lo mismo.

Camarero : Le sirvo la última, porque vamos a cerrar.

Ramón : Paco, ya está bien. Llevamos aquí cinco horas.

Paco : ... Estoy mareado. Me siento mal. ¿Quieres llamar un taxi...?

Ramón : ¡Taxi! ¡Taxi!... ¿Hay algún hospital por aquí cerca...?

In the emergency room

Paco : Oiga, señorita ¿El médico tardará mucho...?

Enfermera : ¡Qué va! Me dijo que venía en seguida.

Paco : ¿Es el mismo que me atendío el otro día...? ¿Un señor más bien alto y con bigote...?

Enfermera : No, no. El del otro día se fue de vacaciones. Hoy asiste a los enfermos otro médico.

Paco telephones his newspaper. He tells Don Raimundo that he doesn't feel well but he doesn't say why.

Paco : ¿Don Raimundo...? ¿Don Raimundo...? Lo oigo muy mal.

Don Raimundo : Dime, dime. Yo tampoco te oigo muy bien.

Paco : Decía que hace unos días le envié el paquete con las fotos y el artículo de Ramón Pérez... ¿Ya lo recibió...?

Don Raimundo : ¡No he recibido nada! ¿Cómo me lo enviaste?

Paco : Certificado, como de costumbre.

Don Raimundo : Bueno, y ¿cómo te fue en la feria...? ¿Hiciste todas las fotos que querías...?

Paco : Me faltó el final. Me puse enfermo y tuve que quedarme en casa todo un día.

Don Raimundo : ¿Un día en cama, tú...? Y ahora ¿cómo estás...?

Paco : Me siento mal. Me duele un poco la cabeza y el médico me ordenó unas pastillas.

Don Raimundo : ¡Oye, Paco! ¿No habrás bebido otra vez...?

LISTEN AND REPEAT
You will find the translation on page 19 of booklet.

1.2.3. Bodegas
4. Bar (Seville)

NOUNS

la copa — wineglass, (alcoholic) drink
el camarero — waiter
el hospital — hospital
las urgencias (fpl) — emergencies
la feria — fair
el artículo — article
la costumbre — custom
la cabeza — head
la pastilla — pill, tablet

---

el jarabe — syrup
la música — music
el dolor — pain
el oído — (inner) ear
la garganta — throat
la rodaja — round (of drinks)
la cortada — cut
la botella — bottle

ADJECTIVES

último(a) — last (in a series)
gordo(a) — fat
certificado(a) — certified
enfermo(a) — ill, sick

VERBS

tomar una copa — to have a drink
ir de copas — to go from bar to bar

probar — to taste, to try
estar mareado(a) — to be light-headed
tardar — to be late (behind)
oír — to hear, perceive
recibir — to receive
ponerse enfermo(a) — to become ill
ordenar — to order
emborracharse — to get drunk

---

casarse — to marry
acostarse — to go to bed
levantarse — to get up
divertirse — to have a good time

MISCELLANEOUS

lo mismo — the same thing
ya está bien — that's enough
ninguno(a) — not any, no (+ noun) *(1)*
¡ qué va! — not at all!
en seguida — immediately *(2)*
más bien — rather *(3)*
el de — the one with (of) *(4)*
de vacaciones — on vacation
hace unos días — a few days ago
nada — nothing
oltra vez — again
fuera — outside
fuera de — outside of

NOTES . . .   *NOTES . . .*   *NOTES . . .*   *NOTES . . .*

(1) Remember, "ninguno" drops its final "o" before a masculine singular noun. — (2) also "enseguida" or "inmediatamente." Note English words beginning with "imm" become "inm" in Spanish. — (3) In the dialogue, expressing degree: "más bien alto . . ." = rather tall. — (4) Choice of article must reflect the number and gender of noun(s) referred to. — (5) "Oído" refers to the inner ear. "Oreja" refers to the outer ear. — (6) "Another" is "otro(a)." The indefinite article is not used.

HOW TO SAY IT

1. ASKING ABOUT SOMEONE'S HEALTH

¿ *Cómo estás? Tienes mala cara* — How are you? You don't look well
¿ *Cómo te sientes?* — How do you feel?
¿ *Qué tienes?* — What's the matter with you?
¿ *Estás mejor hoy?* — Are you better today?
¿ *Qué te duele?* — What hurts you?

2. SPEAKING ABOUT YOUR HEALTH

Me siento mal. Me encuentro mal — I don't feel well
Estoy mareado(a)
Me da vueltas la cabeza — I feel dizzy (light-headed)
Estoy débil — I feel weak
Estoy constipada(o) — I'm constipated
Me duele la cabeza — I have a headache
Me duelen los oídos — My ears ache **(5)**
Tengo fiebre (décimas) — I have a fever
Me puse enfermo(a)
Caí enfermo(a) — I've become ill

3. ASKING WHY AND ANSWERING

¿ *Por qué no tomamos otra copa?* — Why don't we have another drink?
Porque ya hemos tomado demasiadas — Because we've had too much already

4. GIVING ADVICE

Deberías tomarte la temperatura — You ought to take your temperature
Le aconsejo (recomiendo) la merluza — I recommend the hake
Más vale volver a casa — Better to go home
Sería mejor ir a la farmacia — It would be better to go to the pharmacy
Yo en su lugar llamaría al médico — In your situation, I would call the doctor

5. ANSWERING QUESTIONS IN THE NEGATIVE

¿ *Hay algún hospital? No, no hay ninguno* — Is there a hospital? No, there is none
¿ *Sales algunas veces? Nunca* — You leave sometimes? Never
¿ *Quieres beber algo? No, nada* — Do you want something to drink? No, nothing
¿ *Y comer algo? No, tampoco* — And something to eat? Not either
¿ *Ves a alguien? No, no veo a nadie* — Do you see anyone? No, I don't see anyone
¿ *Estás enfermo? ! Qué va!* — You're sick? Not at all!

1. USING THE PRETERITE

[● ●] LISTEN:

1977 (acabar los estudios)
- *En 1977 acabé los estudios*
1978 (comenzar a trabajar)
- *En 1978 comencé a trabajar*

Continue according to the model:
1977 (acabar los estudios) — 1978 (comenzar a trabajar) — 1979 (viajar al extranjero) — 1980 (casarse) — de 1980 a 1981 (vivir en Madrid) — de 1981 a 1982 (trabajar en una empresa francesa) — 1982 (cambiar de trabajo) — 1983 (establecerse en España).

Grammar: See L.

2. ASKING QUESTIONS

[● ●] LISTEN:

ir · tú · ¿Dónde?
- *¿Dónde fuiste?*
venir · él · ¿Cuándo?
- *¿Cuándo vino?*

Continue according to the model using the preterite to ask questions:
ir · tú · ¿dónde?; venir · él · ¿cuándo?; estar · vosotros · ¿dónde?; hacer · yo · ¿qué?; decir · ellos ¿qué?; traer · ella · ¿qué?; estar · usted · ¿cuándo?

Grammar: See G.

3. PRETERITE/IMPERFECT

[● ●] LISTEN:

levantarse · sentirse bien (yo)
- *Me levanté porque me sentía bien*

Continue according to the model putting the first verb in the preterite and the second verb in the imperfect:
levantarse · sentirse bien (yo) — dormir · tener frío (él) — acostarse · estar cansados (ellos) — irse · aburrirse (nosotros) — quedarse · divertirse (tú) — ir · estar enfermo (usted) — llamar · querer salir (vosotros) — comer · tener hambre (ella).

Grammar: See L.

4. FEELING DISCOMFORT

[● ●] LISTEN:

la espalda
- *Me duele la espalda*
los brazos
- *Me duelen los brazos*

Continue according to the model using "meduele" or "meduelen" as needed:
la espalda — los brazos — las piernas — el vientre — los oídos — la garganta — las muelas — el estómago.

5. SPENDING TIME

[● ●] LISTEN:

cinco horas · en el bar (yo)
- *Llevo cinco horas en el bar*

Continue according to the model while changing subjects or persons:
cinco horas · en el bar (yo) — dos años · Tarragona (nosotros) — cinco meses · esta ciudad (Manuel) — un año · la empresa (este empleado) — ocho semanas · España (vosotros) — un mes · el hospital (ellos).

Grammar: See J.

6. "ALGUNO/NINGUNO"

[● ●] LISTEN:

¿Hay algún hospital por aquí cerca? (a 10 minutos)
- *No, no hay ninguno. ¡Ah, sí! Hay uno a 10 minutos de aquí*
¿Hay alguna farmacia por aquí cerca? (100 metros)
- *¡Ah sí! Hay una a 100 metros*

Answer the following questions as in the model:
¿Hay algún hospital por aquí cerca? (a 10 minutos) — ¿Hay alguna farmacia por aquí cerca? (a 100 metros) — ¿Hay algún hotel por aquí cerca? (a la vuelta) — ¿Hay alguna oficina de Correos por aquí cerca? (no muy lejos) — ¿Hay algún estanco por aquí cerca? (bastante cerca) — ¿Hay alguna parada de taxis por aquí cerca? (a 5 minutos) — ¿Hay algún kiosco por aquí cerca? (a la vuelta).

Grammar: See H.

CEREMONIES AND HOLIDAYS

Religious or pagan, national or local, austere or happy, ceremonies and holidays abound in Spain. They attract tens of thousands of tourists throughout the year. Some of them are less famous than others, but no less fascinating.

Religious feasts are undeniably the most elaborate. When we think of Andalusia, we think of Holy Week in Seville, a renowned holiday that hasn't lost (or at least not much) its authenticity. It's astonishing to see the devotion of thousands of Sevillians crowding in close as the "pasos," sculptures of Stages of the Cross (some of them weighing a ton), are dragged pitifully inch by inch through the city streets by "costaleros."

Behind comes a silent line of thousands of hooded pilgrims, some of them barefoot. Each quarter of the city, each fraternal group, has its "paso." As the most famous one — the Virgin of Macarena — goes by the crowd verges between hysteria and ecstasy while cries of "guapa" (beautiful) for the Madonna break out everywhere. Andalusian religious feeling is more full of enthusiasm than awe.

There are a multitude of other holy weeks in Spain. The one in Valladolid is more austere but equally fervent; the Castilian retinue carries itself with Andalusian congeniality. Although not as well known, the feast in Zamora near the Portuguese frontier has kept a charming distinction in its original Spanish ceremonies, unaltered by the centuries.

Two weeks after Holy Week, Seville puts its hoods back in the closet to welcome the Fair. For one week, day and night, they dance the "sevillana" to the sounds of casta-

nets and guitar, fortified by sherry. The celebration centers inside "casetas" (little wooden huts built by the town) while outside. Sevillians in traditional costume walk majestically through the streets beside their horses.

At Pentecost, the Andalusians also celebrate one of the most captivating of Spanish feasts. It's the Rocio pilgrimage in Huelva province that draws almost a million visitors each year. For almost a week, cortèges of richly decorated ox-drawn carts converge across the fields toward the little village of El Rocio, which takes on a Far West atmosphere. Andalusian women, wearing their traditional finery, ride behind horsemen and prancing animals. Throughout Saturday night, in an atmosphere of collective hysteria, a

delirious crowd follows the cortège of the Rocio Virgin through the village streets.

Let's not forget Carnival, which Franco banned for a time, but which has returned with all its vigor. There's one in Cádiz, and the most sumptuous one in Santa Cruz de Teneriffe in the Canary Islands.

Many local and village holidays have not yet been mentioned. An important one, commemorating the battle of the Moors against the Christians at Alcoy in Alicante province takes place in April. On Pentecost, "Caballada" in Atienza near Guadalajara celebrates the war exploits of the city's mule drivers.

The profusion of holidays in the country bears added witness to the conviviality of the Spanish people.

N° 1   ▣▶ LISTEN

Check your knowledge about Spain while listening to the cassette

1. ☐ Santander   ☐ Barcelona   ☐ Sevilla

2. ☐ Barcelona   ☐ Madrid   ☐ Sevilla

3. ☐ 1982   ☐ 1986   ☐ 1985

4. ☐ Valencia   ☐ Sevilla   ☐ La Coruña

5. ☐ Málaga   ☐ Tenerife   ☐ Valencia

6. ☐ 20   ☐ 18   ☐ 17

7. ☐ Cataluña   ☐ Andalucía   ☐ Aragón

Use your intelligence: find 22 words which refer to the human body, reading in a horizontal and vertical direction, from left to right and right to left.

B	R	A	Z	O	T	N	A	P	A	R	P	A	D	O	S
P	S	T	A	M	O	S	B	O	S	T	L	Z	A	M	O
A	E	E	P	L	S	L	A	B	I	O	S	M	M	O	C
N	S	X	A	A	T	C	M	S	O	S	E	O	A	L	U
T	A	T	L	I	O	L	E	U	Z	I	R	A	N	O	E
E	T	R	B	B	E	S	I	J	L	E	P	P	O	G	L
B	O	E	L	A	M	I	L	U	A	B	S	T	I	O	L
R	N	M	E	U	S	P	A	D	A	S	L	E	P	A	O
A	T	I	M	G	A	E	R	O	D	I	L	L	A	S	S
Z	I	D	O	N	E	B	A	N	O	E	O	O	E	E	P
O	L	A	Z	E	B	A	C	A	S	C	U	L	E	I	P
P	L	D	A	L	E	M	A	I	N	R	E	E	M	P	L
O	O	E	S	N	O	T	I	O	E	A	S	T	A	L	O
L	M	S	S	U	L	B	R	E	N	N	U	E	N	I	M
I	A	I	L	Ñ	M	T	S	L	P	E	S	S	G	A	O
P	T	L	N	A	L	E	U	A	L	O	R	E	J	A	S
O	O	J	O	S	O	R	E	L	V	A	C	I	O	S	O

See answers on page 20 of booklet.

🔊 LISTEN

THE MICE!

Soledad and her son are at the pool. Her daughter searches for her toilet kit. The mother is upset because she cannot stop thinking about the noises that kept them awake. She is troubled by stories she's heard about the house.

Pablo : *¿Cuánto tiempo he tardado en atravesar la piscina esta vez, mamá...?*

Soledad : *Tres minutos treinta y eso que el agua está todavía fría.*

Pablo : *Voy a intentarlo nuevamente.*

. . . .

Nieves : *¡Mamá! ¡Mamá! ¿Dónde has puesto la bolsa de aseo? No he podido peinarme...*

Soledad : *Nunca encuentras nada. ¡Qué despistada! Ya deberías saber que la dejo siempre en el cuarto de baño.*

Nieves : *Oye, mamá ¿Por qué no salimos a caminar...? Llevamos tres días aquí y todavía no hemos dado ningún paseo.*

Soledad : *¿Cómo...?*

Nieves : *¿Qué te pasa...? Estás muy distraída.*

Soledad : *Desde que me he levantado no he dejado de pensar en lo que ocurrió ayer. Me tiene preocupada.*

Pablo : *No le des más vueltas, mamá. Ya te lo dije. Esos ruidos que escuchamos, eran los ratones. No tienes porqué alarmarte.*

Soledad : *Mira, hijo; se han contado tantas historias raras de este lugar que no sé qué decirte. La abuela, una noche oyó unos ruidos infernales y desde ese día ya no quiso volver.*

Nieves : *¡Mamá! ¿Ya habéis desayunado...?*

Soledad : *¡No, no! Te estábamos esperando. Desayunaremos ahora mismo y más tarde nos iremos a dar un paseo por el monte.*

Pablo : *Mami... ¿Quién construyó el chalé? ¿El abuelo...?*

Soledad : *No, cariño. Cuando el abuelo lo compró ya estaba construido. De eso hace más de setenta años.*

🔊 LISTEN AND REPEAT
You will find the translation on page 20 of booklet.

Signs of old Spain: 1. Montánchez (Caceres)
2. Ruins of Belchite
3. Avila
4. Salamanca

NOUNS

el ratón — mouse
el minuto — minute
la bolsa de aseo — toilet kit
el monte — mountain
el ruido — noise
la historia — story
el abuelo/la abuela
— grandfather/grandmother
el chalé — villa
la madre — mother
la mamá — mama
la mami — mommy *(1)*
el padre — father
el hermano/la hermana — brother/sister
el tío/la tía — uncle/aunt
el primo/la prima — cousin

_____

el negocio — business
la familia — family
la novela — novel

ADJECTIVES

despistado(a) — scatterbrained
distraído(a) — distracted
preocupado(a) — worried
raro(a) — strange

VERBS

intentar — to try
peinar(se) — to comb
ducharse — to shower
dejar de — to cease, to stop from
pensar en — to think about
ocurrir — to happen
dar vueltas a — to think in circles, obsess
tener porqué — to have reason to
alarmarse — to become worried
contar — to tell
volver — to return
construir — to construct
_____

nadar — to swim
afeitarse — to shave

MISCELLANEOUS

y eso que — and not withstanding
nuevamente — anew
¿ qué te pasa? — What's happening to you?
desde que — since
ayer — yesterday
cariño — dear

HOW TO SAY IT

---

1. GIVING INFORMATION ABOUT TIME

Llevo aquí una hora — I've been here for an hour *(2)*
Llevamos casados cuatro años — We've been married for four years
¿Cuánto tiempo tardas en atravesar? — How long are you taking to cross?
Te espero desde hace tres horas — I've been waiting for you for three hours
Te espero desde las tres — I've been waiting for you since three
Hace mucho tiempo que te espero — I've been waiting for you a long time

---

2. SCOLDING SOMEONE

¡Qué despistada! — What a scatterbrain!
¡Estás (Eres) muy distraída! — You're very absentminded!
¡Estás (Eres) tonto! — You are foolish!
No deberías beber tanto — You shouldn't drink so much
Podrías ser más amable — You could be nicer

---

3. EXPRESSING AN ACTION'S REPETITION

Voy a hacerlo nuevamente (de nuevo/otra vez/una vez más) — I'm going to do it again *(3)*
He vuelto a caer enfermo — I've become ill again *(3)*
Vuelvo a repetirlo — I (will) repeat it once more

---

4. TELLING WHAT SOMEONE HAS DONE

El abuelo ha construido el chalé — Grandfather has constructed the villa. Grandfather had the villa constructed *(4)*
Me he cortado el pelo — I've cut my hair. I've had my hair cut *(4)*
Me han hecho un vestido — I have made a dress for myself
Yo los hago trabajar — I make them work

NOTES . . .   NOTES . . .   NOTES . . .   NOTES . . .

(1) "Mamá" and "papá" have the diminutives "mami" and "papi" (dad/daddy). — (2) "Llevar" is sometimes an equivalent for "estar . . . desde hace" = "to be (here, there) . . . since + time." — (3) The prefix "re," indicating repetition is not used often. "Volver + a + infinitive" would be an appropriate equivalent. — (4) These sentences have a dual interpretation.

1. PRESENT PERFECT

[● ●] LISTEN:

dar un paseo (yo)
- *Hoy he dado un paseo*
salir temprano (nosotros)
- *Hoy hemos salido temprano*

Continue according to the model changing the verbs' tense:
dar un paseo · yo (hoy) — salir temprano · nosotros (esta mañana) — dormir · el niño (esta noche) — nadar · vosotros (esta tarde) — venir · Paquita (este fin de semana) — comer · nosotros (a mediodía) — leer · la abuela (anoche) — ver la televisión · los niños (esta tarde).
Grammar: See L.

2. PRESENT PERFECT

[● ●] LISTEN:

¿Por qué no te peinas?
- *Ya me he peinado*
¿Por qué no se acuesta la niña?
- *Ya se ha acostado*

Answer the questions as in the model:
¿Por qué no te peinas? — ¿Por qué no se acuesta la niña? — ¿Por qué no os ducháis? — ¿Por qué no se afeitan los chicos? — ¿Por qué no te lavas? — ¿Por qué no se levanta, Usted? — ¿Por qué no os bañáis?
Grammar: See L.

3. PRETERITE/PRESENT PERFECT

[● ●] LISTEN:

¿Le has escrito a tus padres? (este fin de semana)
- *Sí, les he escrito este fin de semana*
¿Has visto a Juan? (el año pasado)
- *Sí, lo ví el año pasado*

Answer the questions according to the model. Use the present perfect for recent action and the preterite for an action well in the past:
¿Le has escrito a tus padres? (este fin de semana) — ¿Has visto a Juan? (el año pasado) — ¿Habéis hablado con el profesor? (esta mañana) — ¿Tus padres han ido a Madrid? (el mes pasado) — ¿Has recibido el paquete? (esta semana) — ¿Tu marido ha leído este libro? (hace muchos años).
Grammar: See L.

4. "HACE . . . QUE" . . .

[● ●] LISTEN:

Llevamos tres años viviendo aquí
- *Hace tres años que vivimos aquí*
Llevo dos días trabajando en este proyecto
- *Hace dos días que trabajo en este proyecto*

Change the following sentences as in the model:
Llevamos tres años vivendo aquí — Llevo dos días trabajando en este proyecto — Llevo un año escribiendo esta novela — Llevan un mes viajando por España — Lleváis mucho tiempo haciendo esta película — Llevo un mes descansando aquí — Llevamos dos años pensando en estas vacaciones.
Grammar: See I.

5. "DESDE" "DESDE HACE"

[● ●] LISTEN:

¿Desde cuándo trabaja usted en la empresa? (1966)
- *Desde 1966*
¿Desde cuándo no va al médico? (dos meses)
- *Desde hace dos meses*

Answer the questions according to the model. Use "desde" with a specific date. Use "desde hace" for a period of time:
¿Desde cuándo trabaja usted en la empresa? (1966) — ¿Desde cuándo no va al médico? (dos meses) — ¿Desde cuándo vives aquí? (el año pasado) — ¿Desde cuándo hablas español? (dos años) — ¿Desde cuándo no tenéis noticias de la familia?(el mes pasado) — ¿Desde cuándo no han ido al cine? (tres semanas) — ¿Desde cuándo estudias en la Universidad? (1980) — ¿Desde cuándo no hablas con María? (la semana pasada).
Grammar: See I.

6. THAT WHICH, WHAT = "LO QUE"

[● ●] LISTEN:

¿Qué ocurrió?
- *Dime lo que ocurrió*

Change the sentences according to the model:
¿Qué ocurrió? — ¿Qué dijo? — ¿Qué vais a hacer? — ¿Qué piensan? — ¿Qué estás haciendo? — ¿Qué es? — ¿Qué pintan? — ¿Qué pasó?
Grammar: See F.

THE FAMILY

The Spanish family! It was praised to the skies during the Franco regime. For the country's leader, the family constituted a bond of national unity. In the newspapers of that era, you saw photos of families with 10 or 15 children with beaming smiles, posing alongside politicians. The courageous and worthy father would be shown receiving an award. Unmarried mothers, on the other hand, would be seen covered in disgrace, and they enjoyed practically no rights.

Can the Spanish family, which was the object of such political manipulation during the past regime, adapt to changing times? Its image, in any case, must be reformed to adapt to the democratic winds that now blow over the country.

It has, in fact, changed profoundly — most of all in size. The era of large families has come to an end in Spain, a little later than in neighboring countries, but the change is, without doubt, just as irreversible. It looks like from now on one or two children per family will be the rule. This is even more likely because there is no financial encouragement on a political level to have children. Family aid is extremely limited.

The nature of the family has also changed. The traditional family is no longer held up as an example. Top political powers have stopped thinking that good Spaniards must marry at the town hall or the Church and, in addition, have many children. And, in reaction to an educational system in which the imprint of traditional values remains strong, the younger generation refuses to consecrate family values. Young Spaniards often live together without benefit of marriage.

While the family has not escaped the social upheavals of the last two decades in Spain, it has still not lost all its importance. Especially among those over 40, the family remains the foundation of social life more than in other European countries.

Every self-respecting Spaniard spends Christmas with his family. Even though this is true in many countries, nowhere is it more strictly observed than in Spain. The family's presence also manifests itself in more unusual ways. Going to the doctor, for example, is an activity which usually assumes being accompanied by a squad of relatives for reinforcement. During the summer, large reunions take place with members of the entire tribe. Most Spaniards don't go on vacations to the shore or the mountains, but to visit their close relatives.

The family plays another role, that of cushioning problems. In a country with the highest unemployment rate in Europe, most people without jobs have no means of support. It's in the bosom of the family that young people looking for their first job, or older ones condemned to persistent unemployment, find the protection the state cannot offer them. For that particular task, the Spanish family remains indispensable.

Identify the scenes described by the recording and answer true or false to the questions.

	VERDAD	MENTIRA
1. ¡Lo tengo, lo tengo, soy rico!		
2. ¿Mató el que amenaza a su víctima?		
3. ¿Hablan mucho Doña Julia y Margarita?		
4. Roberto vive un momento de nervios		
5. Se escondió el sospechoso detrás de la cortina		
6. Estamos a 23 de Diciembre		
7. Había una piscina y césped donde estaba Roberto		

Find the signs of the Zodiac in Spanish. Search in different directions: horizontal, vertical, from right to left, from left to right.

	A	B	C	D	E	F	G	H	I	J	K	L	M
1	G	P	T	E	S	C	O	R	P	I	O	O	S
2	E	O	T	B	O	B	E	O	A	S	B	S	M
3	M	R	A	U	T	I	L	R	S	R	S	E	T
4	I	M	U	C	E	M	E	P	A	L	A	I	V
5	N	I	R	A	L	E	P	T	G	N	N	R	Z
6	I	S	O	I	N	R	O	C	I	R	P	A	C
7	S	O	T	V	A	M	I	O	T	M	I	O	B
8	O	C	A	N	C	E	R	E	A	R	S	A	L
9	T	L	B	A	I	V	A	N	R	L	C	B	S
10	V	I	R	G	O	S	U	M	I	C	I	T	A
11	I	A	O	M	S	O	C	A	O	Y	S	U	L
12	M	A	L	I	B	R	A	D	S	A	E	V	M

See answers on page 22 of booklet.

⊙⊙ LISTEN:

TWO LETTERS

Soledad writes to her friends and explains her plans.

Querido Paco :
Desde que regresé a Madrid no he sabido nada de ti ni de Paloma. He pasado unos días con mis hijos en el chalé que tienen mis padres en Galicia. Ahora tengo nuevos proyectos de trabajo que pueden interesaros. No tengo la dirección de Paloma. ¿Podrías tú escribirle o enviarme sus señas…? Me han encargado un reportaje sobre «El turismo en Playa de las Américas», en Tenerife. No nos vendrían mal unos quince días allí. Nos pagan bien. Será ideal para combinar trabajo y playa. ¿Puedes escribirme a vuelta de correo haciéndome saber lo que piensas…?
En espera de tus noticias te envía un cordial saludo.

Soledad

Paco writes to Paloma

Palomita mía :
¡Qué cara más dura tienes! Ni una palabra desde aquella tarde en que nos despedimos. ¡Qué bien lo pasamos en la discoteca de Valencia! ¿Te acuerdas…? Yo no podré olvidarlo. Y desde entonces sin noticias.
Aquí en Sevilla me aburro mucho. Menos mal que Ramón es simpático y que también el trabajo va saliendo. ¿Cómo estás tú…? ¿Cómo es la gente esa del cine…? Soledad me escribió. Nos propone hacer un reportaje en Tenerife, sobre el turismo de aquella isla. A mí me encantaría ir ¿Y a ti…? Lo pasaríamos muy bien en Canarias. Hace días te llamé al Hotel Imperial. Primero decían que no te hospedabas allí y luego que te habías marchado. Por eso ahora te escribo esta carta a la dirección de tus padres. Bueno, preciosa, espero tu carta o tu llamada. Vuelvo a enviarte mi teléfono. ¡Cuidado con los ligues! No me olvides y dime qué quieres hacer. Muchos abrazos y un besote de tu amigo.

Paco.

⊙⊙ LISTEN AND REPEAT
You will find the translation on page 22 of booklet.

Views of Spain:
1. Women embroidering
2. Girl in Seville
3. Windows in Segovia
4. Craftsman in Santiago
5. Youths in Madrid
6. Galician clogs
7. Group in small town (Cáceres)
8. Galician fisherman
9. Town of Cáceres
10. Andalusian shepherd

NOUNS

la carta — letter
el proyecto — project, plan
las señas — address
el turismo — tourism
la palabra — word
la isla — island
los ligues — flirtatious meetings
el abrazo — hug, embrace *(1)*
el beso — kiss
el besote — big kiss *(2)*

---

el alojamiento — lodging
la ventanilla — box office, entrance window
el sello — stamp
el buzón de correos — mailbox
el sobre — envelope
la tarjeta postal — postcard

ADJECTIVES

querido(a)
estimado(a) — dear
apreciado(a) — valued
precioso(a) — precious, splendid

VERBS

encargar — to put in charge
venir bien/mal — doing well/badly
despedirse — to say goodbye, to leave
acordarse — to remember
olvidar — to forget
hospedarse — to give lodging
marcharse — to leave

MISCELLANEOUS

ni — neither, nor
unos quince — about fifteen
a vuelta de correo — by return mail
en espera de — waiting for, awaiting
¡qué cara más dura!
¡qué cara dura! — how shameless!
en que — in which
hace días — some days ago
por eso — therefore, that's why
¡cuidado! — careful!

---

de nuevo — again, anew

HOW TO SAY IT

1. BEGINNING A LETTER

A. Informal

Querido(a) amigo(a): — Dear friend,
Queridísimo Paco: — My very dear Paco,
Amor mío: (Cariño:) — My love,

B. Somewhat formal

Estimado(a) amigo(a): — Esteemed friend,
Apreciado(a) amigo(a): — Valued friend,
Distinguido(a) amigo(a): — Distinguished friend,
Estimado (Apreciado/Distinguido) Señor: — Dear Sir,

C. Very formal

Señor(a) Sánchez: — Mr. (Mrs.) Sánchez:
Muy señor(a) mío(a): — Sir (Madam):
Muy señores míos: — Dear Sirs:
Señor Presidente: — Mr. President:/Mr. Chairperson: *(4)*
Señora Directora: — Madam Director: *(4)*

2. ENDING A LETTER

A. Informal

Un beso — A kiss
Un abrazo — A hug
Muchos besos — Lots of kisses
Cariñosamente — Affectionately

B. Somewhat formal

Cordialmente — Cordially
Amistosamente — In friendship
Un saludo afectuoso — Warm regards

C. Very formal

(Muy) Atentamente — Yours truly, Very truly yours
Aprovecho esta ocasión para saludarlo atentamente — I take this opportunity to send you my sincere greetings.

NOTES . . .　　　*NOTES . . .*　　　*NOTES . . .*　　　*NOTES . . .*

(1) In the sense of "the act of taking someone in your arms." — (2) The suffix "ote," much less common than "-ito(a)," gives the sense of something large or gross. — (3) The salutation of a letter is concluded with a colon and not a comma. — (4) No article in direct address.

1. PAST PERFECT

⊙● LISTEN:

He recibido una propuesta. Por eso te escribo
* *Te escribí porque había recibido una propuesta*
He tenido un accidente. Por eso me llama
* *Me llamó porque había tenido un accidente*
Continue according to the model:
He recibido una propuesta. Por eso te escribo — He tenido un accident. Por eso me llama — No hemos reservado alojamiento. Por eso no vamos a España — No lo han terminado. Por eso no me envían el artículo — No te he escrito. Por eso te enojas — Los habéis invitado. Por eso van al teatro.   Grammar: See L.

2. RECOUNTING: "DIJERON QUE. . . "

⊙● LISTEN:

No se hospeda en el hotel
* *Dijeron que no se hospedaba en el hotel*
Se marchó
* *Dijeron que se había marchado*
Continue as in the model using the imperfect when the verb is in the present and the past perfect with verbs in the preterite and present perfect:
No se hospeda aquí — Se marchó — Cambió de dirección — Vive en Madrid — No lo hemos visto — Se marchó ayer — No están en su habitación — No ha dejado la nueva dirección — Se fue a Madrid.   Grammar: See K, L.

3. RECOUNTING: "DIJO QUE. . . "

⊙● LISTEN:

Nos pagarán bien
* *Dijo que nos pagarían bien*
Lo pasaremos bien
* *Dijo que lo pasaríamos bien*
Tell what you heard beginning with "Dijo que" and using the conditional tense:
Nos pagarán muy bien — Lo pasaremos bien — Empezaremos dentro de una semana — El trabajo durará unos quince días — Haremos un reportaje sobre turismo — Tendremos tiempo para descansar — Podremos combinar trabajo y playa — Nos alojaremos en Tenerife.   Grammar: See H.

4. "VOLVER A" + INFINITIVE

⊙● LISTEN:

Te envío de nuevo mi teléfono
* *Te vuelvo a enviar mi teléfono*
No he visto más a Juan
* *No he vuelto a ver a Juan*
Change the following sentences replacing the expressions that mean repetition with "volver a" + infinitive. Watch the tenses of the verbs!
Te envío de nuevo mi teléfono — No he visto más a Juan — Nos proponen de nuevo un viaje — No han pasado más esa película — Mi amigo me ha escrito de nuevo — Te escribo de nuevo — Os doy nuevamente mi dirección.   Grammar: See J.

5. OF WHOM, OF WHICH . . .

⊙● LISTEN:

chico
* *Este es el chico del que te hablé*
película
* *Esta es la película de la que te hablé*
Continue according to the model using "del/de la/los/las . . . que" as needed:
chica — película — chicas — hotel — compañeros — película — amigo — lugar — carta — amigas — libros — playa — artículos — foto — discoteca.   Grammar: See F.

6. IN WHICH, WHERE . . .

⊙● LISTEN:

En este hotel se hospeda Juan
* *Este es el hotel donde Juan se hospeda*
Cuando nos despedimos, Angela estaba contenta (la tarde)
* *Angela estaba contenta la tarde en que nos despedimos*
Continue according to the model. Remember that with "el día," "el mes," and "el año," you can use "que" all alone:
En este hotel se hospeda Juan — Cuando nos despedimos, Angela estaba contenta (la tarde) — Cuando nació, hubo fiesta en el pueblo (el día) — En esta plaza encontré a María — En esta calle vivían mis padres — Cuando estaba en España, iba a los toros (el año) — Cuando trabajaba en Correos, me aburría muchísimo (la época) — En este colegio estudian mis hijos.   Grammar: See F.

WORK AND THE BUREAUCRACY

Spain has taken a great leap. Yesterday, it was a rural and undeveloped country. Now it has plunged into the computer revolution, going from the nineteenth to the twenty-first centuries without time to catch its breath.

Those who travel to Spain today see that they must give up any preconceptions they had about the country. The image of a disorganized country where things function any which way, with a population that's not inclined toward hard work, is far from the truth. If it ever was that way, Spain is no longer a "Third World" of western Europe.

The Spanish never fail to remind Europeans that the continent stretches to the Strait of Gibraltar, and does not end at the Pyrenees. Spain is rapidly becoming modernized; employers or unions, government or private institutions — each talks only of high technology, research, computerization, and robot-

ics. This is a historic transformation in a country that for too long believed in the famous saying of philosopher Miguel de Unamuno: "¡que inventen ellos!" (let others do the inventing).

Of course, everything does not always go smoothly. Reflexes are still conditioned by decades of protectionist mentality. People have a tendency to count on the protective intervention of the state rather than on their own strength — a state that people never stop damning, but from which, too often, they expect a great deal.

In addition, red tape is more prevalent in Spain than in neighboring countries. Whoever has business with the government can't help seeing its imperfections. Local functionaries judge too often that society must serve the state, rather than the reverse. They have an unfortunate tendency to think that their

work brings more rights than responsibilities. It's often difficult for those under their jurisdiction who finds themselves plunged into Kafkaesque formalities to accomplish the most elementary things. It's not surprising when "gestorias" (offices in charge of administrative proceedings for their clients) go bankrupt in Spain. It's a paradox in a country where informality is generally the rule.

The Spanish are convinced that these rigid earmarks of the past will disappear under the effects of this road to modernization and streamlining the country has embarked upon — a road to modernization that will rank it along with the rest of Europe. Entrance into the European Community symbolizes a leap forward. It is a leap toward the future for a country that has rushed to prove to everyone that it can play the game as well as they. It seems Spain will soon do just that.

141. *ciento cuarenta y uno*

◉◉ LISTEN

La doncella guerrera

Very Old ballad
(Sung and arranged by Joaquín Díaz)

The young woman warrior

En Sevilla a un sevillano siete hijas le dio Dios

todas siete fueron hembras y ninguno fue varón.

A la más chiquita de ellas le llevó la inclinación

de ir a servir a la guerra vestidita de varón.

Al montar en el caballo, la espada se le cayó

por decir «maldita sea», dijo - Maldita sea yo.

Et rey que lo estaba oyendo, de amores se
cautivó :

— Madre, los ojos de Marcos,
son de hembra, no de varón.

— Convídala tú, hijo mío, a los ríos a nadar

que si ella fuese hembra,
no se querrá desnudar.

Toditos los caballeros
se empiezan a desnudar

y el caballero don Marcos se ha retirado a
llorar.

– ¿Por qué llora usted don Marcos?

– ¿Por qué debo de llorar?

Por un falso testimonio
que me quieren levantar.

— No llores alma querida,
no llores mi corazón,

que eso que tú tanto sientes, eso lo deseo yo.

In Seville, God blessed a man with seven daughte

all seven were female and not one a son.

The youngest was moved by the need

to serve in war dressed as a male warrior.

When on horseback, her sword fell to earth

and instead of "cursed it be" she said "cursed
girl, me.

The king hearing it all, became love's prisoner:

— Mother, Marco's eyes are those of a girl,
not a boy's.

— You invite her, my son, to the river to bathe

were she a girl,
she would never disrobe.

But each and every horseman
began to disrobe

and don Marcos went off to weep.

— Why do you weep don Marcos?

— Why must I shed my tears?

Because of an untrue accusation
brought against me.

— Do not cry, dear soul,
do not cry, my heart,

for what hurts you so much, is what I desire.

IDIOMS

CORTARSE LA COLETA

(to cut off one's pigtail)

To quit the "ring"

IR AL GRANO

(Go straight for the grain)

To come to the point

DORMIR A PIERNA SUELTA

(Sleep in a detached-leg fashion)

To sleep soundly

METER LA PATA

(Put one's leg in)

Put one's foot in one's mouth

3.1

COMPLETE with SE or LE : Por la tarde . . . . espera buen tiempo en Granada. En este puesto . . . . . . vende fruta. ¿A quién . . . . . . vendes tu casa? . . . . . . queda bien esa chaqueta. En esta tienda no . . . habla español . . . voy a comprar el coche. ¿Dónde . . . alquilan coches?

TRANSLATE : ¡Qué le vamos a hacer! ¡Qué pena! ¿Qué tiempo hace? En invierno hace mucho frío. ¿Hay alguna oficina de turismo por aquí? No, no hay ninguna.

It will be good weather tomorrow. We are cold. It's very warm (hot). I am very warm (hot). On Sunday, there is no store open.

3.2

PUT the verbs in parentheses in the imperfect tense : Cuando . . . . (ser) (nosotros) jóvenes, ... (salir) (nosotros) todas las noches. Eugenia no . . . . (poder) ir al cine, sus padres no la . . . . (dejar). Y vosotros ¿Qué . . . . (hacer)? . . . . (soler) (nosotros) ir a misa y luego . . . (reunirse) (nosotros) en casa.

TRANSLATE : ¿Quién es aquella chica? ¿Cuál? La de botas. Ese es un hombre inteligente ¿Cuál? El que nos está saludando. A ti te pasa lo mismo que a mí? Lo pasamos muy bien anoche verdad? ¡Qué va! Yo lo pasé fatal.

He went to see her very often. She never used to write to him. Each time he came, he brought flowers for her. He was always happy. From time to time, he received a letter.

3.3

COMPLETE with SE or LE : Mi marido . . . . . . siente mal. . . . . . . duele el estómago; El doctor . . . . ha recetado un calmante. Mi hijo . . . . quedó en la cama porque no . . . . encuentra bien. Este medicamento no . . . . . . sienta bien. Cuando . . . . . . sienta, ... duele la pierna. Manuel . . . . . . pone nervioso porque . . . . . . falta un artículo.

TRANSLATE : Mi mujer se siente débil. Tiene que respirar bien. Debe quedarse en cama. Me falta una medicina. ¿Quieres otra aspirina?

I've become ill. I was not feeling very well. He has a sore throat. Do you want to call another doctor? Everything hurts me. I have been in bed for three days.

3.4

COMPLETE with present perfect tense : ¿Te . . . . (levantarse) (tú) temprano? ¿Donde . . . . (trabajar) (usted)? Los niños no se . . . . (acostarse) todavía. Yo . . . . (decir) nada. Nunca . . . . (vivir) (nosotros) en Francia. ¿ . . . . (ver) (vosotros) ratones?

TRANSLATE : Mis abuelos han venido esta mañana. ¿Quién vino anoche? Mamá está preocupada. No sé lo que ha pasado. ¡Qué despistada! ¡ Qué tonto! ¡Qué loco! ¡Qué inteligente!

My grandmother has been here since last week. The engineers have been here for three days. My cousin has been working in that factory for a year. What happened last night? I don't know what happened to you.

3.5

COMPLETE the sentences with: EL/LA/LOS/LAS QUE AND DEL/DE LA/DE LAS/ DE LOS QUE.

Aquí están los documentos . . . . te hablé. ¿Qué ventanilla es? . . . . está enfrente. ¿Dónde están los sellos? ¿Cuáles?¿ . . . . compraste ayer? Es una actriz . . . . nunca he oído hablar. Te traes ese pedido, ... enviaron nuestros clientes de Roma. Es un tema . . . prefiero no hablar.

TRANSLATE : ¡Menos mal que llegaste! ¡Menos mal que el trabajo no me falta! ¡Cuidado con el ligue! ¡Cuidado con el perro! ¿Puedes contestarme a vuelta de correo?

Today is January 8th. Wednesday, I must go to the airport. I began to work in June of 1980. Tomorrow is May 2d. Dear friend. Esteemed client.

See answers on page 33 of booklet.

MORE VOCABULARY

THE WEATHER

el tiempo — weather

el chaparrón — downpour

la niebla — fog

la bruma — fog, mist

el claro — clearing

la tormenta — storm

la lluvia — rain

el hielo — ice

el trueno — thunder

el relámpago — lightning

el rayo — flash of lightning

el viento — wind

el norte — north

el sur — south

el este — east

el oeste — west

la estación — season

la primavera — spring

el verano — summer

el otoño — autumn

el invierno — winter

helar — to freeze

llover — to rain

suave — mild

húmedo(a) — humid

nublado(a) — cloudy

brumoso(a) — foggy

tormentoso(a) — stormy

lluvioso(a) — rainy

seco(a) — dry

THE BODY

el cuerpo — body

los cabellos (mpl) — hair

el pelo — hair

la cara — face

la frente — forehead

el ojo — eye

la nariz — nose

la boca — mouth

el labio — lip

la lengua — tongue

el diente — tooth (front)

la muela — tooth (molar)

la mejilla — cheek

la barbilla — chin

el cuello — neck

la nuca — nape (of the neck)

el hombro — shoulder

el brazo — arm

el codo — elbow

la muñeca — wrist

la mano — hand

el dedo — finger

el pulgar — thumb

la uña — (finger) nail

la espalda — back

el pecho — chest

el vientre — stomach, abdomen

la nalga — buttock

la pierna — leg

el muslo — thigh

la rodilla — knee

el tobillo — ankle

el dedo del pie — toe

el hígado — liver

el estómago — stomach

el hueso — bone

el nervio — nerve

el músculo — muscle

la piel — skin

HEALTH

la salud — health

la enfermedad — illness

la herida — wound

la tos — cough, cold

el catarro — (head) cold

el resfriado — cold

el constipado — (head) cold

el dolor de cabeza — headache

la fiebre — fever

la diarrea — diarrhea

el estreñimiento — constipation

el esguince — sprain

la quemadura — burn

la medicina — medicine

la receta — prescription

la inyección — injection

la farmacia — pharmacy

la píldora — pill

curarse — to (be) cure(d)

tener mala cara — to look ill

1. REPLACE WITH OBJECT PRONOUNS

— *Si no me cobra mucho, le compro* **el coche** . . . .
— *Si vienes conmigo, te doy* **los libros** . . . .
— *Se pone* **el impermeable** *porque llueve* . . . .
— *¿Os digo* **la verdad***?* . . . .
— *No tenemos prisa, nos devuelves* **el dinero** *otro día* . . . .
— *Me dejé* **las llaves** *en la oficina* . . . .

2. CHANGE THE FOLLOWING SENTENCES AS IN THE MODEL

Quería reservar una habitación. *¿Puedo reservarla ahora?*
Quisiera probar este vino. ¿Puedo . . . . ?
Me gustaría hacer este trayecto. ¿Puedo . . . . ?
Tengo ganas de comprar un libro. ¿Puedo . . . . ?
No tengo tiempo de escribir esta carta. ¿Puedo . . . . *mañana?*
Quiero enviar este paquete. ¿Puedo . . . . *por vía aérea?*

3. COMPLETE WITH THE FOLLOWING PRONOUNS

EL / LA / LO / LOS / LAS QUE · EL / LA / LOS / LAS DE

Esta es una foto de mi oficina. Aquí están todos . . . . *trabajan conmigo.*
¿Quién es el de bigote? Es Raúl. . . . . *está al lado es Francisca.*
¿Cuál? ¿ . . . . *gafas? Es muy bonita. No, ésa es Luisa. Francisca*
es . . . . *está a la derecha. ¿Y tu jefe? ¿Cuál es? Es* . . . . *está*
al lado mío. . . . . *más me gusta es su cara de ogro.*

4. ANSWER THE FOLLOWING QUESTIONS IN THE NEGATIVE

You can use: NADA/NADIE/NINGUN/NINGUNO/NINGUNA

¿Hay algo para beber? No, no hay nada.
¿Queda alguien en la sala de espera? . . . .
¿Usted practica algún deporte? . . . .
¿Quieren algo más? . . . .
¿Conoce a alguien aquí? . . . .
¿Ha trabajado en alguna empresa extranjera? . . . .

5. WRITE THE NAME WHICH CORRESPONDS TO EACH SENTENCE

Pablo va de vez en cuando al cine.   — . . . . . . *va con frecuencia al cine.*
Juana va todos los domingos al cine.   — . . . . *no va nunca al cine.*
Luis no va jamás al cine.   — . . . . *va regularmente al cine.*
Celina va a menudo al cine.   — . . . . *va a veces al cine.*

6. COMPLETE BY USING EN/DESDE/DESDE HACE/HASTA/DENTRO DE

— ¿Cuándo comenzó sus estudios?
— Empecé .... 1973. Estuve en la Universidad .... 1973 .... 1978.
— ¿Cuándo se doctoró?
— En 1980, en Estados Unidos. .... de esto ocho años.
— ¿Y .... cuándo trabaja en Seat?
— .... ocho años. .... 1980 precisamente.
— ¿Cuándo puede comenzar con nosotros?
— .... octubre termina mi contrato. .... de un mes.

7. COMPLETE THE LETTER WITH VERBS IN PARENTHESES

París, 15 de agosto de 1988

Queridos padres :
Ayer ...... (recibía/recibí) el paquete que nos ...... (enviaste/enviasteis).
Los chicos .... (estamos/están) muy contentos con los regalos.
Aquí ha .... (llovido/llovía) toda la semana y ha .... (hecho/hacía)
mucho frío. Ya ..... (llevamos/llevábamos) un año aquí y todavía nos .....
(cuesta/costamos) acostumbrarnos al clima. ¡Cómo nos .... (acordábamos/
acordamos) de Cádiz ahora!
Los niños .... (empiezan/empezaron) las clases la semana pasada. Ya
.... (hablaron/hablan) francés y bien, mejor que nosotros.
Yo he .... (trabajado/trabajaba) mucho estos meses. .... (queremos/
queríamos) comprar un coche de segunda mano para viajar. Laura ....
(empieza/empezó) a trabajar dentro de un mes en un restaurante.
¿Cuándo os .... (vemos/vimos) por aquí? ¿Cuándo os ....
(decidieron/decidis) a venir?

Abrazos a los dos de vuestro hijo

SANTIAGO

8. JOIN THE STATEMENTS THAT GO TOGETHER

1. Tendremos que viajar otro día
2. Me voy de viaje a Francia
3. Me gané un viaje a las Baleares
4. No podré viajar con vosotros
5. Llevo un mes haciendo trámites

A - ¡Qué pena!
B - ¡Qué bueno!
C - ¡Qué rollo!
D - ¡Qué le vamos a hacer!
E - ¡Qué suerte!

See answers on page 34 of booklet.

THE WAY TO EACH OTHER

I'm learning about the city in giant steps. The language is also becoming clearer and clearer to me. Rosa was right about the character of the community's way of life. People from Madrid are gregarious and don't tolerate solitude very well — theirs as well as that of others. That's how I met Pedro and his friends in a neighborhood restaurant where I sat down at a table for dinner. They were four at the neighboring table: Loli, Pedro's wife; Jose Luis, his old friend, and his wife Conchita. Pedro spontaneously came to my aid when he saw I was having trouble ordering. With the few words of French he had learned in school, he tried to help me decide. He ended up by conferring with the waiter himself and a little later I found myself with a completely unexpected dish, which was nevertheless excellent: *angulas al ajillo.*

Dinner went along with conversation from table to table. It became clear that we were going to continue the evening elsewhere. Consequently, I left with the small group looking for a bar for a last drink. In the street they talked loudly, laughed, and, strange, without exactly knowing why, I felt myself completely a part of their group. We left each other after exchanging addresses and telephone numbers. Since then Pedro has introduced me to many others friends. The evenings that we spend together are never alike. Each time a newcomer joins us, and each time it's as though we'd known each other forever.

It's true that all this going out has somewhat turned me away from my search for Rosa. Someone always turns up to suggest something to do.

¿Qué haces esta noche? Hemos quedado con unos amigos para ir a la Fídula. Una amiga de Loli que es pianista toca ahi por las noches. ¿Vienes?''
''¡Si, claro!''

I realize that there's no question of saying no. I couldn't refuse to join them until the day when a bad case of flu nailed me to my bed.

However, dining out at night is not the only ritual in my everyday life. At the office I have formed many other little everyday habits. For example, around eleven o'clock in the morning it's customary to stop *para ir a desayunar.* The company's offices are situated in a super-modern building on Basilica Street, behind *le Corte Inglés de Nuevos Ministerios.* I go out to have *un cortado,* coffee ''with a cloud of milk,'' as the English say. At the counter of *La Cafeteria El Globo,* I find the regulars and the waiter who knows in advance what each one wants. The tables are filled with people who take their time for this morning break.

We begin work at eight o'clock in the morning. I will always be amazed at the promptness with which everyone gets started first thing in the morning. When you've

« La Natividad » El Greco

seen the streets of Madrid so full of life in the middle of the night, you wonder how they all manage to be at work so early the next day. Who would dare to forbid the eleven o'clock break?

My co-workers stop at three o'clock. After that I'm alone with a secretary who doesn't leave the office until six o'clock. I can even ask her to stay a little later when there's urgent business. She willingly agrees to stay late, with a charming smile that has nothing hidden behind it. Paquita has three young children, but she arranges with a neighbor to watch them until she gets home. I believe that she does so without the slightest concern. The friendly solidarity of Madrid guarantees the safety of her offspring.

CONTINUED . . .

NOUVELLE CASTILLE : *Molinos de Consuegra.*

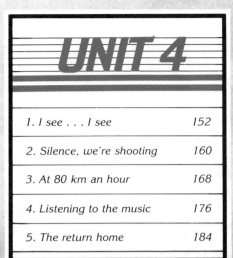

UNIT 4

● ● LISTEN

I SEE . . . I SEE

In Granada, Paloma pays a lot of money to a gypsy who predicts her future.

Paloma : *¡Al Sacromonte!*

Taxista : *¿Quiere que pasemos por la Avenida...?*

Paloma : *Como quiera, ¡es tan bonita la ciudad!*

Taxista : *Qué... lleva pocos días por aquí ¿no?*

Paloma : *No, ya llevo casi una semana.*

Taxista : *¿De vacaciones...?*

Paloma : *No, no. De vacaciones no. Soy actriz y estoy rodando una película.*

Taxista : *¡Ah!... bueno ¿Y cómo se llama usted...?*

Paloma : *Paloma Montes. Es mi primera película.*

. . . .

Gitana : *¡Oye, guapa...! ¿Quieres que te diga la buenaventura...?*

Paloma : *¡Por qué no!*

Gitana : *¡A ver! ¡A ver! La mano. No, la izquierda... Aquí veo algo importante. Creo, niña, que vas a tener mucho éxito*

dentro de poco y que vas a ganar muchísimo dinero.

Paloma : *¿Seguro...? ¿Y en qué voy a ganar tanto...?*

Gitana : *No lo sé con certeza. Tal vez tenga que ver con la televisión o con el teatro.*

Paloma : *¿Qué más? ¿Qué más...?*

Gitana : *¡Ay, niña! Todo no te lo puedo decir. Y aunque yo deseo que seas feliz, siempre hay pequeñas cosas... Ya sabes... Eso sí, tendrás muchos hijos ... Te casarás joven, con un hombre rico: un comerciante.*

Paloma : *¡Cómo! ¿Cómo dice...? ¿Un comerciante?*

Gitana : *¡Sí! Eso se ve claramente. ¿Ves esta línea? Está perfectamente claro. Además harás un viaje muy pronto; lejos de aquí. Quizás a una hermosa playa con sol y árboles...*

Paloma : *¡Qué bien! Seguro que allí conoceré al hombre de mi vida. ¡Oiga! ¿Y cómo ve mi trabajo actual...? ¿Tendré éxito o no...?*

Gitana : *Serás muy famosa, porque te lo mereces.*

Paloma : *¡Ojalá sea pronto! ¿Eso es todo...?*

Gitana : *Eso es todo y son dos mil pesetas.*

Paloma : *¡Dos mil pesetas!... Tenga, tenga.*

Gitana : *Gracias y vete con Dios.*

● ● LISTEN AND REPEAT
You will find the translation on page 24 of booklet.

Andalusia: 1. 2. 3. Rocio fair
4. Bullring (Seville)
5. Flamenco dance

NOUNS

el gitano/la gitana — gypsy
el porvenir — future
el éxito — success
el dinero — money
la certeza — certainty
la incertidumbre — uncertainty
el teatro — theater
la línea — line
el árbol — tree
la vida — life
Dios (m) — God
la moneda — coin, money
la calderilla — small change
la cuenta — bill
el cheque al portador — check payable to the bearer
el cheque cruzado — canceled check
el interés — interest
la bolsa — purse, stock market
la firma — signature
el cajero automático — cash machine
el gasto — expense
la caja de ahorros — savings bank

ADJECTIVES

seguro(a) — sure, safe
hermoso(a) — good looking
famoso(a) — famous
fenomental — extraordinary, super!

---

perfecto(a) — perfect
lento(a) — slow

rápido(a) — rapid
elegante — elegant

VERBS

rodar — to shoot (a film)
tener éxito — to be successful
adivinar — to guess
ganar — to win
desear — to want
merecer — to merit
acabar — to finish *(1)*
irse — to go away

---

dudar — to doubt
tener ganas — to feel like
apetecer — to have a desire (craving) for
prohibir — prohibit
ahorrar — to save
malgastar — squander, to waste (money)

MISCELLANEOUS

muchísimo — very much *(2)*
tal vez
quizás — maybe, perhaps
a lo mejor
¿qué más? — what else? *(3)*
perfectamente — perfectly
aunque — although *(4)*
pronto — soon
¡ojalá! — Oh, let it be so!

HOW TO SAY IT

1. ACCEPTING A SUGGESTION

¿Por qué no? — Why not? (Of course)
Como quiera(s) — As you wish
De acuerdo — Agreed
Es una buena idea — It's a good idea

2. EXPRESSING AN HYPOTHESIS

Quizás (Tal vez/Acaso) vengan — Maybe they would come
A lo mejor vendrán — Maybe they'll come
Puede ser que lleguen tarde — It could be that they are arriving late
Es posible (probable) que no — Possibly (probably) not
Debe ser rico — He must be rich
Creo que vas a tener éxito — I believe you'll be successful

3. EXPRESSING CERTAINTY

Seguro que te casarás — Surely you will marry
Estoy segura que serás feliz — I am sure you'll be happy
Sé con certeza que serás feliz — I strongly believe you'll be happy
Está (perfectamente) claro que serás feliz — It's (perfectly) clear you'll be happy
Eso sí, tendrás muchos hijos — It is certain that you'll have many children

4. EXPRESSING A WISH

Deseo que seas feliz — I want you to be happy
Espero que seas feliz — I hope you'll be happy
¡Ojalá sea pronto! — God grant it be soon!
¡Ojalá fuera cierto! — Oh Heaven, if it were true!

NOTES . . .   NOTES . . .   NOTES . . .   NOTES . . .

(1) Other uses: "acabar con" = "to put an end to," "to finish up"; "acabar de" = "to have just." — (2) Superlative of "mucho" — (3) Also "algo más" = "something more"; "nada más" = "nothing else." — (4) In the indicative it has the sense of "although"; in the subjunctive, the sense of supposition: "even though."

1. "ESPERO QUE" + SUBJUNCTIVE

◉◉) LISTEN:

ganar · dinero (tú)
- *Espero que ganes mucho dinero*
recibir · cartas (ella)
- *Espero que reciba muchas cartas*

Continue as in the model. Remember to make "mucho" agree with the noun that follows:
ganar · dinero (tú) — recibir · cartas (ella) — comprar · cosas (tú) — leer · libros (vosotros) — tener · suerte (nosotros) — vivir · años (usted) — hacer · viajes (ustedes) — tener · hijos (vosotros).
Grammar: See O.

2. EXPRESSING CERTAINTY/DOUBT

◉◉) LISTEN:

¿Estás seguro de que Adela vive en París? (creer)
- *Yo no creo que viva en París*
¿Estás segura de que estos clientes hablan francés? (dudar)
- *Yo dudo que hablen francés*

Continue according to the model:
¿ Estás segura de que Adela vive en París? (creer) — ¿Estás segura de que estos clientes hablan francés? (dudar) — ¿Estás seguro de que aceptan tarjeta de crédito? (creer) — ¿Estás seguro de que comen bien? (dudar) — ¿Estás segura de que tu hijo fuma? (dudar) — ¿Estás seguro de que el avión llega a las ocho? (dudar) — ¿Estás segura de que venden localidades aquí? (dudar) — ¿Estás segura de que regresan mañana? (creer).
Grammar: See O.

3. EXPRESSING A WISH

◉◉) LISTEN:
¿ Viene?
- *¡Ojalá venga!*

Continue according to the model:
¿ Viene? — ¿ Te va bien? — ¿ Hace ese viaje? — ¿ Llegan mañana? — ¿ Os divertís? — ¿ Salimos temprano? — ¿ Me espera? — ¿ Puedes venir?
Grammar: See O.

4. EXPRESSING AN HYPOTHESIS

◉◉) LISTEN:

Vivirá en el extranjero (tal vez)
- *Tal vez viva en el extranjero*
Se casarán dentro de algunos años (quizás)
- *Quizás se casen dentro de algunos años*

Continue according to the model:
Vivirá en el estranjero (tal vez) — Se casarán dentro de algunos años (quizás) — Saldréis en una película cómica (quizás) — Serás muy feliz (tal vez) — Trendrás muchos hijos (quizás) — Conocerá muchos países (tal vez) — Hareis un viaje (quizás) — Recibrás una buena noticia (quizás).
Grammar: See O.

5. EXPRESSING A CONCESSION

◉◉) LISTEN:

Tengo ganas pero no iré
- *Aunque tenga ganas, no iré*

Change the following sentences as in the model using "aunque" + subjunctive:
Tengo ganas, pero no iré — No tenemos mucho dinero pero haremos ese viaje — No me apetece pero comeré — No podemos quedarnos pero pasaremos — No habla francés pero lo contrateremos — Está enfermo pero va a la oficina.
Grammar: See O.

6. FORMATION OF ADVERBS

◉◉) LISTEN:
Ver · perfecto (Usted)
- *Usted ve perfectamente*
Hablar · lento (el profesor)
- *El profesor habla lentamente*

Form sentences as in the model:
Ver · perfecto (usted) — Hablar · lento (el profesor) — Caminar · rápido (tú) — Oir · claro (nosotros) — Comer · abundante (los niños) — Vestirse · elegante (la señora) — Conducir · prudente (el chófer).
Grammar: See E.

MYTHS

Is Don Quixote really dead? Do the Spanish still see themselves in that famous hero created four centuries ago by Miguel de Cervantes? In the eyes of the world, Don Quixote has long symbolized Spain. His altruism, his ineffectual bravery, and his pure idealism in the face of the pitiless realities of the world, were all part of the Don Quixote myth. Are not the Pyrenees the separation between the dreaminess of the south and the logic of the north? For a long time, the history of Spain bore the imprint of Quixote's idealism. Physical courage and epic deeds like those of El Cid, were the most important marks of Spanish heroes. The cloak and sword remained the sole instruments of glory in the popular mind, while business and financial gain were the object of disdain and scorn. El Cid, alone, personified the glory of Spain.

Later, disenchantment set in. The sinking of the Armada, the loss of Spain's great empire in the Atlantic as well as Cuba and the Philippines, and abandonment of its possessions in Morocco, reduced the country to its boundaries on the Iberian peninsula. Then it withdrew into itself, frozen in nostalgia for a great past.

Modernism would finally make its appearance. Rather than remaining reclusive, Spain carefully locked the tomb of El Cid. It knew it must at last integrate itself into the continent of Descartes and Kant, to which it geographically belongs.

Today, the transformation seems to have reached its goal, with Spain becoming part of the European Community. But has the rest of the country followed the broader institutional changes? We are tempted to say it has. Spanish society has

changed profoundly during the last decades. It no longer clings to ancient myths. Memories of a civil war, in which hundreds of thousands of Spaniards on both sides killed one another for their beliefs, weighs heavily on us. Forget valor from now on. The population thinks more of its well-being, of material success. The people have become more middle-class. The country may have lost its idealism, but it is more peaceful.

Business has replaced war as a means to glory. In surveys conducted among young adults, the "greats" of the business world are cited as examples to be followed. Mario Conde, a young banker who,

at 39, became head of the country's most important financial organization, is today's national hero. Spaniards are more passionate about wars between financial groups than of the military. Don Quixote would turn over in his grave!

It's useless to regret the myths immortalized by Cervantes. There's been an inevitable evolution in this country that, in a few decades, has leaped over steps toward modernization that others trudged for a much longer time. Spain has been in a hurry to show that it, too, is capable of European myths. Don Quixote is dead, long live the Common Market and the European Community!

N° 1   🔘🔘 LISTEN:

Listen to the cassette concerning this family and study the drawing. Then complete the exercise by answering the questions.

1. ¿Dónde está la madre de Marta? . . . .

2. ¿Quiénes son Rosario y Rafael? . . . .

3. ¿Qué edad tiene el bebé? . . . .

4. ¿Dónde están el abuelo y la abuela? . . . .

5. ¿Quién es Nuria? . . . .

6. ¿Quién es el 3° de la izquierda? . . . .

7. La Sra. que tiene el bebé en brazos es . . . .

Complete this game. VEO . . . VEO . . . ¿QUÉ VES?

Una cosita que empieze por:

D. . . . . . . / . . . . / . . . .

C. . . . . / . . . . . . / . . . . .

M. . . . . . . / . . . .

Q. . . . . / . . . . . .

D. . . . . / . . . .

C. . . . . / . . . .

C. . . . . / . . . .

V. . . . . / . . . .

C. . . . . / . . . .

U. . . . . / . . . .

See answers on page 25 of booklet.

LISTEN

SILENCE, WE'RE SHOOTING

Paloma is well into the making of a film. It's too bad that the director becomes angry.

Director : *Vamos a filmar el rapto. Tú, Paloma, caminas con tu padre hacia la casa. Estás feliz. Váis charlando y riendo... Y tú, Fernando, la llevas del brazo; al llegar a la palmera, ella se soltará y aparecerán los caballos. ¡Estad atentos! La escena es difícil. Vosotros, los de los caballos, estad preparados. No salgáis ni antes ni después. Escuchad la señal y moveos como ya os he explicado. ¿Estáis listos...? Silencio. Se rueda.*

Director : *¡No! ¡No! ¡Así, no! Ya he dicho tres veces que vayáis rápidamente.*

Paloma : *Es que con estos zapatos no me muevo bien.*

Director : *¡Quítatelos, entonces...! Y no estés pendiente de la cámara; olvida que te están filmando y ven hacia donde yo estoy... Bueno, volvamos a empezar... ¿Listos...? ¡Cámara!*

Paloma : *Espera, espera. Victoria ¿puedes arreglarme el pelo...? Y este vestido se me ha desabrochado otra vez.*

Director : *Bueno, lo dicho. ¡Cámara! ¡Mantén la distancia! Enfoca la escena desde cerca. Quiero un primer plano de los dos . . . ¿ Empezamos . . . ? Tres . . . dos . . . uno. Se rueda.*
Bien . . . bien . . . ¡Gira la cámara a la derecha! Ahí, mantenla ahí. Vosotros, seguid avanzando . . . Muy bien . . . ¡Ese ruido! Paloma, comienza a alejarte de tu padre. ¡Corre! . . . ¡Corre! . . . ¡Los caballos! ¡Los caballos! Ahora, ahora . . . ¡El rapto! . . .

Paloma : *¡Ay!, ¡ay!, ¡ay! mi tobillo... Me he dislocado el tobillo.*

Director : *¡¡Corten!! ¡Corten! ¡Vete al diablo, Paloma!*

LISTEN AND REPEAT
You will find the translation on page 25 of booklet.

Spanish films: 1. Maravillas de Gutiérrez Aragón
2. Mujeres al borde de un ataque de nervios de Almodóvar
3. Moros y Cristianos de Berlanga
4. Amor Brujo de Saura

Una película producida por
Luis MEGINO para ARANDANO s.a.

Maravillas

FERNANDO
FERNAN GOMEZ
CRISTINA
MARCOS

FOTOGRAFIA
TEO
ESCAMILLA
DIRIGIDA POR
MANUEL
GUTIERREZ ARAGON

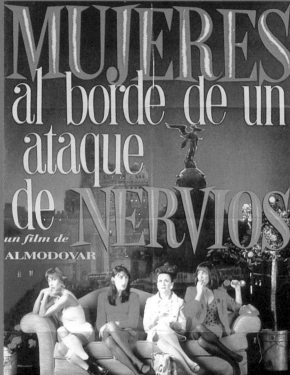

MUJERES
al borde de un
ataque
de NERVIOS

un film de
ALMODOVAR

Carmen Maura • Antonio Banderas • Julieta Serrano
María Barranco • Rossy de Palma • Guillermo Montesinos • Kiti Manver • Chus Lampreave
Yayo Calvo • Loles León • Angel de Andrés López y la colaboración de Fernando Guillén
José Mª de Cossío — Guilles Orthón — Ester García — José Salcedo
Bernarda Bonezzi — José Luis Alcaine — Antonio Lloréns — Agustín Almodóvar
guión y dirección Pedro Almodóvar

MOROS y CRISTIANOS
de Luis G. Berlanga

Fernando Fernán Gómez
Verónica Forqué
Agustín González
Chus Lampreave
José L. López Vázquez
Andrés Pajares
Mª Luisa Ponte
Antonio Resines
Pedro Ruiz
Rosa Mª Sardá

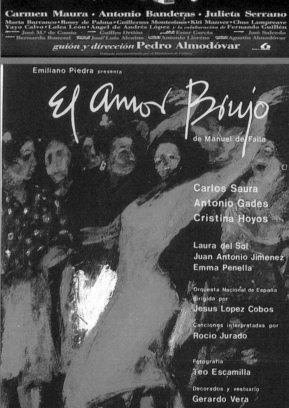

Emiliano Piedra presenta

El amor Brujo
de Manuel de Falla

Carlos Saura
Antonio Gades
Cristina Hoyos

Laura del Sol
Juan Antonio Jimenez
Emma Penella

Orquesta Nacional de España
dirigida por
Jesus Lopez Cobos

Canciones interpretadas por
Rocio Jurado

Fotografia
Teo Escamilla

Decorados y vestuario
Gerardo Vera

Montaje
Pedro del Rey

Banda sonora
distribuida por
EMI

NOUNS

el silencio — silence
el rapto — rape, kidnapping
la palmera — palm tree
el caballo — horse
la escena — scene
la señal — sign, signal
la cámara — camera
la distancia — distance
la entrada — ticket to enter
la localidad — seat (theater)
la sesión — session
la pantalla — screen (movies)
el cartel — poster
la acomodadora — usherette
el documental — documentary

ADJECTIVES

atento(a) — attentive
preparado(a)
listo(a) (1) — ready
enfadado(a) — angry
_____

agotado(a) — used up, none remaining

VERBS

charlar — to chat
soltar(se) — to let go
aparecer — to appear
salir — to go on (2)
mover — to move
moverse — to move oneself, "get around"
explicar — to explain
dirigirse — to address
quitar(se) — to take off, remove (3)
estar pendiente de — to mind, to hang on
(to someone's words)
arreglarse — to prepare oneself (5)
abrochar — to fasten, to button
desabrochar — to unfasten, to unbutton
mantener — to sustain
enfocar — to focus
avanzar — to advance
comenzar — to begin
alejarse — to distance (oneself), to move away
dislocar — to dislocate
_____

gritar — to shout
ser puntual — to be on time
repetir — to repeat
ensayar — to rehearse
hacer cola — to get on line

MISCELLANEOUS

así — in this way, so
así no — not this (or, that) way
rápidamente — rapidly

1. GIVING AN ORDER

¡Quítatelos! — Take them off!
¿Cierras la ventana, por favor? — (Would you) close the window, please?
¿Te callas, sí o no? — Are you going to be quiet?
Te digo que te calles — I'm telling you to be quiet

2. EXPRESSING A PROHIBITION

No salgas — Don't go out
Te digo que no salgas — I'm telling you, don't go out
Te prohibo que salgas — I forbid you to go out
Está prohibido fumar — Smoking is prohibited
Prohibido fumar — No smoking
No pisar el césped — Don't walk on the grass

3. ASKING A REQUEST OF SOMEONE

¿Puedes arreglarme el pelo? — Can you "fix" my hair?
¿Podría decirme la hora?
¿Le molestaría decirme la hora? — Would you tell me the time?
¿Sería tan amable de decirme la hora?
¿Tendría la amabilidad de decirme la hora? — Would you be kind enough to tell me the time?
Le ruego que venga — I urge you to come
Se ruega no fumar — Please do not smoke

4. SENDING SOMEONE ON HIS/HER WAY

¡Vete (Váyase) al infierno!
¡Vete (Váyase) al diablo! (al cuerno!) — Go to hell, (to the devil)!
¡Vete a paseo! — Take a walk!
¡Fuera! — Get out!

NOTES . . .   NOTES . . .   NOTES . . .   NOTES . . .

(1) Also "intelligent," "alert." — (2) Or "salir a escena," literally "to come out upon the scene." — (3) "Quitar el abrigo a alguien"="to remove someone's coat." "Quitarse el abrigo"="to take off one's own coat." — (4) "Estar pendiente del teléfono, de un enfermo"="to be alert for the ring of the telephone, to devote oneself to a sick person." — (5) Without an object pronoun: "to get ready (to go out)." "To straighten one's hair, skirt."="Arreglarse el pelo, la falda." "Arreglárselas"="to straighten things, to clear up, to manage."

1. THE COMMAND (familiar plural)

👁️👁️ LISTEN:

Estoy cansada · Trabajo demasiado
• *Pues trabaja menos*
Estamos mareados · Bebemos demasiado
• *Pues bebed menos*

Give advice as in the model:

Estoy cansada · Trabajo demasiado — Estamos mareados · Bebimos demasiado — Nos duele la cabeza · Fumamos demasiado — Nos duelen los pies · Caminamos demasiado — Estoy agotado · Salgo demasiado — Estamos arruinados · Gastamos demasiado.

Grammar: See O.

2. COMMAND, IRREGULAR VERBS

👁️👁️ LISTEN:

¡Venid hacia mí!
• *Ven hacia mí*

Give commands going from the familiar plural to the singular:

¡Venid hacia mí! — ¡Salid ahora! — ¡Tened cuidado! — ¡Mantened la distancia! — ¡Haced lo que digo! — ¡Poned la cámara aquí! — ¡Dad la alerta! — ¡Id hacia la casa!

Grammar: See O.

3. FORMAL COMMANDS

👁️👁️ LISTEN:

Tengo que correr hacia la casa
• *Sí, corra*
Debemos caminar lentamente
• *Sí, caminen lentamente*

Use the "usted" or "ustedes" commands to answer the following questions:

Tengo que correr hacia las casa — Debemos caminar lentamente — Tengo que gritar — Debo girar la cámara — Tenemos que hablar — Debo ir hasta la fuente — Tengo que cerrar la puerta — Tenemos que venir corriendo — Debo salir por esta puerta — Debemos traer los caballos.

Grammar: See. P.

4. THE NEGATIVE COMMAND

👁️👁️ LISTEN:

¿Puedo fumar? (tú)
• *No, no fumes ahora*
¿Podemos beber? (vosotros)
• *No, no bebáis ahora*

Continue according to the model using the negative command:

¿Puedo fumar? (tú) — ¿Podemos beber? (vosotros) — ¿Puedo comer? (usted) — ¿Podemos leer? (ustedes) — ¿Podemos escribir? (vosotros) — ¿Puedo trabajar? (tú) — ¿Puedo salir? (usted) — ¿Podemos ir? (ustedes) — ¿ Puedo caminar? (tú) — ¿Podemos descansar? (vosotros).

Grammar: See P.

5. EXPRESSIONS OF INSISTENCE

👁️👁️ LISTEN:

Escucha la señal
• *¡Ya te he dicho que escuches la señal!*
Mirad la cámara
• *¡Ya os he dicho que miréis la cámara!*

Insist on these actions as in the model beginning each statement with "Ya te he dicho que":

Escucha la señal — Mirad la cámara — Sea puntual — Haz tu trabajo — Salid corriendo — Atad los caballos — Descansa — Gira la cámara.

Grammar: See P.

6. "PEDIR"/"PREGUNTAR"

👁️👁️ LISTEN:

¿Compras este video? (preguntar)
• *Me pregunta si compro este video*
¡Compra este video!
• *Me pide que compre este video*

Change the following sentences using "pedir" or "preguntar" appropriately responding to a command or a question:

¿Compras este video? — ¡Compra este video! — Ve al cine — ¿Quieres leer este artículo? — Lee este artículo — ¿Fumas? — Fuma estos cigarrillos — ¿Repites esta escena? — Repite esta escena — Toma un aperitivo — ¿Tomas un aperitivo?

NEWSPAPERS
AND TELEVISION

Spaniards today do not read newspapers very much. Newspaper circulation is one-third less here than the European average, fewer than 80 copies per 1,000 people.

The country, nevertheless, has excellent daily newspapers. Many of them sprang up during recent years after 40 years of suppression of the free press by Franco's heavy hand. Dailies like El País and Diario 16 were born when the dawn of democracy began to break on the horizon and rapidly made a place for themselves.

Thirteen years after its birth, El Pais has begun to rival the best European newspapers. It's the daily with the highest circulation in Spain. After having been deprived for 40 years of interparty debate and parliamentary life, Spaniards have fixed their choice on this serious and exacting newspaper. It keeps them informed in luxurious detail about long-forbidden political activity.

Of course, all Spanish newspapers are not top quality. Too often,

journalists tend toward narcissism. They think their problems, their phobias, or their family battles are important enough to merit national attention, and spare the reader no detail. It's a throwback to the time, at the very beginning of democratic rule, when Parliament was not yet fulfilling its duties and political debate unfolded more often in newspaper columns.

Many newspaper writers have held on to the habit of explaining to the government, at length, how it should govern, instead of being content with the more modest but also noble role of informing the public. No doubt, this is part of the reason only a minority of the population is interested in newspapers.

In contrast to the small amount of newspaper reading done, there is a big audience for television and radio. For most Spanish homes — especially in rural areas — they are the only sources of information on what's happening nationally and internationally. It's not surprising that

disputes on who will control future television are very lively.

Spain has only two national public television channels, and three regional public channels (in the Basque country, in Catalonia, and in Galicia). A recent law created three private channels.

The public TV channels, meanwhile, as monopolies, are being pilloried by the press. It is criticizing their dependence on the government (which, of course, undeniably exists). The press is criticizing them even more ferociously since the big newspaper organizations are among the principal candidates for running the new private TV channels, and are trying to rush an end to government monopoly.

The debate is beginning to be outstripped by reality with the appearance of the first dish antennas. The "dishes" allow the Spanish to pick up many programs from neighboring countries, from both public and private television channels.

N° 1   ●● LISTEN

Identify these four individuals and complete their introductions.

1. Soy . . . . de cine y me llamo . . . .

2. Me llaman . . . . pero me llamo . . . .

3. Canto . . . . y me llamo . . . .

4. Hago . . . . y soy . . . .

5. Me mató . . . . en . . . . *(Jaén)*

Complete the first column with the appropriate information on the left.

1. Tengo una mantilla . . . .

2. Soy aficionado a los toros . . . . . .

3. El Valencia es un gran equipo . . .

4. A mi me gusta la marcha y el baile

5. El Prado me encanta . . . .

6. Me gusta mucho J.S. Bach . . . . .

7. Admiro de un actor su personalidad

A. ... por eso voy a los conciertos.

B. ... por eso voy a las discotecas.

C. ... es un museo fantástico.

D. ... no me pierdo ni una corrida.

E. ... por eso amo el teatro.

F. ... para ir a las verbenas de Madrid.

G. ... por eso voy al estadio.

See answers on page 27 of booklet.

◉◉ LISTEN

AT 80 KM AN HOUR

Paco, Paloma and Soledad have gone to Teneriffe to film a commercial. Several incidents happen to them there.

Policía : *Déme su carné de conducir... y acerque el coche a la acera. No ponga en peligro la circulación.*

Paco : *Sí... Discúlpeme, pero el carné se me ha olvidado en casa; siempre lo llevo conmigo, ... pero...*

Policía : *¿Y los documentos del coche...?*

Paco : *¡Un momento! Aquí los tiene.*

Policía : *¿Es suyo este coche...?*

Paco : *¡Claro que es mío! ¿De quién va a ser...?*

Policía : *TF-4530-C. Tenga, sus documentos.*

Paco : *¿Será mucho...?*

Policía : *No. Ya se lo dirán. Lo más probable es que le retiren el carné por unos meses, además de la multa, ¡claro!*

Paco : *¡El carné! ¡Pero no es posible! Pero... ¿Qué pasa? ¿Qué he hecho...?*

Policía : *¡Ir como un loco!...*

Paco : *¿Cómo...? Cómo, como un loco, si iba a 80.*

Policía : *Le parece poco ir a 80 kms por hora en la ciudad.*

On the beach

Paco : *Oye ¿te importa que te deje el bolso?*

Turista : *Déjamelo, si quieres... ¿Tienes un cigarrillo...?*

Paco : *¿Fumas negro...?*

Turista : *Fumo rubio, pero no importa. ¿Son muy fuertes?... Nunca había visto tabaco canario...*

Soledad : *¿Dónde te metiste...? Te hemos estado buscando en el café ¡Vaya plantón que nos has dado!*

Paco : *¡Qué va...! Si estuve allí más de una hora.*

Paloma : *¿En el Topolino...?*

Paco : *¿Pero cómo en el Topolino, si quedamos en el Arga...?*
... Una hora esperando, os equivocáis de cafetería y para postre me ponen una multa.

Paloma : *Pero... ¿qué hiciste...? Seguro que ibas como un loco.*

Paco : *¡No me pongas más nervioso, Paloma!*

Soledad : *Déjalo, mujer.*

◉◉ LISTEN AND REPEAT
You will find the translation on page 27 of booklet.

The Islands 1. Ibiza (Balearic)
2. Menorca (Balearic)
3. Las Palmas (Canary)
4. Lanzarote (Canary)

4

NOUNS

el policía — policeman *(1)*
el carné de conducir — driver's license
el carné de identidad — identification card
el certificado de matrícula — registration certificate
el seguro — insurance
la acera — pavement
el peligro — danger
los documentos — documents
los datos — information, data
la multa — fine
el tabaco — tobacco, cigarettes
la autopista — highway, expressway
la calzada — wide road, causeway
la cuneta — ditch
el cruce — crossing
la arena — sand
la roca — rock
la ola — wave
la marea alta (baja) — high (low) tide
el/la mar (m or f) — sea *(2)*
la orilla — shore
la costa — coast

VERBS

conducir — to drive
acercar(se) a — to approach, to come near
disculpar(se) — to excuse (oneself)
llevar consigo — to carry on alone
entregar — to hand over
retirar — to take back
importar — to be important, to import *(3)*
meterse — to place oneself *(4)*
buscar — to look for
dar un plantón — to keep someone waiting
quedar — to remain, to make an appointment
equivocar(se) — to be mistaken
poner nervioso(a) — to make someone nervous *(5)*
circular — to walk around
ahogarse — to drown
veranear — to spend the summer vacation

———

sentarse — to sit down
llevarse — to take away
detener — to stop
molestar(se) — to bother
regar — to water
arreglar — to arrange, to fix

ADJECTIVES

loco(a) — crazy, mad
fuerte — strong
nervioso(a) — nervous

MISCELLANEOUS

por hora — by the hour
en la carretera — on the road
¿qué pasa? — what's happening?
para postre — for dessert
todo riesgo — at all risk

HOW TO SAY IT

1. EXCUSING ONESELF

Discúlpeme — Excuse me
Disculpe la molestia — Sorry for the bother
Perdone, espero no haberle molestado — Sorry, hope that I haven't bothered you
Le ruego que me disculpe — Please excuse me
Lo siento, todo está completo
Lo lamento, todo está completo — I'm sorry, everything is taken, we're "full-up"

2. ASKING PERMISSION TO DO SOMETHING

¿Te importa que te deje eso? — Does it matter if I leave you that?
¿No le importa que fume? — You don't mind if I smoke?
¿Le molesta el humo? — Does the smoke bother you?
¿Por favor, puedo salir? — Please, may I leave?
¿Me permite? — May I?, Can I?, You allow me?
¿Me permite explicárselo?
¿Me permite que se lo explique? — (Will) you allow me to explain?
¿Me deja que se lo explique? — Let me explain it to you

3. EXPRESSING YOUR SURPRISE

¡No es posible!
¡No puede ser! — It can't be (possible)!
¡Será posible!
¡Qué extraño! — Can it be?, How strange!
Me extraña — I'm surprised
¡Es increible! — It's unbelievable!
¡Qué sorpresa! — What a surprise!
No me lo puedo creer — I can't believe it

NOTES . . .   NOTES . . .   NOTES . . .   NOTES . . .

(1) But "la policía"="the police force." — (2) It is only feminine in poetic language and in expressions: "la mar de gente, de libros"="sea of people, books." — (3) "No importa"="It's not important." "No me importa"="It's not very important to me." "¿Te importa que?"="what does it matter to you?" "¡Y a ti qué te importa!"="What does it matter to you?" — (4) "Meterse en la cama"="to get into bed"; "meterse en todo"="to get mixed up in everything"; "meterse con alguien"="to annoy, worry someone." — (5) Also "poner triste"="to make someone sad"; "poner malo"="to make someone ill."

1. COMMAND + OBJECT PRONOUN

●● LISTEN:

¿Por qué no los compras?
• ¡Cómpralos!
¿Por qué no la miras?
• ¡Mírala!

Continue according to the model, changing the verb to the command form and adding the pronoun:
¿Por qué no los compras? — ¿Por qué no la miras? — ¿Por qué no los vendes? — ¿Por qué no la escuchas? — ¿Por qué no lo crees? — ¿Por qué no la bebes? — ¿Por qué no las acompañas? — ¿Por qué no la lleva? — ¿Por qué no lo piensas?

Grammar: See F.

2. + DOUBLE OBJECT PRONOUNS

●● LISTEN:

¿Quieres que te muestre las fotos?
• Sí, muéstramelas
¿Le importa que le deje este bolso?
• No, déjemelo

Replace the nouns for pronouns as in the model. Remember "le" becomes "se" when followed by another third-person pronoun:
¿Quieres que te muestre las fotos? — ¿Le importa que le deje este bolso? — ¿Quieres que te devuelva el artículo? — ¿Te importa que te lleve las llaves? — ¿Quiere que compre esa máquina? — ¿Te importa que me lleve este documento?

Grammar: See F.

3. + REFLEXIVE PRONOUN

●● LISTEN:

¿Me siento?
• Sí, siéntese

Answer the questions as in the model:
¿Me siento? — ¿Me levanto? — ¿Me acuesto? — ¿Me lavo? — ¿Me afeito? — ¿Me quedo? — ¿Me voy? — ¿Me peino?

Grammar: See F.

4. AFTER GERUND AND INFINITIVE

●● LISTEN:

¿Ya has leído el libro?
• No, estoy leyéndolo
¿Todavía no has hecho las compras?
• No, voy a hacerlas ahora

Continue as in the model using ESTAR + GERUND when you hear "Ya . . ." and VOY A + INFINITIVE each time you hear "Todavía":
¿Ya has leído el libro? — ¿Todavía no has hecho las compras? — ¿Ya has acabado el trabajo? — ¿Todavía no te has acostado? — ¿Ya has regado las plantas? — ¿Todavía no has puesto el café? — ¿Ya has cerrado la tienda? — ¿Todavía no te has levantado? — ¿Ya has arreglado el coche? — ¿Todavía no has pagado la multa?

Grammar: See F.

5. REPEATING WHAT HAS BEEN SAID

●● LISTEN:

«Deténgase» (¿Qué te dice?)
• Que me detenga
«Acercaos» (¿Qué nos dice?)
• Que nos acerquemos

Repeat what they say as in the model:
Deténgase (¿Qué te dice?) — Acercaos (¿Qué nos dice?) — Deme su carné (¿Qué te dice?) — Bajaos del coche (¿Qué nos dice?) — Abrame el maletero (¿Qué te dice?).

Grammar: See O.

6. POSSESSIVE PRONOUNS

●● LISTEN:

¿Es suyo este coche?
• ¡Claro que es mío! ¿De quién va a ser?
¿Son vuestras estas bicicletas?
• ¡Claro que son nuestras! ¿De quién van a ser?

Answer the questions using the possessive pronouns as in the model:
¿Es suyo este coche? — ¿Son vuestras estas bicicletas? — ¿Son tuyos estos cigarrillos? — ¿Es vuestro este carné? — ¿Son tuyos estos documentos? — ¿Es vuestra esta bolsa? — ¿Son suyas estas maletas?

Grammar: See F.

BEACHES

Rock-strewn or sandy, at the foot of an inlet or stretching out beyond a plain or the base of a mountain, the beach is the ultimate Spanish vacation. Madrid's successive governments have based their tourist policies on the beaches for the past 30 years. During this time, tourism has contributed almost 10 percent annually to the national income. The 50 million visitors who come to Spain each year do so mostly in search of "sol y playa," sun and sand.

There's something for every taste, every age, and every budget. Each part of the Spanish coast, which is almost 2,500 miles long, has its own name and attracts a different type of tourist. People gather together by interest, by nationality, and by social class. The broad range includes Arab sheiks and multimillionaires who rendezvous at Marbella, the classy resort just south of Málaga, as well as retirees and masses of tourists who gather in crowded Benidorm, between Valencia and Alicante.

Travelers coming from the north via the Mediterranean coast will discover, after crossing the frontier and before reaching Barcelona, the beautiful "Costa Brava" (rugged coast). It is magnificent but disfigured, wild but domesticated by an uncontroled tourist invasion and unbridled real estate speculation. One can still sense the raw fascination of the Costa Brava between developments that now mark it, at the foot of untamed creeks where mountains descend directly to the sea.

After Barcelona, we reach "Costa Dorada" (the Gold Coast). The steep mountains of Costa Brava give way progressively to tranquil hills, while sand takes the place of rocks and is often bordered by fresh-smelling pine woods. Passing the Ebro River delta, one comes to "Costa del Azahar" (Orange Blossom Coast) — a name that evokes fruit orchards enriching the air with aroma and color — as we approach Valencia. "Costa Blanca" (the White Coast) stretches near Alicante. It takes its name from the blinding light of the region and its constant sun. The mountain is far away from

the sea here, leaving room for wide, sandy beaches where popular seaside resorts draw noisy crowds day and night. The more aristocratic "Costa del Sol" (Sunny Coast) takes over after Almeria. This has become the rendezvous for today's international jet set. Costa del Sol has escaped the tourist invasion of Costa Brava, and enjoys a mild winter, thanks to the Sierra Nevada and Sierra de Ronda which provide natural protection against cold winds from the north.

But the Spanish coast is not only bathed by the peaceful Mediterranean waters. It also has its bit of Atlantic foam, angry winds, and full tides on "Costa Verde" (the Green Coast). Pressed between the Cantabrian cliffs and the Gulf of Gascony, between Santander and Galicia, it lies alongside fertile fields that contrast with the brown plateaus found elsewhere in the country. There is also the jagged Galician coast, nearly all islands and fjords, with waves and fog — far away from the sunny quiet of Costa del Sol on a many-faceted coastland.

Listen to the information and identify each person (1, 2, 3, 4). Then, indicate who has spoken each sentence.

1. El carné se me ha olvidado en casa . . . . □

2. ¡Vaya plantón que nos has dado! . . . . □

3. Claro que es mío este coche . . . . □

4. Lo más probable es que le retiren el carné por unos meses . . . . □

5. Fumo rubio, pero no importa que sea negro . . . . □

6. Te hemos estado buscando . . . . □

7. ¿Y los documentos del coche? . . . . □

Find the answer to this problem.

Pedro tiene un paquete con seis cigarrillos y encuentra reunidos a cinco amigos y una amiga. ¿Cómo es posible dar un cigarrillo a cada uno de sus amigos y tener todavía uno en la caja?

See answers on page 28 of booklet.

DIALOGUE

⊙⊙ LISTEN

LISTENING TO THE MUSIC

The three friends go out for the evening. First they go to a concert, then to a discotheque.

Paco : *Te lo dije, Paloma. Si hubiéramos venido antes tendríamos mejores asientos. Desde aquí, apenas veo.*

Paloma : *No importa. Se les oye bien y al menos estamos los tres juntos.*

Soledad : *Tocan estupendamente ¿ no ?*

Paco : *¡ Claro ! Es uno de los mejores conjuntos de folklore de toda España, al menos para mí.*

Paloma : *Yo los vie el año pasado por televisión. Me encantaron.*

Paloma : *¿ Queréis un chicle . . . ?*

Soledad : *¡ Ni hablar ! Si supieras lo que me dijo el dentista de los chicles, no comerías más.*

Paloma : *A mí me calman los nervios. Pero me pone nerviosa ver masticar a los demás.*

Paco : *Tú siempre estás nerviosa.*

At the discotheque

Soledad : *Yo me voy. Quedaos si queréis. A mí esta música me resulta insoportable.*

Paco : *¿ Qué ?*

Paloma : *¡ Que se va !*

Paco : *Quédate un poco más, mujer.*

Soledad : *Si la música no estuviera tan fuerte me quedaría. Mañana no os olvidéis de estar a las ocho abajo, que la furgoneta pasará a esa hora.*

Paloma : *No te preocupes. Seremos puntuales. ¿ Cuánto tiempo tardaremos en llegar al Sur . . . ?*

Paco : *Una hora más o menos, si no ocurre nada.*

Soledad : *¡ Adiós ! Que lo paséis bien. Y no os acostéis demasiado tarde.*

Paco : *Tú, tranquila...*

Paco : *No te lo he dicho antes pero voy a terminar por enamorarme de ti.*

Paloma : *¿ Qué ? ¿ De mí... ? ¡ Déjate de bromas ! Ya somos mayorcitos. Esto se acabará dentro de quince días. Luego, si te he visto no me acuerdo.*

Paco : *¿ Y no podríamos planificar nuestro futuro juntos ? Si tú quisieras, Paloma, podríamos...*

⊙⊙ LISTEN AND REPEAT
You will find the translation on page 28 of booklet.

Dances: 1. Verbena de San Isidro
2. Tuna
3. Segovianas
4. Sardana (Barcelona)
5. Sevillanas

4.4 VOCABULARY

NOUNS

el asiento — seat
el conjunto — ensemble, group
el chicle — chewing gum
el dentista — dentist
el nervio — nerve
la discoteca — discotheque
la furgoneta — light truck, van
la broma — joke
el espectáculo — spectacle (theatrical)
el público — public
el palco — box seat (theater)
la butaca — orchestra seat
el baile — dance
el baile regional — folkloric dance
el concierto — concert
la orquesta — orchestra
el director de orquesta — conductor
la batuta — baton
el disco — record
el tocadiscos — phonograph
el equipo
el cadena — high fidelity (stereo) system
el altavoz — loud speaker
las costumbres (f pl) — customs
la corrida — bullfight
la tauromaquia — bullfighting
el ruedo — bullring (arena)
el torero — bullfighter
el traje de luces — glittering outfit worn by
the bullfighter (suit of lights)

_____

el humor — humor

ADJECTIVES

estupendo(a) — stupendous, wonderful
insoportable — unbearable
tranquilo(a) — calm
mayorcito(a) — older person, adult (1)
bromista — joker
tradicional — traditional

_____

histérico(a) — hysterical

VERBS

calmar — to calm, to quiet
masticar — to chew
resultar — to become (2)
preocuparse — to worry
enamorarse — to fall in love
dejarse de — to stop from (3)
planificar — to plan
grabar — to record

_____

atrasar — to slow down
avisar — to alert
bailar — to dance

MISCELLANEOUS

apenas — hardly
al menos — at least
los demás — the rest
más o menos — more or less

_____

peor — worse (4)
temprano — early

1. MAKING A SUPPOSITION

Si llueve, no saldremos — If it rains, we will not go out
En el caso de que llueva, no saldremos
Suponiendo que llueva, no saldremos — If it should rain, we won't go out
En el supuesto de que digas la verdad, . . . — Supposing you're telling the truth, . . .
Si por casualidad lo vieras . . . — If by chance you should see him . . .
Si algún día lo ves . . . — If some day you (should) see him . . .

2. EXPRESSING REGRET

Si hubiéramos venido antes, estaríamos mejor — If we had come before, we would be better (off)
¡ Ojalá estuvieras conmigo! — If only you were with me!
Siento (Lamento) no haber llegado a tiempo — I regret not to have arrived on time
Echo de menos el pasado — I miss (regret) the past

3. INDICATING YOUR DISPLEASURE

¡ Déjate de bromas! — Stop joking!
¡ Ya está bien de tonterías!
¡ Basta de tonterías! — That's (enough) nonsense!
¡ Déjame tranquilo(a)! — Leave me alone!
¡ Estoy harto (de oírte)! — I've had enough (of listening to you)!
¡ No seas tan pesado(a)! — Stop bothering me!
¡ No me des la lata! — Don't give me trouble (a hard time)

4. REASSURING SOMEONE

No te preocupes — Don't worry
Tú, tranquilo(a) — Be calm
Confía en mí — Count on me, Trust in me
No hay de qué alarmarse (preocuparse) — There's nothing to worry about
No te hagas mala sangre — Don't be hateful!

NOTES . . .   NOTES . . .   NOTES . . .   NOTES . . .

(1) A familiar diminutive and a bit tongue-in-cheek for "los mayores" = "the big (older) people." — (2) "Resultar" + adjective = "to be, to remain, to become, to be revealed." "Resulta que" = "it turns out that." — (3) "Dejarse de" + noun = "to stop"; "déjate de bromas (tonterías)" = "enough silly jokes." "Dejarse de," "dejar de," + infinitive = "to cease from." — (4) Adjective or adverb, like "mejor."

1. EXPRESSING APPRECIATION

◖●●◗ LISTEN:

hotel (confortable)
* *Este hotel es uno de los más confortables de la ciudad*
plaza (bonita)
* *Esta plaza es una de las más bonitas de la ciudad*

Continue according to the model. Remember the superlative for "bueno" is "mejor" and for "malo" it is "peor."
hotel (confortable) — plaza (bonita) — actriz (buena) — restaurante (elegante) — discoteca (divertida) — cantante (malo) — cine (pequeño) — teatro (viejo).

2. "PONERSE" + ADJECTIVE

◖●●◗ LISTEN:

música (nervioso)
* *A mí esta música me pone nervioso*
bromas (mal humor)
* *A mí estas bromas me ponen de mal humor*

Continue according to the model. Remember to make "ponerse" agree with the noun that follows:
música (nervioso) — bromas (mal humor) — noticias (triste) — trabajo (buen humor) — escándalos (nervioso) — películas (triste).

3. CONJECTURING USING THE FUTURE

◖●●◗ LISTEN:

Juan no ha venido (Estar enfermo)
* *Estará enfermo*
Mis amigos no contestan (haber salido)
* *Habrán salido*

Continue according to the model:
Juan no ha venido (estar enfermo) — Mis amigos no contestan (haber salido) — El tren no ha llegado (estar atrasado) — Los chicos no han llamado (llamar mañana) — El restaurante está cerrado (abrir más tarde) — El teléfono no suena (estar descompuesto).

Grammar: See M.

4. MAKING AN HYPOTHESIS: SI . . .

◖●●◗ LISTEN:

poder (llamar)
* *Si puedes, llámame*

Continue according to the model putting the first verb in the present and the second in the imperative:
poder (llamar) — despertar (avisar) — salir (despertar) — cambiar de idea (telefonear) — venir (escribir) — gustar (decírselo).

Grammar: See K, P.

5. IF I COULD . . .

◖●●◗ LISTEN:

Si puedo, iré a la discoteca
* *Si pudiera, iría a la discoteca*
Si tenéis tiempo, recorreremos la costa
* *Si tuvierais tiempo, recorreríamos la costa*

Continue as in the model, using the imperfect subjunctive for the first verb and the conditional for the second:
Si puedo, iré a la discoteca — Si tenéis tiempo, recorreremos la costa — Si son puntuales, llegarán a tiempo — Si termino el trabajo, saldré de vacaciones — Si me apetece, me quedaré — Si te levantas, te sentiras mejor — Si bebes, te hará bien.

Grammar: See H, O.

6. IF I HAD BEEN ABLE. . .

◖●●◗ LISTEN:

Si saliéramos antes, llegaríamos a tiempo
* *Si hubiéramos salido antes, habríamos llegado a tiempo*

Continue as in the model changing the first verb to the past perfect subjunctive and the second to the conditional perfect:
Si saliéramos antes, llegaríamos a tiempo — Si estuviera enfermo, nos llamaría — Si tuvieras el carné, no te pondrían multa — Si pusieran otra música, me quedaría — Si bailaras, no te aburrirías — Si vinierais, os divertiríais.

Grammar: See N, O.

LOISIRS

LEISURE-TIME ACTIVITIES

What do young Spaniards do with their free evenings? First of all, they go out. They spend a considerable amount of their time this way. For them, a real evening of relaxation must be spent outside the home.

Friday and Saturday evening activities generally consist of a fixed ritual. It begins by "ir de copas," making the rounds of cafés. Evenings that begin this way promise to be long ones. Young people usually go out in groups, rarely in couples; "bandes" remain the foundation of Spanish social life.

The grand tour often includes a visit to one pub or another (when you speak the language of Cervantes, pronounce pub with a soft "v": puf). With its subdued atmosphere, this typical English institution appears to be the very opposite of Spanish taste. It is, however, gaining a foothold, especially since it is the best place for young men to pick up girls and vice versa.

After eating and drinking, the tempo picks up; disco time has arrived. For foreign visitors looking for the exotic, don't be deceived. Young Spaniards do not gather on the dance floor to do the flamenco or sevillano, but dance instead to rock-and-roll and pop rhythms. The names of the discos in Madrid (such as New York, Open Gate, Navy, and even Fifth Avenue) show that the winds blow more strongly from the Hudson than from Guadalquivir.

Some entire sections of Madrid are made up of these night spots. For example, in Orense Street, the new center for the capital's youth, bars and discos are lined up, one after the other, for almost a mile, and popular music blares 'til the wee hours.

If you want to know what has happened to the flamenco, it has taken refuge in "tablaos," Andalusian cabarets where one seeks "el duende," the musical demon that possesses the Andalusian singer. In Madrid, most tablaos are in the central city, in the narrow streets of the old section. But you'll definitely find that tourists are more numerous than local people there.

If you'd like to find the atmosphere of old Spain in a less confining place, try the lanes around Plaza Mayor, such as Cava Baja. The "mesones" or clubs that are lined up next to each other there have tempting tapas. Inside, groups of young people surprise visitors with old local refrains, with everyone joining in the chorus. Then, the most authentic Andalusian you could find grabs a guitar and improvises a "cante" (flamenco song), with everyone clapping hands in accompaniment. It's a far cry from discos and pop music.

I've already said that the nights are long in Spain, and that they go on 'til the wee hours of the morning. That's the time to take part in a last local ritual, "chocolate con churros," a special Spanish hot chocolate in which you dunk doughnuts. That will restore you — even after a night on the town in Madrid.

N° 1 •• LISTEN

After listening to the cassette, match each member of the family with the action depicted below.

1. D. Gustavo . . . .   **A.** ... Se quedó en la cama.

2. Martita (sábado) . . . .   **B.** ... Salieron con unos amigos a dar una vuelta.

3. Antonio . . . .   **C.** ... Se fue al fútbol con Pedro.

4. D. Gustavo y Encarna   **D.** ... Asistió al Concierto de la Banda Municipal.

5. Martita (domingo) . . .   **E.** ... Se quedó en casa viendo el baloncesto.

6. Pedro . . . .   **F.** ... Se fue a una discoteca.

Recipe for "Gazpacho"

INGREDIENTES : *Un puñado de sal — Ajo — Vinagre — Aceite — Media barra de pan — Tomates — Pepinos — Pimientos verdes.*
Sírvase bien frío ; preferiblemente acompañado de : pepino picado — cebolla picada — taquitos de pan — pimiento picado.

¡Que le aproveche!

See answers on page 30 of booklet.

⚫⚫ LISTEN

THE RETURN HOME

Returning from Teneriffe, Paco begins the story of a story . . .

Soledad : *Sentémonos delante, siempre es mejor.*

Paloma : *Cuando vinimos, lo pasé bien, pero el avión iba a tope. ¡ Menos mal que ahora hay poca gente !*

Paco : *Bueno . . . Despidámonos de Tenerife. Quisiera volver otra vez por estas tierras.*

Paloma : *Aunque fue difícil, finalmente yo estoy contenta de la filmación. ¿ No creéis... ?*

Soledad : *¡ Claro! Con experiencia, las cosas salen mejor. Por cierto, ¿ cómo te fue en Granada . . . ?*

Paloma : *Olvídate de Granada. Eso es agua pasada.*

Paco : *Le fue mal. ¡ Fatal !*

Paloma : *¡ Tú siempre tienes que dar la nota, Paco! ¡ Que simpático eres! Anda, déjame el periódico y cállate de una vez.*

Paco : *¡ Un whisky ! por favor.*

Azafata : *¿ Quieren que les sirva algo más ?*

Soledad : *Yo quisiera que me trajera unas postales del avión para mis hijos.*

Paloma : *Yo no quiero nada, gracias.*

Paco : *¿ Queréis que os cuente una historia ?*

Paloma y Soledad : *¡ Cuéntanosla ! Pero que sea divertida.*

Paco : *Érase que se era una vez, en un avión de Iberia, dos mujeres que escuchaban encandiladas a un tonto. Volvían de un trabajo-excursión que los había dejado entusiasmados quince días. El avión se acercaba a la capital y ellas se iban durmiendo poco a poco . . . poco a . . .*

⚫⚫ LISTEN AND REPEAT
You will find the translation on page 30 of booklet.

Art in the 20th century: 1. Tower of Maíz (Madrid)
2. Building in el Paseo de la Castellana (Madrid)
3. La Vaguada (Madrid)
4. Centro Reina Sofía (Miró exposition)
5. Miró Foundation (Barcelona)

NOUNS

la tierra — earth
la filmación — filming
la experiencia — experience
la postal — postcard
la mentira — lie
el diario — newspaper
el semanario — weekly (publication)
la revista — magazine
el anuncio — advertisement
el suceso — event
la suscripción — subscription
la literatura — literature
la obra maestra — masterpiece
el poema — poem
la novela — novel *(1)*
la obra (teatral) — work, play
el asunto — subject, matter
el cuento (de hadas) — fairy tale
el folleto — brochure

VERBS

salir bien — to be successful
salir mal — to be unsuccessful
ir bien (mal) — to go (well) bad
olvidarse — to forget *(2)*
dar la nota — to attract notice
callarse — to be quiet
mejorarse — to get better
empeorarse — to get worse
rogar — to entreat
distraerse — to distract, divert
asomarse — to appear, show
aparcar — to park
estacionar — to park
frenar — to apply the brakes
arrancar — to pull (up, out), unfasten

ADJECTIVES

divertido(a) — amusing
encandilado(a) — intriguing
estupendo(a) — stupendous
maravilloso(a) — extraordinary, "awesome"
magnífico(a) — magnificent
fantástico(a) — fantastic
entusiasmado(a) — enthusiastic
pensativo(a) — pensive
sorprendido(a) — surprised

MISCELLANEOUS

a tope — crammed ("end to end")
por cierto — by the way, for certain
fatal — very bad
¡ anda ! — get on!
de una vez — at one time
érase que se era una vez — there once really was
poco a poco — little by little
en voz alta (baja) — in a loud (soft) voice

1. REFUSING AN OFFER

No quiero nada, gracias — I don't want anything, thank you
No necesito nada
No me hace falta nada — I don't need anything
Eso no me apetece
Eso no me dice nada — That doesn't appeal to me
De momento, no. Quizás más tarde — Right now, no. Maybe later

2. QUIETING SOMEONE

Cállate de una vez — Be quiet, for once and for all
¡ Cierra la boca !
¡ Cierra el pico ! (5) — Shut your mouth!
¡ Guarden silencio ! — Keep quiet!
¡ Chit ! ¡ Silencio ! — Hush! Be quiet!

3. EXPRESSING SATISFACTION OR JOY

Estoy contento(a) de la película — I'm happy with the film
Estoy satisfecho(a) de los resultados — I'm satisfied with the results
Me siento orgullosa de mis hijos — I'm proud of my children
¡ Qué bien ! — How nice!
¡ Qué felicidad ! — What happiness!
¡ Qué alegría de verte ! — What a joy to see you!

4. ASKING SOMEONE FOR NEWS

¿ Cómo te fue el viaje ?
¿ Qué tal te fue el viaje ? — How did your trip go?
¿ Lo pasaste bien ? — Did it go well for you?
¿ No tuviste problemas ? — Did you have any problems?
¿ Qué tal dormiste ? — How did you sleep?

NOTES . . .   NOTES . . .   NOTES . . .   NOTES . . .

(1) "novel" as for a work of literature; "news" = "noticias." — (2) Often reflexive with the same sense as "olvidar." — (3) In another sense, "to pull, to tear away." — (4) Literally "up to the very limit." "Fecha tope" = date limit — (5) Familiar. "El pico" = "the beak."

1. "¿CÓMO TE/LE ... FUE?"

[● ●] LISTEN:

¿Cómo te fue? (muy bien)
• Me fue muy bien
¿Cómo le fue? (mal)
• Le fue mal

Continue as in the model. Remember to change the pronouns according to the persons:
¿Cómo te fue? (muy bien) — ¿Cómo le fue? (mal) — ¿Cómo os fue? (de maravilla) — ¿Cómo les fue? (fantástico) — ¿Cómo te fue? (horrible) — ¿Cómo os fue? (bastante mal) — ¿Cómo te fue? (estupendo).

Grammar: See F.

2. EXPRESSING A WISH

[● ●] LISTEN:

descansar (tú)
• ¡Que descanses!
pasarlo bien (vosotros)
• ¡Que lo paséis bien!

Express the wishes as in the model with the help of "que" + subjunctive:
descansar (tú) — pasarlo (vosotros) — mejorarse (tú) — divertirse (vosotros) — tener buen viaje (ustedes) — divertise (usted).

Grammar: See O.

3. "DEJAR" + ADJECTIVE

[● ●] LISTEN:

Excursión · entusiasmado (yo)
• Esta excursíon me ha dejado entusiasmado
película · pensativa (ella)
• Esta película la ha dejado pensativa

Continue as in the model. Remember agreement with the adjective and subject.
excursión · entusiasmado (yo) — película · pensativa (ella) — isla · encantados (nosotros) — noticia · triste (vosotros) — viaje · impresionado (él) — reacción · sorprendida (yo).

4. "PERO QUE" + SUBJUNCTIVE

[● ●] LISTEN:

¿Os cuento una historia? (ser divertida)
• Cuéntala, pero que sea divertida
¿Reservo una habitación?
• Resérvala, pero que tenga cuarto de baño

Continue as in the model.
¿Os cuento una historia? (ser divertida) — ¿Reservo una habitación? (tener cuarto de baño) — ¿Pido una cerveza? (estar bien fría) — ¿Saco una localidad? (no ser cara) — ¿Compro un libro? (ser para niños) — ¿Traigo frutas? (estar maduras).

Grammar: See O.

5. TENSE AGREEMENT

[● ●] LISTEN:

Quería que leyeras este informe
• Quiero que leas este informe

Continue according to the model. Put the first verb in the present indicative, and the second verb in the present subjunctive:
Quería que leyeras este informe — Deseaba que escucharas este casete — Esperaba que me escribieran — No creía que vinieras — Dudaba que trabajáramos bien — Deseaba que nos encontráramos otra vez.

Grammar: See K, O.

6. TENSE AGREEMENT

[● ●] LISTEN:

Tu padre dice que trabajes
• Tu padre dijo que trabajaras
Los niños me piden que les escriba
• Los niños me pidieron que les escribiera

Continue according to the model. Change the first verb to the present indicative and the second to the imperfect subjunctive:
Tu padre dice que trabajes — Los niños me piden que les escriba — El médico me aconseja que descanse — El director le ruega que vaya — El jefe te prohibe que fumes — El profesor te ordena que te calles.

Grammar: See K, O.

MOVING FORWARD
"LA MOVIDA"

"Madrid, the New York of La Mancha." The headline - was sprawled across the front page of a weekly newspaper in the capital a short time ago. Madrid natives are very proud of this flattering reputation held by their city; it's become one of the great centers of novelty, change, and discovery. The most enthusiastic among them like to compare it to the U.S.A.

A long road has been traveled since the era when the Spanish capital, under Franco, symbolized the heavy hand of government. Madrid was the personification of official culture imposed from on high. In contrast, at that time Barcelona was the center of nonconformity. It was in that latter Catalonian metropolis that every antiestablishment artist felt he had to triumph. Barcelona used to embody the city that looked toward Europe and the fu-ture, while Madrid represented the present as well as the allure of the past.

Nowadays, the Spanish capital is taking its revenge and sowing its wild oats. Currently, it's known as the "in" city, the trendy city. Madrid is the place where everything is happening, the city of "movida," which means everything that changes and moves forward.

"Movida" is a comprehensive cultural phenomenon. Musical offerings, painting, theater, and cinematography have increased spectacularly in a few years. Foreign artists who formerly ignored Madrid and even Spain in their European tours are certain to include them now. From ballet to pop music and experimental theater, Madrid is definitely part of the most fashionable travel circuit.

But "movida" should also be seen as a fundamental impetus. Madrid natives seem to want to make up for lost time, put behind them the authoritarian atmosphere that filled their city for so long. Didn't Philip II establish the seat of the Spanish capital in Madrid in 1561 because he was seduced by the site's austere and ascetic surroundings in the middle of the tawny plateau of la Mancha?

That's long past. Philip II would never recognize the same city with its groups of jean-clad teenagers, girls and boys mingling together and noisily celebrating throughout the night. With green punk hairdo's and bottles of beer in their hands, they crowd the dark discos.

Sex, which used to be practiced in hidden alcoves, now has a place of its own in the capital — to the consternation of the older generation that not long ago was raging against bikinis and women in slacks.

Madrid is exploding. This explosion characterizes all of Spain, which seems to be ridding itself in a few short years of the yoke it had been subjected to for so long, and throwing itself headlong into the twenty-first century.

● ● LISTEN

El frente de Gandesa

Popular song of the Civil War (Sung and arranged by Joaquín Díaz)

Gandesa's front

Si me quieres escribir
ya sabes mi paradero (bis)

If you want to write me
you know my whereabouts (repeat)

En el frente de Gandesa
primera línea de fuego (bis)

On Gandesa's front
frontline of fire (repeat)

Si tu quieres comer bien
para huír en buena forma (bis)

If you wish to dine well
to run off in good order

En el frente de Gandesa
allí tienes una fonda (bis)

On Gandesa's frontline
you have an inn (repeat)

A la entrada de esa fonda
hay un moro Mohamed (bis)

At the entrance of that inn
there's a Moor, Mohammed (repeat)

Que te dice pasa, pasa,
¿qué quieres para comer? (bis)

Who says come on, enter
what do you want to eat? (repeat)

El primer plato que te dan
son granadas rompedoras (bis)

For a first course they serve
exploding grenades (repeat)

El segundo de metralla,
para recordar memoria (bis)

And the second is of shrapnel
For your memory to remember (repeat)

Si me quieres escribir
ya sabes mi paradero (bis)

If you want to write to me
you know my whereabouts (repeat)

En el frente de Gandesa
primera línea de fuego (bis)

On Gandesa's front
frontline of fire (repeat)

IDIOMS

LEER LA CARTILLA

(Read the military book)

Read the riot act

ESTAR EN EL AJO

(Be in the garlic)

To be in the "thick" of things

LLAMAR A CAPITULO

(Call to chapter)

To take to task

HILAR FINO

(Spin a fine thread)

To split hairs

4. WRITTEN PRACTICE

CHANGE the verbs in parentheses to the subjunctive : *Quiero que* . . . . *(ir) (tú) al teatro. Espero que* . . . . . . *(poder) (él) venir. Tal vez te* . . . . . . *(escribir) (yo). No creo que* . . . . . . *(hacer) (nosotros) ese viaje. ¡Ojalá* . . . . . *(tener) (él) suerte! Dudo que* . . . . . *(llegar) (ellos) mañana.*

TRANSLATE : *Como usted quiera. ¡Ojalá llegue a tiempo! Quizás reciba una buena noticia. Espero que aceptes esta propuesta. A lo mejor llama por teléfono. No me asuste.*

4.2

CHANGE the verbs in parentheses to the imperative : . . . . *(trabajar) (tú) menos. No* . . . . *(fumar) (usted) demasiado.* . . . . *(venir) (vosotros) conmigo. No* . . . . *(ir) (ustedes) solos. No* . . . . *(comer) (tú) tanto.* . . . . *(hablar) (usted) en voz baja.*

TRANSLATE : *¿ Estáis listos? ¡Estad atentos! ¡No, así no! Volvamos a empezar. Interpreten la escena otra vez. Silencio, se rueda.*
She wants to know if you are ready. He asks you to wait. I asked you if you had this newspaper. I ask you not to move. He asks you the time. He asks you to go to see him.

ANSWER the questions changing the underlined words to the object pronoun: : *¿ Le limpio el <u>parabrisas</u>? Sí,* . . . .*¿Le arreglamos <u>el neumático</u>? Sí,* . . . . . . *¿Le lleno <u>el tanque</u>? Sí,* . . . . *¿Llamo a la policía? Sí,* . . . . *¿Le reviso <u>el motor</u>? Sí,* . . . .

TRANSLATE : *¿ Es suyo este vehículo? ¡ Claro que es mío! ¿ De quién va a ser? He tenido un accidente en la carretera. ¡ Pero no es posible! No puede ser. Estas historias me ponen nerviosa.*
Can I park my car here? Where is the closest garage? Can you send me a mechanic? Do you have any (loose) change for the parking meter? The horn doesn't work. The car doesn't start.

4.4

COMPLETE the sentences using the verbs in parentheses : *Si* . . . . *(estar) (ella) enamorada, me llamaría. Si* . . . . *(ser) (ellos) amigos, no se pelearían. Si me* . . . . *(querer) (tú), no dirías estas tonterías. Si lo* . . . . . . *(abandonar) (yo), se pondría muy triste. Si* . . . . . . *(tener) (vosotros) menos prisa, podríamos charlar un rato.*

TRANSLATE : *Esta música me resulta insoportable. Este conjunto es famoso. Para mí es uno de los mejores de la ciudad. Este chico me pone nerviosa. Espero que nos volvamos a ver. Voy a terminar por discutir con ella.*
If you wish, we can go to a discotheque. If I had time I would reserve seats for Friday night's performance. If you liked bullfights, I would take you on Sunday.

4.5

CHANGE the verbs in parentheses to the subjunctive, present, or preterite as needed : *Espero que el jefe* . . . . *(llegar) a tiempo. No creí que* . . . . *(venir) tanta gente. Dudo que* . . . . *(viajar) todos. ¿Quieren que la azafata les* . . . . *(traer) una copa? La dirección deseaba que los empleados* . . . . *(presentarse) a primera hora.*

TRANSLATE: : *¡ Menos mal que salimos! ¿Cómo te fue ayer? De maravilla. Pide una bebida pero que no sea whisky. Despídeme del jefe.*
We said goodbye at the airport. I did not have the time to say goodbye to my friends. This country has fascinated me. Although the filming may have ended, I will remain here a few days.

See answers on page 34 of booklet.

MORE VOCABULARY

THE AUTOMOBILE

la matrícula — registration

el techo — roof

el volante — steering wheel

el asiento trasero — backseat

la puerta (de coche) — car door

el tablero — panel

el salpicadero — splashguard

el/la testigo (m/f) — witness

la bocina — horn

el claxon — horn

el intermitente — flashing signal

el retrovisor — rearview mirror

la palanca de cambio — shift (gear)

la caja de cambios — gear box

el freno de mano — hand brake

el parabrisas — windshield

el limpiaparabrisas — windshield wipers

la ventanilla — car window

la luneta trasera — rear window

el maletero — trunk

la rueda — wheel

el neumático — tire

la cámara de aire — inner tube

la rueda de recambio — spare tire

el gato — jack

el tubo de escape — muffler

el pedal — pedal

el parachoques — shock absorber

el faro — headlight

la luz larga — headlights

la luz de cruce — signal light

la antiniebla — fog light

el antivaho — de-icer

el motor — motor

la batería — battery

la bujía — sparkplug

el radiador — radiator

el depósito de gasolina — gasoline tank

el tapón — plug

el empleado de gasolinera — gasoline-pump attendant

el cinturón de seguridad — seat belt

el ventilador — fan

el carburador — carburetor

el embrague — clutch

el encendido — ignition

la señal de tráfico — traffic signal

la dirección prohibida (f) — no thoroughfare

dirección única (f) — one way

preferencia de paso (f) — right of way

piso resbaladizo (m) — slippery road

paso a nivel (m) — grade crossing

precaución obras — work in progress

apagar las luces — to turn off headlights

quitar el contacto — to turn off

tener una avería — to have a breakdown

dar marcha atrás — to go in reverse

llenar el depósito — to fill (the tank) up

cambiar de marcha — to change speed

pinchar una rueda — to have a flat

atropellar — to knock down, to run over

chocar — to collide, to hit

adelantar — to go forward

SPORTS AND LEISURE ACTIVITY

el deporte — sport

el fútbol — football, soccer (outside USA)

el campo de fútbol — soccer field

el partido — match

el árbitro — umpire

el pito — whistle

la portería — goal

el portero — goalie

el descanso — rest, time out, halftime

el empate — tie (game)

la pista de tenis — tennis court

la red — net

el saque — service (tennis)

la pelota — ball

el marcador — scoreboard

el gimnasio — gymnasium

el estadio — stadium

el esquí — ski

la vela — sail

la carrera de caballos — horse race, race track

la apuesta — bet

el boxeo — boxing

el ajedrez — chess

el tablero — chessboard

la ficha — token, coin

el crucigrama — crossword puzzle

la pesca — fishing

la caza — hunting

la pintura — painting

la cerámica — ceramics, pottery

las bellas artes (f pl) — fine arts

4. TEST YOURSELF

1. "TU" OR "USTED"?

	TÚ	USTED
¡No me pongas nervioso!		
¡Salga por la ventana!		
¡No nos mientas!		
¡Ven aquí!		
Ve a la Oficina de enfrente		
¡No ponga la música tan fuerte!		
Entre por esta puerta		
¡No grites!		
Llene esta ficha		

2. MATCH EACH QUESTION WITH ITS ANSWER

1. ¿ De quién es este billete?
2. ¿ Esta tarjeta es tuya?
3. ¿ Es vuestro este pasaporte?
4. ¿ Estas llaves son las tuyas?
5. ¿ De quién son estos bolsos?
6. ¿ Estas maletas son las vuestras?
7. ¿ Este es tu hotel?

A. Sí, son las nuestras
B. No, no es el nuestro
C. Es mío
D. No, no es el mío
E. Sí, es mía
F. Sí, son las mías
G. Son míos

3. CHANGE EACH SENTENCE ACCORDING TO THE MODEL

¿Me pasas los documentos del coche? ¿Puedes pasármelos? Pásamelos, por favor.

¿Le abres la puerta? . . . .
¿Nos prestas el coche? . . . .
¿Les mandas un telegrama? . . . .
¿Le pago la multa? . . . .
¿Nos sirves la cena? . . . .
¿Me traes una copa? . . . .

4. COMPLETE EACH SENTENCE

1. Si sigues pasando los semáforos en rojo . . . . **A.** podrías ver mejor
2. Si viniera el agente . . . . **B.** sacarás el carné de conducir
3. Si hubieras respetado el límite de velocidad . **C.** no te hubieran detenido
4. Si vas a esa auto-escuela. . . . . **D.** muéstrale el permiso
5. Si encendieras los faros. . . . . **E.** te cobrarán una multa
6. Si hubieras cerrado las ventanillas . . . . **F.** no te habrías resfriado

5. CHANGE EACH SENTENCE TO THE INDIRECT FORM

beginning with: "Le dijo que . . ."

«Usted ha tenido muchos problemas» . . . .

«He vivido en el extranjero» . . . .

«Estuvo de secretaria en una empresa española» . . . .

«Hizo también de periodista» . . . .

«Ahora está enamorado pero tenga cuidado» . . . .

«Tiene que esperar un poco» . . . .

«Dentro de unos meses, todo irá bien para usted» . . . .

6. COMPLETE THIS DIALOGUE

with the following verbs: ACABAR / IR / DEJAR / IMPORTAR / PONER

¿Te . . . . que me siente aquí?

¡Oh, Ramón! ¡Qué sorpresa! ¿Cuando llegaste?

. . . . de llegar. Sabía que te iba a encontrar en la discoteca.

¿Y cómo te . . . . ?

De maravilla. Este viaje me . . . . muy contento. He hecho muchos contratos. Oye, esta música me . . . . nervioso. ¿Por qué no vamos a un lugar más tranquilo?

See answers on page 34 of booklet.

THE WAY TO EACH OTHER

It's strange. I have the impression that I've always lived in Madrid, that I've always understood and spoken Spanish. My memories of Paris are more and more distant. And yet it is only yesterday that I celebrated my second year here with my pals. I had a two-year contract and there are only a few days left to get ready for my return to France. I'm sad at the thought of having to leave this little world.

Last week my car was being fixed and I had to take a taxi to go to the Alcobendas factory outside of town. The cab driver didn't take me for a tourist. We talked about the news and we both complained about the traffic getting worse and worse. When we went by Guzman el Bueno Street, he showed me a building, telling me that he had lived there when he was a kid.

"Antes, en este barrio habia tanto campo que no nos faltaba lugar donde jugar al fútbol. Mi madre me mandaba a comprar leche a une vaquería, del otro lado de Cea Bermúdez. Los dueños tenian a las vacas detrás mismo del local. ¿Se imagina?"

Actually, in less than fifty years, the city has known the greatest changes in its history. It is, however, taking on the look of a great European cultural and economic center. El Paseo de la Castellana, for instance — who would have believed it? From a quiet promenade bordered with trees and peaceful middle-class houses, it is today crowded with large banks, both Spanish and international. Since only the most prominent architects have been commissioned, the avenue is a virtual museum of modern architecture and sculpture. Overlooked until now by its European neighbors, this little world is in the process of becoming a great metropolis.

And with all that, I see this soft, filtered light that clearly silhouettes the already numerous towers, sharpening their height even more against the intense blue background of the Madrid sky! People live faster than before, but they still live. While the traffic light is red, they still take the time to listen to the noise of the water in the great fountains. Sitting at the terrace of a café, they can still watch the light steps of the passing women who, without turning around, let it be known that they know they're being admired. How I recognize Rosa! Without ever having found her, I meet her every day in the street, in the stores, at the movies — in the theater and on the screen — at the Prado Museum in the charming country scenes of Goya. I also imagine her walking by my side on the banks on the Manzanares River; and I go with her to the Chapel of San Antonio to find her again in the faces of the angels painted on the frescoes of the cupola. I would never have guessed that it was the best way to get to know her better.

I was thinking about all that tonight coming home. As always, the concierge was at her post.

Se le murió su amante y se ba al comb.

«Se le murió el amante y se va al convento» Goya

"Buenas noches, Adelino. ¿Ha habido correo para mi esta tarde?"

Adelina gave me several envelopes. Statements, several bills, and a letter sent to my Paris address that had been forwarded. A French stamp, mailed in Paris, a familiar handwriting. Nervously I tore open the envelope.

"Querido mio:

He vuelto a Paris hace poco. Me encantaria verte. Espero tu llamada.

Rosa

THE END.

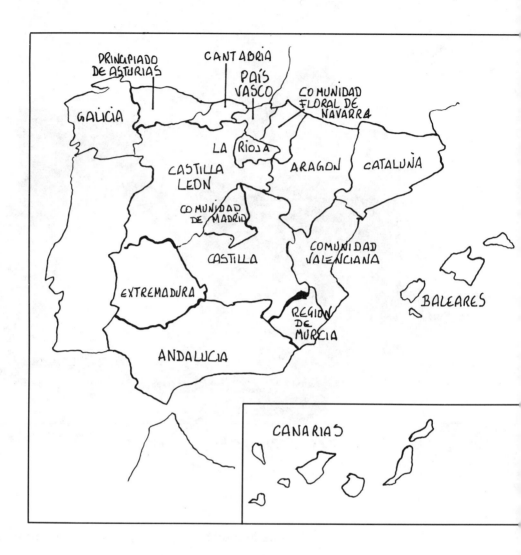

PRINCIPIADO
DE ASTURIAS

CANTABRIA

PAÍS
VASCO

COMUNIDAD
FLORAL DE
NAVARRA

GALICIA

LA RIOJA

CASTILLA
LEON

ARAGON

CATALUÑA

COMUNIDAD
DE MADRID

CASTILLA

COMUNIDAD
VALENCIANA

EXTREMADURA

BALEARES

REGION
DE
MURCIA

ANDALUCIA

CANARIAS

Telegraph

Most of the post offices offer telegraph services, as well as telex and telegraphed money orders, on both a national and international basis.

Postal Service

The Spanish postal service has more than 6,000 offices distributed throughout the country, including those in small towns, in railroad stations, ports, and airports. All types of services are available, and performed in a modern and efficient fashion.

The main offices in Madrid, Barcelona, and Bilbao, as well as those in international airports, are open 24 hours a day.

Two types of service are available. One purely postal service concerns itself with different types of correspondence. The other provides banking service in the form of postal money orders and telegraph money orders.

Every post office has a general delivery service, where it's possible to register to receive letters, packages, or money orders. These, of course, can also be sent to hotels or any other address.

In addition, postage stamps are sold in post offices and authorized tobacco shops (estancos) throughout the country.

To find out about the various postal services available, call: 221-40-04/91.

Telephone

Almost everywhere in Spain, there are public telephone booths from which you can phone anywhere in the world by following instructions posted in the booth and translated into several languages. These phones function with 5-, 25-, 50-, and 100-peseta currency, and can be used for any length of time. In the largest cities, there are also telephone centers that remain open throughout the day.

To call from Spain by telephone to anywhere in the world, you must dial 07. After hearing the dial tone, dial the area code of the country, the exchange of the city you wish to reach, and finally the number of the party you wish to speak to. The area code for Spain, which you need to know to receive calls from other countries, is 34. The caller would then have to dial the exchange for the province, and then the specific telephone number.

For general information, dial 003.

Spanish currency is the peseta.

Notes and Coins

Bank notes come in denominations of 100, 200, 500, 1,000, 2,000, 5,000, and 10,000 pesetas.

Coins come in denominations of 1, 2, 5, 10, 25, 50, 100, 200, and 500 pesetas.

Exchange of Currency

Every bank offers foreign currency exchange against the peseta. Most hotels and many travel agencies also offer this service. In addition, most hotels and restaurants — as well as a wide range of businesses — accept the most common international credit cards and travelers' checks.

Banks

Banks are open to the public from 9 A.M. to 2 P.M., except on Saturday when the schedule is 9 A.M. to 12:30 P.M.

Certain offices are open in the afternoon and, in those cases, are closed Saturday.

The hours of pharmacies are established by the government of each town, but generally they are open from 9:30 A.M. to 2 P.M., then again between 4:30 and 8 P.M. At other times, pharmacy service is guaranteed by establishments that take turns staying open. Every pharmacy posts a list with the addresses of those that are open; and it is customary to indicate which pharmacies that are open are the closest. The entire list is published each day in the newspapers.

PRACTICAL INFORMATION

Hotels

Spain has a hotel system noted for the number, variety, and quality of its hotels. Distributed throughout the country, they are capable of answering every need.

Spanish hotels are divided into five categories, with one to five stars awarded to each hotel according to the services and features offered. In addition, there are a small number of exceptional five-star hotels that are considered "deluxe."

Residence hotels are governed by the same criteria as others. They have no restaurants, but do serve breakfast, have room service, and a bar or cafeteria.

"Hostal" is similar to a hotel, but more modest. Hostales are rated from one to three stars.

Guest houses, known as "pensiones," are yet another type of lodging. They are welcoming and convenient places, in which service and amenities can range from plain to relatively luxurious. Generally run by the family that owns the house, meals are included in the price and are often excellent. Guests pay separately for showers. Pensiones are ideal for visitors who want to learn about Spain, away from the roads most often traveled by tourists.

Paradores

Paradores are the most original and most interesting type of lodging offered to tourists. The word "parador" is found in a number of classic Spanish texts. At a time when the "posada" or inn was a place used at night to board animals, and most travelers were not treated as guests, the parador was used to lodge those who were considered important. It was based on this tradition that, in 1926, the Marquis of Vega-Inclán, Royal Commissioner of Tourism, created a series of Government Paradores. King Alphonse XIII personally approved the project. The first parador was built in Sierra de Gredos to be used during hunting, "the sport of kings." Then, gradually, as the idea of tourism and travel became more important, paradores were built at distances from one another that could be easily traveled in a day by automobiles of that era. This gave rise to the paradores in Manzanares, Bailén, Oropesa, and Mérida. Now, the system includes 86 inns.

The fundamental philosophy of the parador was and continues to be based on two things. The government favors putting them in areas the private sector finds unprofitable and therefore neglects. The second important point is, whenever possible, to take advantage of historic sites, ancient places of refuge, palaces, mansions, and convents in which paradores can be situated. That way, the traveler will have the pleasant experience of sleeping in the same room in which Charles V spent the night in Jarandilla de la Vera while waiting for his suite to be readied in a nearby monastery. Or one might eat in rooms belonging to Compluto University, founded by Cardinal Cisneros at Alcalá de Henares — or spend a few days at the Castle where the Prince of Condé fought 300 years ago.

A trip through Spain staying at paradores is also a voyage into its history, tracing it from the Middle Ages to the twentieth century.

For information and reservations, write: Paradores del Turismo, Calle Velazquez, num. 18, 28001, Madrid. Telephone: 435-97-00 or 435-97-44.

Apartments

Renting a furnished apartment is another interesting lodging possibility. Offers of tourist apartments exist for the entire Spanish coast, but are concentrated especially on Costa Brava, Valencia, the Balearic Islands, and Costa del Sol. These can be especially convenient when you travel in a group. Prices, which vary according to the place and season of the year, are calculated per person or per group.

Travel agencies generally offer apartment rentals as one of their services.

Spanish cuisine is good and as varied as the country itself. As a producer of fine quality food, of popular traditional dishes, and many new offerings that fine chefs have brought there recently, the prestige of Spanish cuisine has attained a top place in Europe.

In broad terms, one can divide the Spanish peninsula into six types of predominant cuisine.

• **The north** is one of the most notable areas for dining. Fish and shellfish from Galicia, among the best in the world, are prepared in a manner unequaled anywhere. Basque cuisine is celebrated internationally and its recipes of codfish with "pil-pil" or Biscay fashion, and its delicious eels are among the best Spanish dishes. In Asturia, a must is "fabada," a magnificent bean dish; there are also excellent local cheeses and cider.

• **The Pyrenees** is the region for "chilindrones." Aragon offers an unlimited number of dishes prepared with this flavorful sauce, and good ham from Teruel.

• **Catalonia** is known for "cazuelas" (casseroles). These dishes are set off by pork sausages and cheeses, as well as regional sauces. One sauce in particular, "ali-oli," has an international reputation.

• **The Valencia** region is considered the home of rice dishes. In addition to the celebrated "paella," Valencians can prepare marvelous rice with any sort of ingredient at all — meat, chicken, shellfish, green vegetables, or fish. "Caldero" or rice from Murcia is also wonderful.

• **Andalusia** is known for fried foods. The fried fish is especially good. In addition, remember "gazpacho" (cold soup with tasty vegetables) and Jabugo ham from Huelva province — truly delicious.

• **Central Spain** is where you'll find roast meat. Lamb, veal, suckling pig, baby lamb, and other meats are roasted slowly in wood-burning ovens, acquiring a delicious texture and flavor. Good hams, cheeses, and the best pork in Spain complete this region's offerings. Madrid, with its close ties to Castile, merits its own mention. Without creating a specific cuisine, Madrid's strong personality is expressed in a large number of typical native dishes. Madrilenian "cocido," an all-in-one dish with vegetables and different kinds of meat; tripe, Madrid style; and wonderful sweet dishes are outstanding.

Two island cuisines constitute a special place in Spanish cooking.

• **The Balearic Islands** created a well-known specialty that's been exported worldwide: mayonnaise originated in Mahón on Minorca. Majorca has "ensaimadas," a light cake made of puff pastry, and "sobrasada," a very flavorful pork dish.

• **The Canary Islands** offers a very imaginative cuisine that tries to go beyond limitations imposed by native-grown foods. Of the many dishes based on fish and a famous piquant sauce, "mojo picón" distinguishes itself from the rest with its magnificent tropical fruits — banana, avocado, and papaya produced on the islands.

DRINKING

Wine

Wine is the preeminent Spanish drink. Spain, with France and Italy, is one of the three biggest wine producers in the world. It offers an immense variety of quality vintages from more than 57 different regions, among which there are some truly exceptional wines.

• **Rioja** is the king of Spanish wines. Its producers, knowing they control the destiny of one of the world's best wines, protect its quality and trade name with strict official standards. This makes fraud impossible and assures the prestige of this exquisite wine, whose color, aroma, and flavor cannot be confused with any other.

• **Sherry** (wine from Jerez) is the most international of all the Spanish wines; it is exported each year to more than 120 countries. There are five different varieties of this Andalusian wine foreigners call sherry in honor of the city of Jerez de la Frontera, where the first cellars were established. The five varieties are manzanilla (very dry), fino (pale, very dry), amontillado (moderately dry), oloroso (slightly sweet), and dulce (sweet), also called cream sherry.

- **Catalonian wine** cellars, which evolved in the Penedes region, have an excellent sparkling wine, whose value for the money enables it to rival French champagnes on the most demanding international market.

- **Cariñena** wine from Aragon has a strong aroma and flavor, and goes well with meat and spicy dishes.

- **Valdepeñas** wine from La Mancha is a very popular drink of good quality, smooth, dry, and not sour.

- **Jumilla** wine from Murcia is aged in oaken barrels; there are also some young wines. Both have a high alcohol content.

- **Ribeiro** wine from Galicia, both white and red, is light, a little sour, and goes well with Galician cuisine.

- **Sangria** is a refreshing wine-based drink mixed with fresh fruit.

Beer

There is not a long tradition for beer drinking in Spain, but it is currently becoming widespread. There are many breweries that produce beer for the national market.

Spanish beer is very cheap and, with rare exceptions, has very little alcohol. It is served cold. It is not customary to drink it at meals. One usually has it before dinner, to complement those wonderful hors d'oeuvres served at bars in most Spanish regions.

• Spirits

The famous Spanish brandy is the best known of Spanish spirits. In this category, as well, each region of Spain has its specialty. Spirits made from plants in Galicia and Iviza — "pacharan" from Navarre, absinthe from Levante, Andalusian "cazalla," and anise from Chinchón near Madrid — are some examples. "Orujo" or brandy made in several northern regions is particularly well liked.

In general, the visitor will find Spanish spirits an excellent value for the money.

Schedules

The Spanish, perhaps because of their mild climate and long daylight hours, generally get up a little later and go to sleep much later than is the custom in most other European countries.

Stores stay open from 9 A.M. to 1:30 P.M., and from 4:30 or 5 P.M. to 8 or 8:30 P.M. Generally, they close one and one-half days a week, usually Saturday afternoon and Sunday — although a number of stores only close on Sunday. In tourist areas in summer, hours are usually extended to 10 or 11 P.M., and stores stay open every day.

Restaurants have very varied schedules. The most common one is to serve meals from 1:30 to 3:30 P.M., and dinner from 8:30 to 11 or 11:30 P.M. In summer, the hours are usually longer. There are some restaurants with continuous hours, as well as an equal number that serve meals until the early hours of the morning. Bars are generally open all day long and a good part of the night.

In general, night life in Spain is very intense, and bars and discos stay open most of the night. In summer, they often don't close until after 3 or 4 A.M. In large cities like Madrid and Barcelona, there are many local bars that don't close until dawn — even in winter.

Tipping

Tipping is traditional in Spain. Even though nowadays all bars include a surcharge for service on the bill, it is customary to leave additional money as a tip. This custom, which was always practiced in bars and restaurants, usually includes hotel bellboys, theater and movie ushers, and, less often, taxi drivers. None of these are absolutely required; no one will demand a tip if you prefer not to give one.

HOLIDAYS

Popular Holidays

The richness and age of Spanish cultural traditions, the different heritages that have blended into it, and the variety of its regions create beauty and originality in fiestas celebrated each year in cities and villages. More than 200 are considered of tourist interest, and some have gained an international reputation.

In February, all Spain celebrates Carnival. The most exciting festivities take place in Cádiz and Teneriffe. The music, humor, and color display the intensity with which they are celebrated in these two cities where Carnival turns daily life upside down.

The "fallas" of Valencia take place in March. During that month, the city is filled with enormous cardboard sculptures — satiric and amusing depictions of real people and events. They are burned in great bonfires on March 19, to the joy of the local inhabitants.

Holy Week is a time for traditional religious processions of great beauty. The most original and most important are in Valladolid, Cuenca, and Zamora in Castile, and in Seville and Malaga in Andalusia. During April, the Seville fair is held. The central city is transformed into a miniature Seville with a life of its own. Singing and dancing go on all day and all night in the fiesta's wooden sheds.

The Rocio pilgrimage, a traditional Andalusian procession, is celebrated in May. People go on horseback or by cart to the El Rocio sanctuary near Doñana Park in Ayamonte, Huelva province.

From July 6 to 14, in Pamplona, the famous feast of San Fermin takes place, during which young men join in the "running of the bulls" through the city streets.

HANDICRAFTS

Varied Spanish handicrafts are the legacy of old traditions, kept intact over the course of centuries. They are an important tourist attraction.

An active craft district exists in almost every city in Spain; they are most numerous in places visited by tourists. There is usually no fee to enter places where handicrafts are sold, and they follow the usual business hours.

Outstanding among traditional products is leatherwork. There is a great deal of it, especially Andalusian leather, which combines excellent quality of skins with well-made and up-to-date designs. The impetus given recently to the fashion industry has contributed to its prestige, and influenced the distribution of other craft products, such as shoes, an industry located mostly in Alicante and the Balearic Islands. Couturiers and designers in Ibiza in the Balearics merit special mention. They've created a special style based on Balearic traditions, and are very successful. Their collections are handmade in most cases, and use handmade fabrics.

As for decorative arts, Spain also offers a large variety of schools and products. First, thanks to its wide distribution, we should mention ceramics. Each region of the country specializes in at least one special type of ceramic. Sargardelos in Galicia has strived for many years to create new styles and is in the forefront of Spanish ceramic centers. Talavera de la Reina, more conservative, stems from a very old tradition. Its immense production has made it the hub of the ceramics industry with the broadest distribution. The Manises school in Valencia is also significant. It is known for the metallic brilliance of its glass.

Glassmaking is centered in the Balearic Islands. Traditional wood furniture is well represented in artisan workshops around Valencia. Castile and León also stand out in this field, creating their indigenous styles. Cáceres, Granada, and Murcia bring beautiful vividly colored handwoven carpets to market. Finally, there's wrought iron, one of the most Spanish of decorative arts and of which there are many schools and traditions. Castilian wrought iron is superior, as much for its ancient tradition as for its quality.

REGIONS OF SPAIN

History and the Future

Historically, Spain enjoyed a splendid beauty and an absolutely unique geographic and strategic position between Europe, to which it belonged, and Africa toward which it faced. Since antiquity, this has made Spain a crossroad, a meeting place between East and West. Diverse peoples, races, and civilizations that gazed upon Spain could not resist the temptation to live there, leaving behind a unique culture.

Spain has been Greek, Phoenician, Jewish, Roman, Gothic, Arabic, and finally Christian and European. It has been conquered and conqueror, and has learned to integrate its various heritages into a modern and strong country, whose inhabitants, proud of the long history of their land, have taken a decisive stake in the future.

General Geography

Spain is a large and varied country. References to Spain's diversity are common because the natural climatic and cultural differences of its many regions are plain to see.

One can distinguish broadly among northern Spain, which is humid and green; Mediterranean Spain, which is fertile and sunny; southern Spain or Andalusia — perhaps the most famous — which is warm and dry and as resplendent as the limestone with which its houses gleam; and the two island groups — sisters, but very different. These are the Balearic Islands, which has kept all the old wisdom of "Mare Nostrum", and the Canary Islands — a dreamlike volcanic chain of striking beauty in the Atlantic Ocean.

Autonomous Communities

The Spanish constitution, approved in 1978, recognized the strong individualism of the various regions of Spain by instituting "autonomous communities." These are regionally administered areas that collaborate with the central government, but assume specific responsibilities. In certain cases, those responsibilities can be very broad.

Verdant Spain

- **The Basque Country**

Called Euskadi in the Basque language, and Vascongadas in Spanish, this area occupies the eastern section of the Cantabrian mountain range, and is one of the most industrialized in the country. Over the course of the centuries, its inhabitants have been able to conserve their very ancient indigenous culture whose most precious joy is the language. It's a pre-Indo-European tongue whose origins are still a mystery.

—**Bilbao,** founded at the beginning of the fourteenth century, is the largest city in the region. There is a beautiful old section with an outstanding cathedral and town hall.

—**San Sebastián** (whose Basque name is Donostia) is the capital of Guipúzcoa province and not far from France. During the last century, it was one of the summer places most frequented by the Spanish aristocracy because of its beauty and the quality of its beaches. It has kept a cosmopolitan and distinguished air up to the present day.

—**Vitoria** (or Gasteiz) is the Basque capital. The old section of the city is quite beautiful. There are two cathedrals, a Gothic cathedral finished in the fifteenth century and another, which was begun in the twentieth century but is not yet completed.

- **Cantabria**

Green and maritime, the lovely countryside hides evidence of the oldest prehistoric inhabitants of the Iberian peninsula. Among these, the most significant are the Altamira cave paintings near the pretty village of Santillana del Mar. They are, without doubt, one of the most important archeological finds of their type in the world. Toward the interior of the region, there are very lovely mountain views.

—**Santander** is the capital of this region. High up, facing a picturesque bay flanked by wide beaches, this stable and elegant city suffered considerably from a great fire in 1941. However, reconstructed with care, it has recaptured all of its charm. The very handsome palace of Magdalena is the setting every summer of an important international university program. The museum has an excellent painting collection from the seventeenth and eighteenth centuries.

- **Asturias**

Capital of a Christian kingdom that, over the centuries, fought against the Islamic kingdoms in the south, Asturias is bordered on the east by Cantabria and on the west by Galicia. This very mountainous region still proudly preserves its old title of Principality.

—**Oviedo** is the region's capital. This very beautiful city is known for a cathedral that is a handsome example of late Gothic architecture, as well as the churches of Santa Mariá del Naranco and San Miguel del Lillo, exemplifying the height of the magnificent pre-Romanesque Asturian style that flourished in the ninth century.

• **Galicia**

Occupying the northwest end of the peninsula, this region was called Finis Terrae by the Romans, who thought it was the western edge of the world. During the Middle Ages, it was famous for being the main route taken by European pilgrims to Santiago de Compostela. A mountainous and humid area, its remarkable coastline is shaped by a succession of rocky, vast estuaries abounding in shellfish. Galicia has an original culture, rich folklore, and its own language — Galician.

—**Corunna** (known as A Courune in Galician and La Coruña in Spanish) is the largest Galician city. Of ancient origin, it has preserved its considerable heritage of historical sites. Outstanding among these are several Romanesque churches and a lighthouse of Roman origin. Perhaps its most beautiful and distinctive characteristics are the glass-enclosed porticos which grace the facades of the houses.

—**Santiago de Compostela** is the current capital of Galicia, and one of the loveliest cities in Spain. Early destination of world-renowned pilgrimages, the Romanesque cathedral with its Baroque façade is the center of city life. There are other interesting monuments, such as the old university, the Romanesque college of Santa María del Sar, the Palacio de Gelmirez, and the magnificent Hostal de los Reyes Católicos, now transformed into a deluxe Parador.

—**Lugo,** capital of the province of the same name, has completely preserved its thick Roman walls and fine Romanesque cathedral.

—**Vigo** is second in size to Lugo in Galicia, and is a very important port. Despite its spectacular growth, it has kept intact its picturesquely charming old quarter.

Mediterranean Spain

• **Catalonia** (Catalunya)

Sheltered by the Pyrenees and bathed by the Mediterranean, this region occupies the northeast end of the peninsula. Its strong individuality is recognized in its culture and in its own language. It is a very developed and dynamic region. With six million inhabitants, it's the most populous part of Spain after Andalusia.

—**Barcelona** is the historic capital of Catalonia, and the second largest and most important city after Madrid. It's one of the most important ports on the Mediterranean. This splendid city has great monumental heritage. There's the Gothic quarter with its cathedral, City Hall, Episcopal Palace, and splendid Palacio de la Generalidad, current seat of the Catalonian government. The city is also known for the works of the brilliant modern artist and architect, Antonio Gaudi. Barcelona is the recipient of most of his masterpieces, among them the uncompleted Sagrada Familia Church, Parque Güell, Palacio Güell, and Casa Batlló and Casa Milá apartment buildings. In addition, Barcelona has many museums, among them the Picasso Museum and the Catalonia Art Museum. The city has been designated the site of the 1992 Olympic Games.

—**Costa Brava** is the coastal region that begins about 25 miles north of Barcelona and includes the entire provincial coast of Gerona. The picturesque landscape has a succession of steep cliffs, alternating with small coves of fine sand. Some of the villages have been massively exploited by tourism, but others, such as Tossa de Mar, have preserved their original seaside ambience.

The main tourist centers on the Costa Brava are: Rosas, San Pedro Pescador (Sant Pere Pescador), San Martin de Ampurias (Sant Marti de Ampurias), La Escala, Estartit, Bagur (Begur), Palafrugell, Palamós, Playa de Aro (Platja d'Aro), S'Agaró, San Felíu de Guixols, Tossa de Mar, Lloret de Mar, and Blanes.

—**Costa Dorada** (Costa Daurada) begins south of Barcelona and extends to Tarragona. It is made up of lovely, wide beaches, which are well cared for.

The principal centers of tourism are: Calella de la Costa, Arenys de Mar, Castelldeféls, Sitges, Calafell, Torredembarra, Tarragona, Salou, Cambrils, Miami Playa, Hospital del Infante, and Sant Carles de la Rapita.

- **Valencian Region**

The Mediterranean region that extends below Catalonia is known for the magnificent spectacle of its endless orange groves and for the beauty of its beaches. Its Mediterranean traditions merge harmoniously with a deep Hispanic-Arabic heritage, the result of a lengthy Muslim presence.

—**Valencia** is the regional capital. It is known universally for its fiestas, especially "fallas," which take place on St. Joseph's Day in March. On March 19, local residents burn enormous cardboard effigies satirizing real people and events. Valencia has a precious monumental heritage from the Gothic period, outstanding of which are the "Lonja" (Exchange) and Miguelete (the cathedral belltower).

—**Costa de Valencia** is near the capital, and has two large beaches. It also includes other tourist centers like Cullera, Gandía, and Oliva.

—**Costa del Agahar** (Orange-Blossom Coast) extends to the north of the Valencian coast, along Castellón province. Its most important tourist centers are Vinaroz, Benicarló, Peñíscola, Alcocebar, Oropesa, and Benicasim. Especially notable are:

—**Peñíscola,** a market town located on a rocky spur of land that is dominated by a medieval castle. Its streets and homes are well suited to the narrow and broken terrain.

—**Oropesa,** which has preserved its Torre del Rey (King's tower), a sixteenth-century monument.

—**The Carmelite Monastery of Desierto de las Palmas** (Desert of Palms), located away from the coast on the heights at Benicasim.

—**Alicante,** capital of the province of the same name, is the second most important city in the Valencian Region. Situated south of the city of Valencia, it has two large beaches and is dominated by the Arabic castle of Santa Bárbara, from which one can view the entire palm-strewn city.

—**Costa Blanca,** which coincides with the provincial coast of Alicante, is one of the most visited areas of Spain — thanks to its excellent accommodations and magnificent broad beaches of fine sand.

Important tourist centers on Costa Blanca are Denia, Javea Moraira, Calpé, Santa Pola, Guardamar de Segura, Torrevieja, and Campoamor. Notable here is Peñon de Ifach (Ifach Rock) in Calpé, an enormous rocky spur that juts into the sea, one of the most remarkable natural attractions on the Mediterranean coast.

- **Murcia**

The Murcia region, located between Andalusia and the Valencian Region, had powerful Carthaginian and Roman enclaves during antiquity. Then a long Muslim presence marked its history during the Middle Ages. Famous for the early fruits and vegetables it produces, it's an important tourist area.

—**Murcia,** the region's capital, is away from the coast. It's a university city, and has a lovely cathedral.

—**Cartagena** is the most important port in the region. Founded in 221 B.C. by the Carthaginians (who called it Carthago nova), it has remained important to this day. Its museum has excellent Roman and pre-Roman collections that bear witness to the historic role of the city.

—**Costa Calida** (warm coast) extends along the coast of Murcia province. The climate is particularly mild, and there are fine sandy beaches. Mar Menor is a salt-water lagoon that connects with the Mediterranean, and is especially good for water sports. The region's most important tourist centers are Santiago de la Ribera, La Manga del Mar Menor, La Union, Carboneras, Puerto de Mazarrón, Aguilas, and Cartagena itself.

Southern Spain

- **Andalusia**

Noted for its sun, its poets, its traditions, original folklore, and long history, Andalusia is also known for the unique heritage it received from its Arabic ancestors.

—**Seville** is the Andalusian capital and the third largest Spanish city in size. Bathed by the Guadalquivir River, Seville has a unique character; its working-class quarters, such as Santa Cruz, are as interesting as its great monuments. The most shining examples of the latter are the Alcazar (an ancient Moorish fortress), la Giralda (the minaret of a twelfth-century mosque that was incorporated 300 years later as a bell tower in the grandiose Gothic cathedral), and Torre del Oro (golden tower), which was part of the old wall protecting the city.

—**Cordova,** also crossed by the Guadalquivir River, is situated northwest of Seville. For several centuries, it was the capital of the independent Muslim Caliphate founded by Abd-er-Rahman in the eighth century. It has kept some splendid vestiges from that epoch, particularly a glorious mosque, one of the most beautiful monuments imaginable. The city also has, among other historic sites, a beautiful Jewish quarter with a handsome Mudéjar-style synagogue.

—**Granada,** well-situated on a slope of the Sierra Nevada, was the seat of one of the last Muslim realms in Spain. In the fourteenth century, its rulers completed the Alhambra there, a marvelous palace of graceful beauty with large patios surrounded by porticos and graceful pavilions. Splendid gardens such as those of the Generalife can also be found, adorned with lovely fountains and peaceful ponds.

—**Málaga,** located on the coast, is a pleasant city with an extraordinarily clement climate, even in winter. It is dominated by a majestic Alcazaba (Moorish fortress).

—**Costa del Sol** (sunny coast), near Málaga, is one of the most important tourist areas of Spain. Besides famous places like Marbella and Torremolinos, the best-known tourist centers are Calahonda, Torre del Mar, Fuengirola, San Pedro de Alcantara and Estepona, plus the city of Málaga.

The most interesting places here are:

—**Mijas,** one of the most charming Andalusian villages, with sloping streets bordered by sparkling whitewashed houses.

—**Ronda,** in the interior of Málaga province, is a historic city of exceptional beauty located on the edge of a rocky precipice.

—**Almeria,** at the eastern end of Andalusia, has preserved its Arabic heritage with a great deal of purity. Situated opposite a beautiful bay beneath the shadow of the Moorish fortress, Alcazaba, it is the center of the Andalusian beach area.

—**Costa de Almeria** Alongside places exploited by tourism, there are some tranquil and relatively solitary beaches of great beauty. The most important tourist centers are Adra, Aguadulce, Cabo de Gata, Mojácar, and Roquetas de Mar.

—**Costa de la Luz** (light-filled coast) is the Andalusian Atlantic coast in the provinces of Cádiz and Huelva. The most important tourist centers are Barbate, Algeciras, Tarifa, Conil de la Frontera, Chiclana de la Frontera, Cádiz, Puerto de Santa Maria, Rota, Chipiona, Sanlúcar de Barrameda, Torre la Higuera, Mazagón, Punta Umbria, El Rompido, La Antilla, and Isla Cristina.

—**Jerez de la Frontera,** cradle of the universally known wine that bears its name (sherry), is, in addition, the home of a famous school for thoroughbred racehorses.

On the North African coast, opposite the Andalusian coast, are two cities that are free ports. They are part of Spain's national territory.

—**Ceuta,** on the North African side of the Mediterranean, has preserved the remains of its ancient fortress. The city is dominated by Africa Square and by a cathedral.

—**Melilla,** also on the North African side of the Mediterranean, is administered by Málaga. It is essentially a modern city; however it has preserved some interesting historic monuments.

Interior Spain

• **La Rioja**
This small region, located in the northeastern part of the peninsula, is the most important wine-growing center in the country. Rioja wine, which is produced there, is undoubtedly among the world's best wines.

—**Logroño** is capital of the region.

—**Haro,** around which are found most of the wine cellars, is the most important wine-growing center in the region. Its life revolves almost exclusively around wine. On the day of the local fiesta, inhabitants happily pour wine on one another in a "wine battle."

- **Castile/León**

This large area is on a unique tableland with unusual topolographic characteristics. It includes the old kingdom of León and the northern half of the old kingdom of Castile. It joins a majestic, infinitely flat countryside with splendid monuments and a historic heritage.

—**Segovia** has a superb Roman aqueduct, the best existing example of its period and style. In addition, there are other important examples of various historical eras. One is the large Gothic cathedral; another is a splendid Alcazar — a fortress of Arabic origin which has incorporated elements of other periods.

—**Avila,** birthplace of Saint Teresa, preserves its old medieval walls and impressive fortifications from the Romanesque period in exceptional condition. There are also magnificent examples of Romanesque art, such as the San Vicente basilica. The Cistercian Cathedral is embedded in the city walls.

—**Burgos** In addition to the honor of being the birthplace of El Cid, Burgos has one of the most beautiful Gothic cathedrals in Spain. The old quarter has also preserved some lovely churches and palaces from medieval days and the Renaissance.

—**Valladolid,** the current capital of Castile, is the area's largest city. Famous for its beautiful gardens and the solemnity of its Holy Week celebration, Valladolid has two glorious Plateresque buildings — the College of Santa Cruz and the College of San Gregorio. The Museum of Sculpture has an unequaled collection of sixteenth- and seventeenth-century Spanish artists. The Berruguete collection is one of the most important in the nation.

—**León,** capital of the old kingdom of the same name, has three highly important historic buildings. The twelfth-century San Isidoro Church has a crypt decorated with excellent Romanesque frescoes. The Gothic cathedral was constructed with singularly lovely workmanship; its numerous stained-glass windows are compared to those in Chartres. The San Marcos Convent is a Renaissance structure that is currently a deluxe Parador.

—**Salamanca** was famous during the Renaissance because of its university, which was considered one of the best in Europe. It is a pretty city that has preserved some wonderful historic buildings. Among these are a Gothic-style cathedral with Plateresque elements, and an older Romanesque cathedral. The city's Plaza Mayor is surrounded by arcades and Renaissance buildings. Nearby is the university with its magnificently decorated façade.

- **Castile/La Mancha**

This large region extends south of Madrid, and is the southern part of the old kingdom of Castile. It includes the countryside called La Mancha, which is universally known as the setting of Miguel Cervantes' novel, Don Quixote.

—**Toledo,** the regional capital, may have the world's greatest density of historic monuments. Almost all periods of Spanish art are represented. The city has preserved Arabic and Mudéjar structures, Jewish temples such as the Transito Synagogue and Jewish Synagogue, and the Gothic Renaissance Cathedral. In the sixteenth century, Toledo was the home of El Greco. Of his many paintings remaining in the city is his masterpiece, The Burial of Count Orgaz, now in Santo Tomé Church. The museum now housed in the old Santa Cruz Hospital is outstanding among several in the city.

—**Cuenca** is enclosed by a countryside of natural and fantastic beauty, and has a clearly medieval charm. Its "Casas Colgadas" (hanging houses), suspended above a narrow gorge, are quite famous. There is a magnificent Gothic cathedral, and the Museum of Abstract Art is among the best of its kind.

—**Ciudad Real** is the traditional capital of La Mancha. Near the city, one can still look at the lovely spectacle of the windmills that Don Quixote attacked in Campo de Criptana, mistaking them for giants.

- **Estremadura**

Although one of the prettiest, it is perhaps the least known region of the Spanish interior. Most of the conquerors of the American continent were born in its cities, which at various times came under Roman, Moorish, medieval, and aristocratic rule.

—**Cáceres** is the capital of upper Estremadura. Its old city, surrounded by its Almohad-built walls with their superb towers, has remained intact since the Golden Age. Within it are magnificent palace and dwellings from the sixteenth and seventeenth centuries.

—**Trujillo,** Pizarro's birthplace, contains one of the most captivating plazas in Spain, a medieval castle, and aristocratic mansions emblazoned with coats of arms.

—**Badajoz** is the capital of lower Estremadura. It has preserved various monuments from the Muslim era, from which the Alcazaba — with its ramparts and towers — stands out.

—**Mérida,** current capital of the region, was one of the most important cities in Roman Spain. Remaining from that era is one of the most handsome classical theaters ever preserved, an amphitheater, two aqueducts, a bridge, various churches and other buildings. The Museum of Roman Art has collections from the classical period.

• **Madrid**
The life of this region, comprised of one province located in the geographic center of the peninsula, revolves around the city that has been the country's capital since the sixteenth century.

—**Madrid,** founded by the Arabs in the ninth century, is now a modern and lively city with numerous tourist attractions. Its legacy of historical monuments is extensive. The layout of the medieval city has been preserved around Plaza de la Paja. The old quarter, called "Madrid de los Austrias," near Puerta del Sol (traditional center of the city), was built in the Golden Age. In its immediate vicinity is lovely Plaza Mayor, surrounded by arcades, as well as the Plaza de la Villa with its handsome City Hall, a baroque building from the seventeenth century. The Royal Palace, surrounded by gardens that are partially open to the public, is a wonderful example of eighteenth-century art. The city also has many examples of interesting and distinct artistic styles from the nineteenth and twentieth centuries. There are numerous parks and gardens in Madrid. Outstanding among these is Retiro Park, a botanical garden founded by royal order in the seventeenth century, and Casa de Campo Park. Of the vast number of museums and galleries, the Prado emerges as one of the best in the world. Its annex, Casón del Buen Retiro, houses Picasso's Guernica. The Archeologic Museum is also of interest.

—**San Lorenzo del Escorial,** in Sierra Guadarrama, was built as a monastery/palace by Philip II. Work of Juan de Herrera, Spanish Renaissance architect, it was the largest Spanish artistic undertaking of the time.

—**Alcalá de Henares,** birthplace of Cervantes, was an important university city in the sixteenth and seventeenth centuries. The most interesting historic site in its old quarter is the university.

—**Aranjuez** was created to hold the royal country home, which is surrounded by a superb park on the banks of the Tagus River.

• **Navarre**
Medieval kingdom on the French frontier, Navarre has preserved much evidence of the important role its strategic location enabled it to play in the past. It contains many picturesque mountainous areas in the Pyrenees.

—**Pamplona** is the capital of Navarre. Universally famous for its "encierros," the running of the bulls that takes place every year during the Feast of San Fermin, it is a peaceful and pleasant city.

• **Aragon**
This ancient kingdom that came to dominate the Mediterranean is now a lovely area of contrasting and impressive landscapes. It has kept its rich folklore.

—**Saragossa** is the Aragonese capital. Bathed by the waters of the Ebro River, it is one of the chief Spanish cities. Important in the Roman and Muslim periods, its museum houses some important collections. The medieval cathedral stands out among its monuments.

—**Huesca** is located in the foothills of the Pyrenees, in a site of majestic beauty.

—**Teruel,** which was under Arab domination for a long time, offers magnificent examples of the Mudéjar school of art. Three of them are the bell towers of the churches of San Martin, San Pedro, and San Salvador.

Island Spain

• Balearic Islands

The Balearic archipelago is located in the Mediterranean opposite the east coast of Spain, some 150 miles east of Valencia. Famous for their natural beauty, beaches, and excellent climate, the islands are one of the strongest tourist attractions in Spain. There are five islands: Majorca, Minorca, Iviza, Formentera, and Cabrera. Thanks to their climate, their beaches, and their tourist accommodations of every type, they are undoubtedly one of the most prestigious and attractive vacation areas in the Mediterranean.

—**Palma de Majorca** is the capital of the island chain. Its port is one of the principal ports in the Mediterranean. The city has many valuable monuments, including the Bellver Castle, dating from the fourteenth century and known for its square layout. The Gothic cathedral, the former Exchange, the archbishop's palace, the San Francisco Monastery, plus some striking mansions built by families made wealthy through commerce, are others.

—**Mahón** is Minorca's capital. Among the city's charms are its Town Hall, Santa María and San Francisco churches, and its beautiful port.

—**Ciudadela** was the former capital of Minorca. It's a small, fascinating city with palatial homes and medieval churches.

—**Iviza** (Ibiza) is the capital of the island of the same name. Famous for its working-class quarters whose style spawned the term, "Iviza architecture," the city is dominated by a medieval fortress. The Punic cemetary of the ancient city of Puig des Molins is nearby.

• The Canary Islands

The Canary Island chain is located in the North Atlantic Ocean, opposite the western coast of Africa. They are a natural paradise of volcanic origin, characterized by imposing geologic formations and luxuriant vegetation. Outstanding among the latter are indigenous species and some unusual examples of flora from the Tertiary geologic era. The climate, which is warm and dry even in winter, and the magnificent beaches have made these islands a true tourist haven. There are seven islands, which are divided administratively into two provinces. Teneriffe includes the islands of Teneriffe, Palma, Gomera, and Hierro. Grand Canary includes Fuerteventura, Lanzarote, and Grand Canary.

—**Santa Cruz de Teneriffe** is the capital of the island and province of Teneriffe. Rich in museums and intriguing buildings, it competes with such attractions outside the city as Mt. Teide, the highest point in Spain. Two other cities on the island are Puerto de la Cruz, the main tourist center, and La Orotava in a lovely valley of the same name, whose typical houses are the model for a style quite popular in Spanish America.

—**Las Palmas de Grand Canary** The old city has preserved its lovely Gothic cathedral and other historic buildings. A riot of flowers and diversely colored plants form a permanent display. Grand Canary Island is also known for its magnificent wide beaches, Inglés, and Maspalomas.

—**Arrecife** is the capital of Lanzarote, an island of many natural beauties whose volcanic remains have sculpted grandiose lunar landscapes. Timanfaya National Park is a prominent example of this.

A

¿a dónde?—where?
a la derecha—on the right
a la izquierda—on the left
a lo mejor—perhaps
a menudo—often
a nombre de—in the name of
a pie—on foot
¿a qué hora?—at what time?
a tope—end to end
a veces—sometimes
a ver—let's see
a vuelta de correo—by return mail
abajo—below
abogado (M)—lawyer
abrazo (M)—embrace
abrigo (M)—overcoat
abril (M)—April
abrir—to open
abrochar—to fasten, to button
abuelo (M)/abuela (F)—grandfather, grandmother
aburrirse—to become bored
acabar—to end
acabar con—to finish, to end in
acabar de—to have just
aceite (M)—oil
aceituna (F)—olive
acera (F)—sidewalk
acercar(se) a—to approach
acomodadora (F)—usherette
acompañar—to accompany
aconsejar—to advise
acordarse—to remember
acostarse—to go to bed
actor (M)/actriz (F)—actor/actress
actual—now, present
actuar—to play (a role)
acuerdo (M)—agreement
adelantar—to go ahead, to pass
además—besides

adiós—goodbye
adivinar—to guess
aeropuerto (M)—airport
afeitarse—to shave oneself
agencia (F)—agency
agencia de cambio (F)—exchange office
agente de tráfico (M)—traffic policeman
agosto (M)—August
agotado(a)—used up, sold out
agradable—pleasant
agua (F)—water
aguja (F)—needle
ahí—there
ahogarse—to drown
ahora—how
ahora mismo—right now
ahorrar—to save
ahorro (M)—savings
aire (M)—air
ajedrez (M)—chess
ajo (M)—garlic
al—to the
al lado de—beside, on the side of
al menos—at least
alcanzar—to reach
alarmarse—to become upset
alegre—happy, gay
alejarse—to move away, to distance oneself
alfombra (F)—rug
algo—something
algodón (M)—cotton
algún/o(a/os/as)—some, a few
alguna cosa—something
algunas veces—sometimes
alimentos (MPl)—foodstuff
almendra (F)—almond
almuerzo (M)—lunch
alojamiento (M)—lodging

alquilar—to rent
altavoz (M)—loudspeaker
alto(a)—tall
allí—there
amable—amiable, nice
amarillo(a)—yellow
amigo (M)/amiga (F)—friend
amplio(a)—ample, full
¡anda!—go ahead!
andaluz(a)—Andalusian
animado(a)—animated
antes—before
antes de—in front of
antiguo(a)—old
antiniebla (F)—foglight
antivaho (M)—defroster
anuncio (M)—announcement, advertisement
apagar (las luces)—to turn
aparcar—to park
aparecer—to appear
apartamento (M)—apartment
apellido (M)—last name
apenas—hardly
apetecer—to find appetizing
apreciado(a)—expensive
aprovechar—to benefit from
apuesta (F)—bet, wager
aquel(aquella)—that . . . there
aquí—here
aquí tiene(s)—here is
árbitro (M)—umpire
árbol (M)—tree
arena (F)—sand
armario (M)—closet
arquitecto (M)—architect
arrancar—to pull, to snatch
arreglado(a)—arranged, fixed
arreglar—to arrange, to fix
arreglarse—to get oneself ready
arreglárselas—to clear things up
arriba—above

arroz (M)—rice
artículo (M)—article
artista (M or F)—artist
ascensor (M)—elevator
aseo (M)—cleanliness
así—in this way
así no—not like that
asiento (M)—seat
asiento trasero (M)—backseat
asistir—to attend to
asomarse—to appear
asunto (M)—subject
atender—to take care of
atento(a)—attentive
atrás—behind
atrasar—to be late
atravesar—to cross
atropellar—to run down
aunque—although
autobús (M)—bus
automático(a)—automatic
autopista (F)—expressway, freeway
avanzado(a)—advanced
avanzar—to advance, to propose
avenida (F)—avenue
avería (F)—breakdown, failure
avión (M)—plane
avisar—to warn
ayer—yesterday
azafata (F)—flight attendant
azúcar (M)—sugar
azul—blue
azulejo (M)—tile

bailar—to dance
baile—dance
baile regional (M)—regional dance
bajar—to go down, to get off
bajo(a)—below
banco (M)—bank
bañador (M)—bathing suit
bañarse—to bathe
baño (M)—bath
barato(a)—cheap
barbilla (F)—chin
barco (M)—boat
barra (F)—bar, beam
barrer—to sweep
barrio (M)—district
bastante—enough
bata (F)—bathrobe
batería (F)—battery
batuta (F)—baton, bread, rod
beber—to drink
bebida (F)—drink

bellas artes (FPl)—fine arts
bello(a)—good-looking
beso (M)—kiss
besos—kisses
besote (M)—kiss/large
bien—well
bigote (M)—mustache
billete (M)—ticket
blanco(a)—white
blusa (F)—blouse
boca (F)—mouth
boca de metro (F)—subway entrance
bocina (F)—horn
bolsa (F)—bag, purse
bolsa de aseo (F)—toilet kit
bolso (M)—handbag
bonito(a)—pretty
bota (F)—boot
botella (F)—bottle
botón (M)—button
boxeo (M)—boxing
bragas (FPl)—woman's undergarment
brazo (M)—arm
brisa (F)—breeze
broma (F)—joke
bromista—joker
bruma (F)—haze, mist
brumoso(a)—hazy
buenas—hello (eve or afternoon)
buenas noches—good evening, night
buenas tardes—good afternoon, good evening
buenaventura (F)—fortune
buenísimo(a)—very good
bueno—good
bueno(a)—good
buenos días—good morning
bufanda (F)—scarf
bufete (M)—office
bujía (F)—candle
buscar—to look for
butaca (F)—orchestra seat
buzón de correos (M)—mailbox

C

caballero (M)—man, gentleman
caballo (M)—horse
cabellos (MPl)—hair
cabeza (F)—head
cada vez—each time
cada vez más (menos)—less/each time
cadena (F)—chain, set of audio components
café (M)—café, coffee

café con leche (M)—half coffee, half milk
caja (F)—cashier
caja de ahorros (F)—savings box
caja de cambios (F)—gearbox
cajero automatico (M)—ticket dispenser
calamar (M)—squid
calcetín (M)—stocking
calderilla (F)—small change
caldo (M)—broth, sauce
calefacción (F)—heat(er)
calmar—to calm down
calor (M)—heat, warmth
calzada (F)—causeway
calzoncillo (M)—men's undershorts
callarse—to become silent
calle (F)—street
cama (F)—bed
cámara (F)—camera
cámara de aire (F)—inner tube
camarero (M)—waiter
cambiar—to change
cambiar de marcha—to change speed
cambio (M)—change
caminar—to walk
camino (M)—road
camisa (F)—shirt
camisón (M)—nightshirt
campo (M)—country, field
campo de fútbol (M)—soccer field
canción (F)—song
cansado(a)—tired
cantante (M or F)—singer
capital (F)—capitol
cara (F)—face
cara de pocos amigos (F)—frowning face
caramelo (M)—caramel (candy)
carburador (M)—carburetor
cariño—dear, honey
carne (F)—meat
carné de conducir (M)—driver's license
carné de identidad (M)—identification
caro(a)—dear, expensive
carrera (de caballos) (F)—racetrack
carretera (F)—road, route
carta (F)—letter
cartas (FPl)—cards (game)
cartel (M)—poster, sign
casa (F)—house
casado(a)—married
casarse—to marry
casi—almost

castaño(a) —chestnut
Cataluña (F) —Catalonia
catarro (M) —cold
catedral (F) —cathedral
cautivo (M) —captive, prisoner
caza (F) —hunt
cazadora (F) —jacket
cebolla (F) —onion
cena (F) —dinner, supper
cenar —to have supper
cenicero (M) —ashtray
centro (M) —center, downtown
cerámica (F) —ceramic
cerca (de) —near
cerdo (M) —pig
cereza (F) —cherry
cerrajería (F) —locksmith store
cerrar —to close
certeza (F) —certainty
certificado de matrícula (M) —registration
certificado(a) —certified
cerveza (F) —beer
césped (M) —lawn
cielo (M) —sky
cigarrillo (M) —cigarette
cine (M) —movies
cinturón (M) —belt
cinturón de seguridad (M) —seatbelt
circulación (F) —traffic
circular —to circulate, to roll
ciruela (F) —plum
ciudad (F) —city
claro (M) —clearing
¡claro! —of course!
claro(a) —clear, light
claxon (M) —horn
cliente (M) —client
cocina (F) —kitchen
coche (M) —car
codo (M) —elbow
coger (el autobús) —to take (the bus)
col (F) —cabbage
cola (F) —line (of people)
colaborador (M) —collaborator
coleccionar —to collect
colegio (M) —high school
colgar —to hang
coliflor (F) —cauliflower
colocar —to place, to put
color (M) —color
combinado(a) —combined
combinar —to combine
comedor (M) —dining room
comenzar —to begin
comer —to eat
comerciante (M or F) —merchant
comida (F) —dinner, meal

¿cómo? —how? what did you say?
¿cómo estás? —how are you?
completo(a) —complete, full (e.g. hotel, theater)
complicado(a) —complicated
compra (F) —purchase
comprar —to buy
comprender —to understand
comunicar —to communicate, to make known
con —with
con cheque —by check
con frecuencia —often
concierto (M) —concert
concretar —to make concrete
concurrido(a) —frequented
conducir —to drive, to conduct
conejo (M) —rabbit
conferencia (F) —telephone call
confusión (F) —confusion
congelado(a) —frozen
conjunto (M) —ensemble, (performing) group
conmigo —with me
conocer —to know, to meet
conocido(a) —famous, well-known
conserje (M) —concierge
constipado (M) — (head) cold
construir —to construct
contable (M) —accountant
contar —to tell, to relate
contento(a) —content, happy
conversación (F) —conversation
convertir(se) —to change (into)
copa (F) —(wine) glass
copiar —to copy
corazón (M) —heart
corbata (F) —tie
cordelería (F) —cordmaking, rigging
cordelero (M) —cordmaker, dealer
cordero (M) —lamb
cordial —cordial
correos (MPl) —post office
correr —to run
corrida (F) —bullring
cortada (F) —cut, installment
cortado (M) —coffee with a little milk
cortar —to cut
corto(a) —short, brief
cosa (F) —thing
costa (F) —coast, side
costumbre (F) —custom
costumbres (FPl) —customs
crédito (M) —credit

creer —to believe
cristiano (M) —Christian
cromo (M) —picture
cruce (M) —crossing, crossroads
crucigrama (M) —crossword (puzzle)
cruzar —to cross
cuaderno (M) —notebook
cuadro (M) —painting, picture
¿cuál? —what, which one?
cuando —when
¿cuánto(a)? —how many? how much?
¿cuánto tiempo? —how long?
¿cuánto vale? —how much is it (worth)?
cuarto(a) —fourth, room
cuarto de baño (M) —bathroom
cubierto(a) —cover(ed)
cuchara (F) —spoon
cuchillo (M) —knife
cuello (M) —neck
cuenta (F) —account, bill
cuento (de hadas) (M) —fairy tale
cuero (M) —leather
cuerpo (M) —body
cuestión (F) —question, matter
¡cuidado (con)! —be careful (with)
cuneta (F) —ditch, drain
curarse —to cure

chalé (M) —villa, chalet
chaleco (M) —vest
chandal (M) —track suit
chaparrón (M) —downpour
chaqueta (F) —jacket
charlar —to chat
cheque al portador (M) —bearer, endorsee (of check)
cheque cruzado (M) —check/canceled
chicle (M) —chewing gum
chico (M) —young child
chimenea (F) —chimney
chocar —to collide, to shock
chotis (M) —typical dance
chubasco (M) —downpour
chuleta (F) —cutlet, chop

dar —to give
dar la nota remarquer —to be noticed

dar marcha atrás—to walk back
dar un paseo—to take a walk
dar un plantón—to keep someone waiting
dar una vuelta—to take a walk
dar vueltas a—to keep going over the same thing
datos (MPl)—data, information
de acuerdo—agreed
de nuevo—again
de parte de—on behalf of . . .
de una vez—at one time
de vacaciones—on vacation
de viaje—traveling
décimo(a)—tenth
decir—to say, to tell
dedo (M)—finger
dedo del pie (M)—toe
dejar—to let
dejar(se) de—to cease
del—of the
delante (de)—in front (of)
deletrear—to spell
demás—the others, rest
demasiado—too much
demasiado(a)—too
dentista (M)—dentist
dentro—inside, within
dentro de—inside of
deporte (M)—sport
depósito de gasolina (M)—gasoline tank
derecho(a)—right
desabrochar—unfasten
desayuno (M)—breakfast
descansar—to rest
descanso (M)—rest
descolgar—to take off the hook
descuidado(a)—negligent
desde—from, since
desde que—since
desear—to desire
despacho (M)—office
despedirse—to say goodbye
despejado(a)—clear
despertador (M)—alarm clock
despertar(se)—to wake up
despistado(a)—scatterbrained
después—after, later
detener—to slop
detrás (de)—behind
devolver—to become, change
día (M)—day
diario (M)—newspaper
diarrea (F)—diarrhea
dibujo (M)—design, picture
dibujos animados (MPl)—cartoons
diciembre (M)—December
diente (F)—(front) tooth

difícil—difficult
¿diga(me)?—what are you saying?
dinero (M)—money
Dios (M)—God
dirección (F)—address
dirección prohibida (F)—no entrance
dirección única (F)—one way
director (M)—director
director de orquesta (M)—conductor
dirigirse—to direct oneself, to address
disco (M)—record
discoteca (F)—discotheque
disculpar(se)—to excuse (oneself)
disculpe—excuse me
discutir—to argue, discuss
dislocar—to dislocate, displace
distancia (F)—distance
distraerse—to be distracted
distraído(a)—distracted
divertido(a)—amusing
divertirse—to have a good time
divorciado(a)—divorced
documental (M)—documentary
documentos (MPl)—official papers
doler—to ache
dolor (M)—pain
dolor de cabeza (M)—headache
domingo (M)—Sunday
¿dónde?—where?
dormir—to sleep
dormitorio (M)—bedroom
ducharse—to take a shower
dudar—to doubt
durante—while

---- **E** ----

edad (F)—age
Edad Media (F)—Middle Ages
ejecutivo (M)—executive
ejercicio (M)—exercise
el de—that (one) of
el mes próximo—next month
el que—he who
el viernes próximo—next Friday
elegante—elegant
elegir—to choose
embarque (M)—shipment
emborracharse—to get drunk
embrague (M)—connecting gear
embutido (M)—sausage
emisora (F)—broadcasting station

emitir—to broadcast
empate (M)—tie (game)
empeorarse—to worsen
empezar—to begin
empleado (M)—employee
empleado de gasolinera (M)—gas station worker
empresa (F)—undertaking
empresario (M)—empresario
en—at, in
en efectivo—in cash
en el medio—in the midst
en espera de—waiting for
en frente (de)—opposite
en la carretera—en route
en que—where
en seguida—immediately
en tu lugar—at your place
en voz alta (baja)—in a loud (low) voice
enamorarse—to fall in love
encandilado(a)—fascinated
encantado(a)—pleased
encantar—to charm
encargar—to entrust
encendido (M)—lighted
encima—on top, over
encima de—on, above
encontrar—to find
encuentro (M)—meeting
enero (M)—January
enfadado(a)—angry
enfermedad (F)—illness
enfermo(a)—ill
enfocar—to come to the point, focus
engordar—to get fat, to fatten
ensalada (F)—salad
ensayar—to rehearse
enseñar—to show, to teach
entonces—then
entrada (F)—(entrance) ticket
entrar—to enter
entregar—to hand over
entusiasmado(a)—enthusiastic
entusiasmar—to be enthusiastic
enviar—to send
equipaje (M)—luggage
equipo (M)—set of stereo components
equivocar(se)—to be mistaken
érase que se era una vez—there was a time; once upon a time
escaparse—to escape
escena (F)—scene
escribir—to write
escritor (M)—writer
escuchar—to listen (to)
escuela (F)—school
escultor (M)—sculptor

ese (esa)—that
esfuerzo (M)—effort, force
esguince (M)—sprain
espalda (F)—back, shoulder
España (F)—Spain
español(a)—Spanish, Spaniard
espectáculo (M)—show
espejo (M)—mirror
espera (F)—waiting, stay
esperar—to hope, wait (for)
esquí (M)—ski
esquina (F)—(street) corner
esta noche—tonight
esta tarde—this afternoon, evening
establecerse—to establish
estación (F)—station
estacionar—to park
estadio (M)—stadium, racecourse
estado (M)—state
estancia (F)—stay
estanco (M)—tobacco stand
estar—to be
estar mareado(a)—to be dizzy
estar pendiente de—to be dependent on
estátua (F)—statue
este (M)—east
este (esta)—this
estimado(a)—dear
estómago (M)—stomach
estreñimiento (M)—constipation
estudiante (M or F)—student
estudiar—to study
estupendo(a)—wonderful
excursión (F)—excursion
éxito (M)—success
experiencia (F)—experience
explicar—to explain
exterior—exterior
extranjero(a)—foreigner

 F

fábrica (F)—factory
falda (F)—skirt
faltar—to lack
familia (F)—family
famoso(a)—famous
fantástico(a)—extraordinary
farmacia (F)—pharmacy
faro (M)—headlight
fatal—deadly
febrero (M)—February
fecha (tope) (F)—deadline
feliz—happy
fenomenal—extraordinary
feo(a)—ugly
feria (F)—fair

ficha (F)—chip
fiebre (F)—fever
fiesta (F)—party
filete (M)—steak
filmación (F)—filming
filmar—to film
fin (M)—end
final (M)—end
firma (F)—signature
firmar—to sign
folleto (M)—brochure, pamphlet
foto(grafía) (F)—photograph
fotógrafo (M)—photographer
Francia (F)—France
francés(esa)—French (man, woman)
frecuencia (F)—frequency
frenar—to brake
freno (de mano) (M)—handbrake
frente (F)—forehead
fresco(a)—fresh
frío(a)—cold, cool
frito(a)—fried
fruta (F)—fruit
fuera—outside
fuera de—outside of
fuerte—strong
fumar—to smoke
furgoneta (F)—cart, wagon
fútbol (M)—soccer
futuro (M)—future

 G

gabardina (F)—raincoat
gafas (FPl)—eyeglasses
galleta (F)—biscuit
gana (F)—desire
ganar—to earn
garbanzos (MPl)—chickpeas
garganta (F)—throat
gas (M)—gas, vapor
gaseosa (F)—soda
gasolina (F)—gasoline
gasolinera (F)—gas station
gastar—to spend
gasto (M)—expense
gato (M)—cat
gente (F)—people
gimnasio (M)—gymnasium
girar—to film, to turn
gitano (M)/gitana (F)—gypsy
gordo(a)—fat, heavy
gótico(a)—Gothic
grabar—to record
gracias—thank you
grado (M)—degree
grande/gran—large, great
gris—gray

gritar—to shout
guante (M)—glove
guapo(a)—good looking
guardia (M)—police officer
guisantes (MPl)—peas
guerra (F)—war
gustar—to please
gusto (M)—pleasure, taste

H

habitación (F)—room
hablar—to speak
hace (unos) días—a few (some) days ago
hacer—to do, to make
hacer de—to act as
hacer la cola—to line up
hacia—toward
hada (F)—fairy
¡hala!—get going!
hambre (F)—hunger
harto(a)—full, fed up
hasta—until
hasta el viernes—until Friday
hasta la noche—until tonight
hasta la tarde—until this afternoon, evening
hasta la vista—see you soon
hasta luego—until then
hasta mañana—until tomorrow
hasta pronto—see you soon
hay—there is, are
hay que—one must
heladería (F)—ice cream parlor
helado (M)—ice cream
helar—to freeze
herida (F)—wound
hermano (M)—brother
hermana (F)—sister
hermoso(a)—good looking
hielo (M)—ice
hígado (M)—liver
hija (F)—daughter
hijo (M)—son
hijos (MPl)—children
hilo (M)—thread
histérico(a)—hysterical
historia (F)—history, story
histórico(a)—historical
hola—hi, hello
hombre (M)—man
hombro (M)—shoulder
hora (F)—hour
horchata (F)—popular Spanish drink
horror (M)—horror
hospedarse—to give lodging
hospital (M)—hospital

hotel (M)—hotel
hoy—today
hueso (M)—bone
húmedo(a)—humid
humor (M)—humor, disposition

ida (F)—going
idea (F)—idea
ideal—ideal
identidad (F)—identity
iglesia (F)—church
iluminado(a)—lighted
imperial—imperial
importante—important
importar—to be important
incertidumbre (F)—uncertainty
indio (M)—Indian
infernal—infernal
infierno (M)—Hell
información (F)—information
ingeniero (M)—engineer
insoportable—unbearable
intentar—to try, to rehearse
interés (M)—interest
interesante—interesting
interesar—to interest
interior—interior
intermitente (M)—blinking
   (sign)
invierno (M)—winter
inyección (F)—injection
ir—to go
ir a dormir—to go to sleep
ir bien (mal)—to go well (badly)
ir de compras—to go shopping
ir de copas—to "hit" watering
   holes (bars)
irse—to go away
isla (F)—island
izquierdo(a)—left

jamón (M)—ham
jarabe (M)—syrup
jardín (M)—garden
jersey (M)—pullover
joven—young
judías verdes
   (FPl)—stringbeans
jueves (M)—Thursday
jugar—to play (a game)

julio (M)—July
junio (M)—June
junto a—next to, beside
juntos(as)—together
jurista (M)—juror

la mar de—great deal of
la mar de bien—very well
la semana próxima—next week
la semana que viene—next
   week
labio (M)—lip
laboratorio (M)—laboratory
labo (M)—side
lámpara (F)—lamp
lana (F)—wool
largo(a)—long
leche (F)—milk
lechuga (F)—lettuce
leer—to read
lejos—far
legumbres (FPl)—vegetables
legua (F)—tongue
lentejas (FPl)—lentils
lento(a)—slow
levantarse—to get up
libre—free
libro(M)—book
ligero(a)—light
liques (MPl)—chance flirtatious
   meetings
limón (M)—lemon
limpiaparabrisas
   (M)—windshield wipers
línea (F)—line
lista (de pasajeros) (F)—list
   (of passengers)
listo(a)—ready, intelligent
literatura (F)—literature
litoral (M)—coastal
lo mismo—the same (thing)
localidad (F)—seat (in a
   theater)
loco(a)—crazy
los demás—the others, the rest
luego—then, following
lugar (M)—place, site
lunes (M)—Monday
luneta trasera (F)—rear mirror
luz (F)—light
luz de cruce (F)—headlights
luz larga (F)—headlights

LL

llamada (F)—(telephone) call
llamar—to call
llamarse—to be called, to be
   named
llave (F)—key
llegar—to arrive
llenar el depósito—to fill up
   (with gas)
llevar—to carry, to lead
llevar consigo—to bring with
   oneself
llevarse—to take (in)
llover—to rain
lluvia (F)—rain
lluvioso(a)—rainy

M

maceta (F)—flower pot
madre (F)—mother
madrugada (F)—early morning
magnífico(a)—wonderful
mal—bad(ly)
maleta (F)—suitcase
maletero (M)—trunk
malgastar—to misspend
malísimo(a)—very bad
malo(a)—bad
mamá (F)—mom(my)
mami (F)—mommy
mano (F)—hand
mantener—to maintain
mantequilla (F)—butter
manzana (F)—apple
mañana—tomorrow
mañana (F)—morning
mañana por la
   mañana—tomorrow morning
mañana por la
   tarde—tomorrow afternoon
   (evening)
mar (M or F)—sea
maravilloso(a)—marvelous
marca (F)—mark
marcador (M)—bulletin board
marcharse—to leave
marea alta (baja) (F)—high
   (low) tide
mareado(a)—dizzy
marejada (F)— surge,
   visible sea undercurrent
marejadilla (F)—calm sea
marrón—maroon
martes (M)—Tuesday

marzo (M)—March
más—more
más bien—rather
más o menos—more or less
masticar—to chew
matrícula (F)—registration I.D.
mayo (M)—May
mayor—older
mayorcito(a)—(young) adult
mayores (MPl)—old people
medias (FPl)—stockings
medicina (F)—medicine
médico (M)—doctor
medieval—medieval
medio(a)—half
mediodía (M)—noon
mediterráneo(a)—Mediterranean
mejilla (F)—cheek
mejillón (M)—mussel
mejor—better
mejorarse—to get better
melocotón (M)—peach
menor—smaller, younger
menos—less
menos mal—fortunately
mentira (F)—lie
merecer—to merit
merienda (F)—light meal
merluza (F)—lake
mes (M)—month
mesa (F)—table, (large) desk
meteorológico(a)—meteorologic
meterse—to "butt" in, to become
meterse con—to "pick" a
   quarrel, fight
método (M)—method
metro (M)—metro, subway
mi (mis)—my
miércoles (M)—Wednesday
mineral—mineral
minuto (M)—minute
mirar—to look (at)
mismo(a)—same
mixto(a)—mixed
modelo (M or F)—model
moderno(a)—modern
molestar(se)—to (be) annoy(ed)
momento (M)—moment, instant
moneda (F)—money
monte (M)—mountain
moreno(a)—brunette,
   olive-complected
moror (M)—Moor
mostrar—to show
motor (M)—motor
mover—to move

moverse—to (be) move(d)
mozo (M)—waiter, bellhop
muchas gracias—thank you
   very much
muchísimo—very much
mucho—much
mucho(a)—a lot of
mucho gusto—very pleased
mueble (M)—furniture
muela (F)—tooth
mujer (F)—woman
multa (F)—fine, penalty
mundo (M)—world
muñeca (F)—doll, wrist
músculo (M)—muscle
museo (M)—museum
música (F)—music
muslo (M)—thigh
muy—very

nacer—to be born
nada—nothing
nadar—to swing
nalga (F)—buttock
naranja (F)—orange
naranja—orange (adj.)
nariz (F)—nose
negocio (M)—affair (business)
negro(a)—black
nervio (M)—nerve
nervioso(a)—nervous
neumático (M)—tire
nevar—to snow
ni—neither
ni hablar—no question
niebla (F)—fog, mist
ningún/o(a)—no (not one)
niño (M)—child
no—no, not
no se retire—don't go
no todavía—not even
noche (F)—night
nombre (M)—name, first name
norte (M)—north
nosotros—we
noticias (FPl)—news
novela (F)—novel
novela corta (F)—short novel
noveno(a)—ninth
noviembre (M)—November
nube (F)—cloud
nublado(a)—cloudy
nuca (F)—nape

nuestro(a)—our
nuevamente—newly
nuevo(a)—new
nuez (F)—nut
número (M)—number

o—or
obra (teatral) (F)—(theatrical)
   work
obra maestra (F)—masterpiece
octavo(a)—eighth
octubre (M)—October
ocurrir—to happen
oeste (M)—west
oficina (F)—office
oficio (M)—craft, job
oído (M)—(inner) ear
¡oiga!—listen!
oír—to hear
¡ojalá!—Heaven grant that . . . !
ojo (M)—eye
ola (F)—wave
olvidar(se)—to forget
ordenar—to command, to order
oreja (F)—(outer ear)
orilla (F)—shore
orquesta (F)—orchestra
oscuro(a)—dark
otoño (M)—Autumn
otra vez—again
otro(a)—(an)other
¡oye!—listen!
oyente (M)—listener

padre (M)—father
padres (MPl)—parents
pagar—to pay
palabra (F)—word
palanca de cambio
   (F)—gearshift
palco (M)—boxseats (theater)
pálido(a)—pale
palmera (F)—palm tree
pantalón (M)—pants
pantalla (F)—screen (movies)
pañuelo (M)—handkerchief
papel (M)—role, paper
paquete (M)—package
para—for
para mí—for me

para postre—for dessert
parabrisas (M)—windshield
parachoques (M)—shock absorbers
parada (F)—stop
paraguas (M)—umbrella
parecer—to seem
pareja—pair
parque (M)—park
pared (F)—wall
parte (F)—part
partido (M)—match, game
pasado mañana—day after tomorrow
pasajero (M)—passenger
pasaporte (M)—passport
pasar—to happen
pasarlo bien (mal)—to have a good (bad) time
pasear—to take a walk
paseo (M)—promenade, walk
paso a nivel (M)—level crossing
pastilla (F)—pill
patata (F)—potato
patatas fritas (FPl)—French fries
pato (M)—duck
pavo (M)—turkey
pecho (M)—breast, chest
pedal (M)—pedal
peinar(se)—to comb one's hair
pelado(a)—hairless, penniless
película (F)—film
película del oeste (F)—western
peligro (M)—danger
pelo (M)—hair
pelota (F)—ball
pena (F)—ache, trouble
pendiente de—dependent on
pensar—to think
pensar en—to think about
pensativo(a)—pensive
peor—worse
pepino (M)—cucumber
pequeñito(a)—very small
pequeño(a)—small
pera (F)—pear
perdone—pardon me
perfectamente—perfectly
perfecto(a)—perfect
periódico (M)—newspaper
periodista (M or F)—journalist, newspaper person
pero—but
perro (M)—dog
pesca (F)—(live) fish

pescado (M)—fish
peseta (F)—peseta, Spain's official monetary unit
picar—to nibble on (snacks)
pico (M)—beak
pie (M)—foot
piel (F)—skill
pierna (F)—leg
píldora (F)—pill
piloto (M)—pilot
piña (F)—pineapple
pinchar una rueda—to have a flat (tire)
pintar—to paint
pintor (M)—painter
pintura (F)—painting
piscina (F)—pool
piso (M)—(house) floor
piso resbaladizo (M)—slippery thoroughfare
pito (M)—whistle
plan (M)—plan, project
planificar—to plan
plano (M)—plan
planta (F)—floor
planta baja (F)—ground/floor
plátano (M)—(green) banana
plato (M)—plate, dish
plato combinado (M)—combination plate
playa (F)—beach
playeras (FPl)—tennis
plaza (F)—plaza
pobre—poor
poco—little
poco a poco—little by little
poco (a)—little + noun
poder—to be able
poema (M)—poem
policía (F)—police
policía (M)—police officer
pollo (M)—chicken
pomelo (M)—grapefruit
poner—to place, to put
poner malo—to make ill
poner nervioso(a)—to make nervous
poner triste—to sadden
ponerse enfermo(a)—to become ill
por—by, for
por aquí—over here
por cierto—à propos, about, on the subject of
por eso—therefore
por favor—please

por hora—by the hour
por qué?—why?
por supuesto—of course
portería (F)—porter's lodge
portero (M)—concierge, porter
porvenir (M)—future
posible—possible
postal—postal
postal (F)—postcard
postre (M)—dessert
precaución obras—caution; work in progress
precioso(a)—delightful
preferencia de paso (F)—right of way
preferir—to prefer
preguntar—to ask (a question)
prendas de vestir (FPl)—garments
prensa (F)—news media
preocupado(a)—worried
preocuparse—to be worried
preparado(a)—prepared
primavera (F)—spring
primer/o(a)—first
primero—at first
primo (M)/prima (F)—cousin
probable—probable
probador (M)—fitting room
probar—to taste, to try
profesor (M)—professor, teacher
programa (M)—program
prohibir—to prohibit
pronto—quick, soon
proponer—to propose
propuesta (F)—proposition
próximo(a)—next
proyecto (M)—project
publicidad (F)—publicity
público (M)—public
pueblo (M)—village, town
puente (M)—bridge
puerro (M)—leek, scallion
puerta (F)—door
puerta (de coche) (F)—(car) door
puerto (M)—port
pues—well then
pulgar (M)—flea
pulsera (F)—bracelet
puntual—on time

que—what, who, that
¿qué?—what (who) is it?

¡qué!—what a . . .!
¡qué bien!—that's terrific!
¡qué cara (más) dura!—what nerve!
¡qué confusión!—what a mess!
¿qué hora es?—what time is it?
¡qué horror!—how awful!
¡qué interesante!—how interesting!
¡qué le vamos a hacer!—What are we going to do with him, her!
¿qué más?—what else?
¿qué pasa?—what's happening?
¡qué pena!—what a pity!
¡qué suerte!—what luck!
¿qué tal?—how goes it?
¿qué te pasa?—what's the matter?
¡qué va!—no problem! Let's go on
quedar—to remain
quedar bien (mal)—to acquit oneself well (badly)
quedarse—to remain
quemadura (F)—burning
querer—to want
querido(a)—dear
queso (M)—cheese
¿quién?—who?
quinto(a)—fifth
quitar(se)—to remove something
quitar el contacto—to cut off contact
quizás—perhaps

R

rábano (M)—radish
ración (F)—portion
radiador (M)—radiator
radio (F)—radio
rambla (F)—avenue, boulevard
rápidamente—quickly
rápido(a)—rapid
rapto (M)—kidnapping, rape
raro(a)—strange
ratón (M)—mouse
rayo (M)—lightening, thunder
rebajas (FPl)—sales
receta (F)—prescription, recipe
recibir—to receive
recorrer—to travel around
recto—straight ahead
red (F)—net

referirse—to refer to
refrescar—to refresh oneself
refresco (M)—cool drink
regalo (M)—gift
regar—to irrigate, water
regional—regional
reír—to laugh
relámpago (M)—lightning
reloj (M)—clock, watch
reloj de pared (M)—wall clock
reloj de pulsera (M)—wristwatch
reloj de sol (M)—sundial
relleno(a)—filled, stuffed
repetir—to repeat
reportaje (M)—(news) report(ing)
reservar—reserve
resfriado (M)—(head) cold
restaurante (M)—restaurant
resto (M)—change, rest
resulta que—it turns out that
resultar—to be, to remain, to turn out (become)
retirar—to retire, to withdraw
retrovisor (M)—driving mirror
revista (F)—magazine
rico(a)—delicious, rich
riesgo (M)—risk
rioja (M)—a Rioja region wine
rizado(a)—curly
roca (F)—rock
rodaja (F)—(small) wheel
rodaje (M)—filming
rodar—to "shoot" a film
rodilla (F)—knee
rogar—to plead
rojo(a)—red
ropa (F)—clothing
rosa—rose
roto(a)—broken, not working
rubio(a)—blond
rueda (F)—wheel
rueda de recambio (F)—spare wheel, tire
ruedo (M)—arena, rotation
ruido (M)—noise

S

sábado (M)—Saturday
saber—to know
sacar—to take out
sacar fotos—to take pictures
sal (F)—salt

salchichón (M)—sausage
salir—to go out, to appear in a scene
salir bien—to go well, to be successful
salir mal—to fail
salón (M)—salon, meeting room
salpicadero (M)—splashguard
salsa (F)—sauce
salud (F)—health
saludo (M)—greeting
sandía (F)—watermelon
sangre (F)—blood
sano(a)—healthy, sound
santo(a)—saint
saque (M)—service (tennis)
sección (F)—section
seco(a)—dry
secretario (M)—secretary
seda (F)—silk
seguir—to continue, to follow
segundo(a)—second
seguridad (F)—security
seguro (M)—assurance, insurance
seguro(a)—certain, sure
sello (M)—stamp
semáforo (M)—traffic light
semana (F)—week
semanario (M)—weekly
sentar bien—to agree well with, to fit well
sentar mal—to go badly with, to fit badly
sentir—regret
sentirse mal—to feel ill
señal (F)—signal
señal de tráfico (F)—traffic signal
señas (FPl)—address, whereabouts
señor (M)—mister, sir
señora (F)—ma'am
señorita (F)—miss
sentarse—to sit
separado(a)—separate(d)
septiembre (M)—September
séptimo(a)—seventh
ser—to be
ser puntual—to be on time
servicio (M)—bathroom
servilleta (F)—napkin
servir—to serve
sesión—session
seto (M)—fence, enclosure
sexto(a)—sixth

si—if
sí—yes
siempre—always
silencio (M)—silence
silla (F)—chair, seat
simpático(a)—pleasant, "nice"
sin—without
sitio (M)—place
sobre—on, over
sobre (M)—envelope
sol (M)—sun
soler—to be accustomed to
sólo—only
solo(a)—alone
soltar(se)—to untie, to unfasten
soltero(a)—unmarried person
sombrero (M)—hat
sopa (F)—soup
soplar—to blow
sorprendido(a)—surprised
sorpresa (F)—surprise
soso(a)—insipid, tasteless
soy yo—It is I
su (sus)—your (their)
suave—soft, mild
subir—to go up, to get on
suceso (M)—event, happening
suéter (M)—pullover, sweater
sujetador (M)—bra
supermercado (M)—supermarket
sur (M)—south
suscripción (F)—subscription

T
---

tabaco (M)—cigarettes, tobacco
tablero (M)—chessboard
taco de jamón (M)—"snack" of ham
tal vez—perhaps
talla (F)—size
taller (M)—workshop
también—also
tampoco—either, neither
tan—so
tan . . . como—as . . . as
tanto—so much
tapas (FPl)—appetizer, hors d'oeuvre
tapón (M)—cork, plug
tardar—to be late, to tarry
tarde—afternoon, late
tarde (F)—afternoon, evening
tarjeta (F)—card
tarjeta postal (F)—postcard
tarta (F)—tart
tauromaquia (F)—bullfighting
taxi (M)—taxi
taxista (M)—taxi driver

teatral—theatrical
teatro (M)—theater
techo (M)—roof
tejido (M)—tissue, fabric
tele(visión) (F)—television, T.V.
telefonear—to telephone
telefónica (F)—telephone company
telefónico(a)—telephonic
teléfono (M)—telephone
temperatura (F)—temperature
temprano—early, soon
tenedor (M)—fork
tener—to have
tener dolor—to feel bad (pain)
tener éxito—to be successful
tener ganas—to feel like
tener mala cara—to look ill
tener por qué—to have a reason
tener que—to have to
tener una avería—to have a (car) breakdown
tenga—take it
tenis (M)—tennis
tercero(a)—third
terminar—to finish
termómetro (M)—thermometer
ternera (F)—veal
terraza (F)—terrace
testigo (M)—witness
tía (F)—aunt
tiempo (M)—time, weather
tienda (F)—shop, store
tierra (F)—earth, land
tijeras (FPl)—scissors
tinto—red (wine)
tío (M)—uncle
toalla (F)—towel
tobillo (M)—ankle
tocadiscos (M)—record player
tocar—to play
todavía—still
todavía no—not yet
todo(a)—all
todo el mundo—everyone
todo recto—straight ahead
todo riesgo—at all risk
tomar—to take
tomar el autobús—to take the bus
tomar una copa—to drink a glassful
tomate (M)—tomato
tonto(a)—silly, stupid
tope (M)—limit
torero (M)—bullfighter
tormenta (F)—storm
tormentoso(a)—stormy
torre (F)—tower
tortilla (F)—Mexican pancake
tos (F)—cough

trabajar—to work
trabajo (M)—work
tradicional—traditional
traer—to bring
tráfico (M)—traffic
traje (M)—suit, dress
traje de luces (M)—bullfighter's attire
tranquilo(a)—tranquil, calm
transbordo (M)—transfer
trasero(a)—rear
tratar—to try
tratar de—to attempt, to try to
tratar de tú (usted)—to use the familiar tú, the formal usted
tratarse—to be a question of
tren (M)—train
triste—sad
trueno (M)—thunder
tú—you (fam.)
tu (tus)—your (fam.)
tubo de escape (M)—muffler
turismo (M)—tourism

¡uf!—interjection denoting annoyance or fatigue
último(a)—last
un poco—a little
universidad (F)—university
unos(as)—a few, some
unos quince—about fifteen
uña (F)—fingernail
urgencias (FPl)—obligations, emergencies
usted, ustedes—you (formal)
uva (F)—grape

V
---

vaca (F)—beef
vacaciones (Fl)—vacation
¡vale!—agreed, "right on"
valer—to be worth
vaquería (F)—dairy
vaqueros (MPl)—jeans
vaso (M)—glass
¡vaya!—there you go!
¡vaya confusión!—what confusion!
vela (F)—sail
vender—to sell
venir—to come
venir bien/mal—to be becoming/unbecoming
ventana (F)—window
ventanilla (F)—car window
ventilador (M)—ventilator (fan)

ver—to see
veranear—to spend the summer vacation
verano (M)—summer
¿verdad?—right?
verde—green
verduras (FPl)—vegetables
vermut (M)—vermouth
vestido (M)—dress, suit
vez (F)—time
viajar—to travel
viaje (M)—trip
vida (F)—life
viejo(a)—old
viento (M)—wind

vientre (M)—stomach
viernes (M)—Friday
vino (M)—wine
visitar—to visit
víspera (F)—evening before
vista (F)—view
vivir—to live
volante (M)—flying, unsettled
volver—to return
volver a—to do . . . again
vosotros—you
voz (F)—voice
vuelo (M)—flight
vuelta (F)—return
vuestro(a)—your

y—and
y eso que—and nevertheless
ya—already, now
ya está bien—that's enough
yo—I, me

zanahoria (F)—carrot
zapatilla (F)—slipper
zapato (M)—shoe
zumo (M)—(fruit) juice

VOCABULARY

KEY TO PRONUNCIATION

SPANISH LETTER(S)	SOUND IN ENGLISH	EXAMPLES
c (before a, o, u)	hard k sound (<u>c</u>at)	campo *(KAHM-poh)* cosa *(KOH-sah)* Cuba *(KOO-bah)*
c (before e, i)	soft s sound (<u>c</u>ent)	central *(sehn-TRAHL)* cinco *(SEEN-koh)*
cc	hard and soft cc (ks sound) (a<u>cc</u>ept)	acción *(ahk-see-OHN)*
ch	hard ch sound (<u>ch</u>air)	muchacho *(moo-CHAH-choh)*
g (before a, o, u)	hard g (<u>g</u>o)	gafas *(GAH-fahs)* goma *(GOH-mah)*
g (before e, i)	breathy h (<u>h</u>ot)	general *(hehn-eh-RAHL)*
h	always silent	hasta *(AHS-tah)*
j	breathy as in h sound (<u>h</u>ot)	José *(ho-SAY)*
l	English l sound (<u>l</u>amp)	lámpara *(LAHM-pahr-ah)*
ll	as in English y (<u>y</u>es)	pollo *(POH-yoh)*
n	English n (<u>n</u>o)	naranja *(nah-RAHN-ha)*
ñ	English ny (ca<u>ny</u>on)	señorita *(seh-nyoh-REE-tah)*
qu	English k (<u>k</u>eep)	que *(kay)*
r	trilled once	caro *(KAH-roh)*
rr (or r at beginning of word)	trilled strongly (operator saying th<u>r</u>ee)	rico *(RREE-koh)* perro *(PEH-rroh)*
s	English s (<u>s</u>ee)	rosa *(ROH-sah)*
v	Approximately as in English b (<u>b</u>ook)	primavera *(pree-mah-BEHR-ah)*
x	English s, ks (<u>s</u>ign, so<u>cks</u>)	extra *(ES-trah)* examinar *(ek-sah-mee-NAHR)*
y	English y (<u>y</u>es) (by itself y = i)	yo *(yoh)* y *(ee)*
z	English s	zapato *(sah-PAH-toh)*

VOWELS

SPANISH LETTER(S)	SOUND IN ENGLISH	EXAMPLES
a	ah (y*a*cht)	taco *(TAH-koh)*
e	ay (d*a*y)	mesa *(MAY-sah)*
	eh (p*e*t)	perro *(PEH-roh)*
i	ee (m*ee*t)	libro *(LEE-broh)*
o	oh (*o*pen)	foto *(FOH-toh)*
u	oo (t*oo*th)	mucho *(MOO-choh)*

DIPHTHONGS

Common Vowel Combinations

SPANISH LETTER(S)	SOUND IN ENGLISH	EXAMPLES
au	ow (c*ow*)	causa *(COW-sah)*
		auto *(OW-toh)*
ei	ay (d*a*y)	aceite *(ah-SAY-tay)*
ai	y (t*y*pe)	baile *(BY-lay)*
ie	yeh (y*e*t)	abierto *(ah-BYEHR-toh)*
ue	weh (w*e*t)	bueno *(BWEH-noh)*

The above pronunciations apply to the Spanish that is spoken in Central and South America, and that is also spoken in parts of southern Spain. The remaining areas of Spain use the Castilian pronunciation:

SPANISH LETTER(S)	SOUND IN ENGLISH	EXAMPLES
ll	ly sound as in mi*ll*ion	llamo *(LYAH-moh)*
c (before *e* or *i*) z	a th sound instead of an s sound	gracias *(GRAH-thee-ahs)* lápiz *(LAH-peeth)*

PHOTO CREDITS